Incredibly Interesting Facts for Smart Kids

Fun Trivia and Quiz Book for Children With 1500+ Awesome Facts About Space, Science, Human Body, Animals, Technology, & Everything

(Trivia Book for Kids)

PUBLISHED BY

Theo Reese

Table of Contents

Introduction

Did you know that Brachiosaurus was as tall as a four-story building? (Hilfrank, 2014b) Or that Mars has a volcano twice the size of Mt. Everest? (Stein, 2022) Have you ever heard that the Ancient Greeks believed redheads were vampires? (Liles, 2020)

In this book, you will learn all that and more as we cover topics ranging from plants to the paranormal. You will have an arsenal of 1,500 + facts you can use to impress your friends, family, or anyone you can get to listen. Your go-to phrase after you read these facts is going to be, "Did you know?"

Why Learn Facts Anyway?

Fact learning is a great way to make friends and learn new conversation topics! While reading this book, you may find that whale facts interest you, and if you share them around school, you may find someone else with the same interest.

Or, while your parents are making burgers for dinner, you'll be able to tell them when the burger was invented. This gives you something to talk about with those you care about and build common interests.

Who knows! Maybe our space facts will capture your imagination, and in the future, you'll be on the first human mission to Mars.

Knowing facts can make us feel smarter and more confident. They are a great way to start finding interests you will have your whole life. Facts are our way to know our world just a little bit better.

For Parents

You may have purchased this book as a gift for your curious kid or as a way to pass long hours on a road trip. Whatever the case, you're helping your child engage more with the world around them.

Most kids spend their time on phones or other electronics, so encouraging them to engage with topics of science or history will help them later in life. Maybe try telling them a fact a day, or read this book together before bed. Together, you and your child can become experts on over fifty topics.

Positive reviews from wonderful customers like you help others feel confident about choosing this book. Sharing your happy experience will be greatly appreciated!

I hope you enjoy the Incredibly Interesting Facts for Smart Kids!

Happy Learning!

Food

Fruits

1. Fruits like strawberries and raspberries aren't really berries, but bananas and kiwis are!

2. Pineapples got their name when Christopher Columbus brought them back from the West Indies to Europe and named them for their resemblance to pine cones.

3. Lemons float while limes sink; this is because of their density. At home, try this for yourself! Then, see if different things affect the experiment, like peeling the fruits or cutting them up.

4. Rhubarb grows so quickly that it creaks when it grows.

5. People used to think tomatoes were poisonous when really it was the acidity of the tomatoes that made the lead trickle off pewter silverware.

6. Though blackcurrants are a popular fruit in many European countries, they were banned in the United States in the early 1900s because they threatened pine trees.

7. Oranges are a hybrid fruit that was created 4,000 years ago in Southeast Asia as a cross between a pomelo—a large citrus fruit—and a mandarin.

8. Though the durian fruit is known to smell like rotting sewage and turpentine, it is a popular fruit around the world, but it is banned on some airlines and in hotels.

9. If you were to microwave a grape, it would create a plasma explosion as the microwave rays come into contact with the water; don't try this at home!

Snacks

10. Peanuts can be turned into diamonds! Scientists in Germany have discovered it is possible by extracting oxygen and applying a tremendous amount of pressure.

11. French fries may not be French, and they may not even be Belgian, but they could actually be Spanish because the Spanish brought back Incan potatoes and then fried them.

12. Doritos were invented in Disneyland after stale tortillas were taken out of the garbage and fried into chips.

13. Pizza was invented in the 1500s in Naples as a poor person's food because people thought tomatoes were poisonous so that made it cheap to make.

14. Americans consume 1.2 billion pounds of chips each year, with plain Lay's being the most popular chip (Specialists in Potato Chips Projects, 2018).

15. The first modern pizza was made in 1889 and was named for Queen Margherita of Savoy.

16. The average American spends $1,200 on fast food each year, which works out to eating fast food twice each week (Daily Mail Reporter, 2014).

Carnivore Corner

17. Americans and Australians eat the most meat in the world, while Indians eat the least (Ritchie, 2019).

18. The phrase *bringing home the bacon* comes from a church in medieval England, which promised a side of bacon to any man who had not fought with his wife for a year and a day.

19. The modern hamburger is thought to have originated in the late 1880s as meat patties coming from Hamburg, Germany became a popular on-the-go food.

20. Joey *Jaws* Chestnut has won the Nathan's hot dog eating contest for the past few years with his current record at 76 hot dogs (Skiver, 2023).

21. Kobe beef is the most expensive meat around at anywhere from $100–$300 a pound because only a few farms in Japan are certified to sell it (Kolikof, 2023).

Breakfast

22. *Breakfast is the most important meal of the day* was a marketing campaign by General Foods to sell more cereal.

23. During the Middle Ages, breakfast was seen as a luxury, so only those who really needed it ate breakfast, such as laborers and farmers.

24. Breakfast became a staple meal in the 17th century as more social classes were able to afford it.

25. China consumes the most eggs in the world, with each citizen eating an average of 1,553 eggs a year (Sophia, 2020).

26. The Romans are credited with the first pancakes, which were made from eggs, spices, flour, and milk.

27. Though associated with France, the croissant was invented in Austria and brought to France through Austrian bakeries.

28. The world record for the most eggs cracked open with 1 hand in 1 minute is 32 (*Most Eggs Cracked*, 2011). That's a lot of broken eggs and probably a very messy kitchen!

29. In Italy, the largest muffin in the world was created, weighing 323 lbs—146.65 kg— which is about the weight of 2 people (*Largest Muffin*, 2015).

Sweets

30. If you like sweets, you're not alone. Americans eat, on average, 25 lbs of candy a year, which is about 113 chocolate bars (Gaille, 2017).

31. It's a myth that gum will stay in your body forever. If you swallow it, your body will digest it like anything else; it just has no nutritional value.

32. The first candy was made in Ancient Egypt by combining honey and fruits. You could probably make something similar in your kitchen right now!

33. Snickers is the most popular candy bar on Earth, and the name comes from the Mars family's favorite horse (Blake, 2018).

34. M&M's stands for Forrest Mars and Bruce Murrie, who were the individuals who invented the candies.

35. Cacao beans used to be used as a form of currency in Mesoamerica, and the Aztecs are credited with inventing hot chocolate.

36. It is true that 7.3 billion skittles are produced every year, which is enough to make a trail to the Moon! (*Fun Candy Facts*, 2023)

37. In 2012, Sees Candy created the largest lollipop in history: 7,000 lbs (3,175 is the size of a car (Blazenhoff, 2012).

Space

38. On Earth, we can only see 46 billion light years of the universe (Staff, 2021, October 15).

39. That may seem like a lot, but when the known universe is 23 trillion light years, it means we're looking at it with our eyes practically shut, not even 1%! (Staff, 2021, October 15)

Solar System

40. Our solar system is one of 3,916 solar systems in the Milky Way, which is our home galaxy.

41. You can see the Milky Way from Earth on cloudless and moonless nights far away from cities, but what parts of it you see will depend on where you live.

42. In 2015, scientists theorized that there is a massive planet just beyond Neptune based on weird gravity readings in the region—or it may be a black hole.

Sun

43. Our Sun is the largest thing in our solar system; 1.3 million Earths could fit inside it! (National Geographic, 2014c).

44. Imagine! 99% of the mass of the solar system is taken up by the Sun, and its gravity is 27.9 times as powerful as Earth's (Boeckmann, 2023).

45. Without the Sun, Earth could be as cold as -523°F (-273°C), which is 10 times colder than Antarctica (*No Sun*, 2023).

46. The light from the Sun takes 8 minutes and 20 seconds to reach us, traveling 93 million miles—148 million km—through our solar system (NASA Science Editorial Team, 2020).

47. Our Sun orbits other bigger stars and moves at a rate of 503,311 mph—810,000 kph—and it takes it 230 million years to go around the Milky Way galaxy once (Boeckmann, 2023).

Moons

48. All of the planets but Mercury and Venus have moons, with Saturn taking the lead at a whopping 146 (Bolles, 2023).

49. Moons are formed when asteroids, meteors, or other space rocks collide with larger planets and get sucked into their gravity.

50. Blood moons are caused when the only sunlight reaching the Moon travels through Earth's atmosphere, creating a rusty color.

51. In the Middle Ages, it was thought the Moon caused insanity and delusions, which is where the word *lunatic* comes from.

52. Our Moon is slowly drifting away from us at the rate of 1.5 in.—3.78 cm—a year, which is about the same rate your fingernails grow (Bolles, 2023).

Planets

53. We have 8 planets in our solar system ever since scientists decided in 2006 that Pluto was a dwarf planet and not really part of the family.

54. On Mars, there is a 72,000-ft—21945.6 m—tall volcano, which is the size of the State of Arizona and twice as high as Mt. Everest (Stein, 2022).

55. The winds on Neptune are 1,200 mph—1,931 kph—which is faster than the speed of sound (Howell, 2015).

56. The atmosphere of Venus is 867—464℃—which is hot enough to melt lead (Osterloff, 2020).

57. Mercury is only 3,030 miles—4,876 km—in diameter, which is the same length as the United States (Kramer, 2015).

58. If you were able to put the planet Saturn in a bathtub, it would float because the gases it is made of, hydrogen and helium, are lighter than water.

59. The *Great Spot* on Jupiter is a storm the size of two Earths with wind speeds of 270–425 mph (430–680 kph) (NASA, 2016).

Stars

60. Though it is impossible to know how many stars there are, right now, the estimate is 2 trillion stars in the universe, which is 5 times the amounts of trees in the Amazon rainforest (Jackson, 2021).

61. Only with perfect conditions can we see the 1,400 stars that are visible to the naked eye, which is less than 0.1% of all stars (Zuckerman, 2019).

62. UY Scuti, a star in the middle of the Milky Way, is the largest star currently known to us, and its size is 5 billion times that of our Sun (Tillman, 2018).

63. Because the stars are so far away, the light we see is millions of years old, and some of those stars have since disappeared.

64. At 1303 square degrees, Hydra is the largest constellation in the sky, taking up 3.16% of the night sky, and it's 65 times bigger than the Big Dipper (*Hydra Constellation*, 2019).

Rockets

65. The first rockets were invented in China in the 9th–10th centuries with the introduction of gunpowder.

66. Rockets need to be able to travel 7 mi—11.26 km—a second to be able to break through Earth's atmosphere, which would be as fast as you running 120 football fields in 1 second (*Top 10 Weird Facts*, 2023).

67. On October 4, 1957, the Soviet Union used a rocket to launch the first satellite into space, and now in 2022, a record was set with 180 successful rocket launches into orbit.

68. Starship, launched by SpaceX in April 2023, is the largest rocket ever built, with a height of 194 ft—59 m—making it as tall as a 20-story building (Kluger, 2023).

69. At the peak of the original mission to the moon in the 1960s, the Apollo mission accounted for 4.4% of the federal budget, or $162 billion in total (Harwood, 2019).

70. SpaceX's Falcon 9 has pioneered reusability technology in rockets with a first stage that can be reused in multiple launches.

71. The Parker Solar Probe, launched by NASA in 2018, holds the record for the fastest human-made object relative to the Sun with speeds up to 430,000 mph—700,000 kph (Frazier, 2018).

72. Launched in 2006, the New Horizons space probe completed a historic fly-by of Pluto in 2015, giving us access to the first images of the dwarf planet.

Animals

Pets

73. Most animals, like cows, sheep, and pigs, were domesticated between 8000 B.C.E and 2500 B.C.E.

74. Dogs and cats were domesticated 15,000 years ago and around 10,000 years, ago respectively.

Dogs

75. Dogs are the most popular pets on earth, with around 471 million pet dogs around the world (National Geographic, 2022a).

76. On average, they can learn over 100 words and commands, and they are sensitive to human emotions (National Geographic, 2022a).

77. Globally, there are 360 dog breeds, with the most popular one being the French Bulldog (Bauhaus, 2018).

78. Bloodhounds have the best sense of smell of any dog, with over 300 million scent receptors in their nose and the ability to follow scents over 130 m—209 km (*The 10 Dog Breed*, 2015).

79. Dogs sweat from their paws and have to cool off through panting, so watch out for hot ground in summer.

80. Mastiffs are the largest dog breed, averaging 31 in.—78 cm—and they're so big they were once used for bear fighting (Purina, 2023a).

81. Currently, there are around 500,000 service dogs working in the United States (*Must Read Service* Dog, 2021).

82. Tibetan mastiffs are currently the most expensive dog breed, with one going for $1.4 million a few years ago (Webgo Admin, 2021).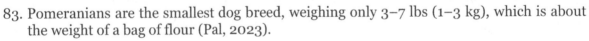

83. Pomeranians are the smallest dog breed, weighing only 3–7 lbs (1–3 kg), which is about the weight of a bag of flour (Pal, 2023).

84. The Norwegian Lundehund is the rarest dog, as they almost went extinct after World War II (*5 of the World's Rarest*, 2021).

85. Napoleon Bonaparte's wife used to use a pug as a bed warmer because it would sit still for so long.

86. Border Collies are considered the smartest dogs because they can learn new commands in under 5 seconds and remember them 95% of the time (Purina, 2023c).

87. Greyhounds run faster than any other dog at 45 mph—72 kph—and some zoos use them as companions for cheetahs (HK9 Staff, 2021).

88. Gunther the German shepherd is the richest dog on Earth with a fortune of $400 million, which his owner left him (Bender, 2023).

89. It was discovered that dogs have evolved to manipulate their eyebrows to make humans do what they want.

90. The breed of the dog Scooby-Doo is probably a Great Dane, known for its large size.

Cats

91. The Ancient Egyptians worshipped cats and would shave off their eyebrows in mourning if a pet cat died.

92. Cats can make up to 100 different sounds, while dogs can make only 10 (01 Amazing Cat Facts, 2018).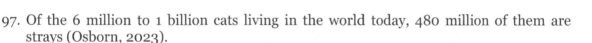

93. Some scientists believe that cats developed their meow to sound like babies crying, so humans would help them more.

94. If your cat gives you a slow blink, kneads you, or drapes its tail over you, then it trusts you.

95. Cats sleep 15–16 hours a day, which is 70% of their lifespan (Purina, 2023b).

96. Ashera cats are the most expensive pet cats at $125,000 a kitten because only 5 kittens are born a year (Gilbert, 2018).

97. Of the 6 million to 1 billion cats living in the world today, 480 million of them are strays (Osborn, 2023).

98. The Prophet Muhammed had an affinity for cats, so it is considered disrespectful in Islam to threaten them.

99. Maine Coons are the largest domestic cat breed weighing about 17 lbs—8 kg—which is the weight of an average 1-year-old child (Omlet, 2017).

100. House cats have 95.6% of the same DNA as tigers, and they share many of the same behaviors (Purina, 2023b).

101. It's a myth that orange cats are dumber than other cats—cat intelligence depends on factors like genetics or socialization, not color.

102. Cats have an internal balancing system that allows them to right themselves, but it's not true they'll always land on their feet.

103. The most followed cat on Instagram, with 4 million followers, is also the richest cat, with a fortune of $100 million (ere are the richest cats, 2023).

104. In the United Kingdom, the Prime Minister's residence has an official mouser, the current one is named Larry.

105. Siamese cats are currently the most popular cat breed on Earth, but they're known for their territorial behavior (The Spruce Official, 2012).

Birds

106. There are over 11,000 species of birds in the world, and there are between 50 billion and 430 billion birds on Earth (*Birds*, 2022).

107. Birds are the only animals with feathers, and unlike most warm-blooded creatures, they lay eggs.

108. Owls are able to turn their head 270° and see in total darkness.

109. Ostriches are the largest birds on Earth, weighing 229 lbs—104kg—with a height of 6.8 ft— 2m (*The 10 Biggest Birds*, 2020).

110. Chickens' number is around 22.67 billion, which means there's enough for 2 chickens per person on Earth (*The Most Common Birds*, 2018).

111. There were 32 birds that served in the World Wars and were awarded the Dickin Medal, which is an animal medal of valor.

112. Peregrine falcons are the fastest fliers with a speed of 242 mph—389 kph—which is twice as fast as a sports car (*17 Amazing Facts*, 2023).

113. Hollow bones were an adaptation birds inherited from the dinosaurs.

114. Penguins have evolved to *fly* in water and keep themselves warm with weighty fat deposits.

115. Bee hummingbirds are the smallest birds on earth, and they're only a bit larger than their insect namesake, weighing only 1.9–2.6 g (Bird Note, 2018).

116. Around 50,000 cormorants are killed each year because they steal fish and food, which makes them the most disliked bird (Wires, 2015).

117. *Birdbrained* is a bit of a misnomer as most birds are able to converse, solve problems, and remember patterns.

118. Sixty percent of all the puffins in the world live in Iceland (Viktoria, 2023).

119. Some male species of penguins give female penguins rocks to win their affection.

120. Due to conservation efforts, the American Bald Eagle population has quadrupled to 300,000 since 2009 (Taylor, 2021).

121. Hummingbirds visit around 1,000 flowers a day, and they never forget where they're fed (Wecker, 2022).

122. Hawks are able to see their prey from 2–4 miles (3.21–6.43 km) away, and their vision is 4–8 times better than a human's (Humaira, 2021).

123. Charles Darwin developed his theory of evolution using the 17 species of finches that live on the Galapagos islands.

124. Bearded vultures are the only birds known to primarily eat bones.

125. Owls are the most common mascot for schools because they symbolize wisdom and power (Admin Hogtown Mascots, 2020).

126. Blue-Fronted Amazons are the most talkative birds, and with extroverted personalities, they make great pets (Lewis, 2021).

127. Canaries really used to be brought into coal mines as early detectors for toxic gases like carbon monoxide. v

128. Doves became symbols of peace because of the Jewish story of Noah in the ark, where a dove symbolizes the end of the flood.

129. Some species of albatrosses have been recorded traveling over 10,000 m—16,000 km—in a single journey (Johnston, 2013).

130. Known for their endurance, common swifts are able to stay in the air for the 10 months of their migration (Yong, 2016).

Reptiles

131. There are 8,000 species of reptiles, and they can be found anywhere but Antarctica (*10 Fun Reptile Facts*, 2017).

132. Reptiles have the longest lifespans of any animal on Earth, with the Aldabra tortoise being able to live 150 years (*10 Fun Reptile Facts*, 2017).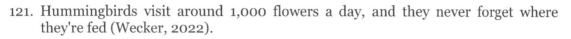

133. Alligators' eyes glow in the dark, which is why they glow red when you point a flashlight at them.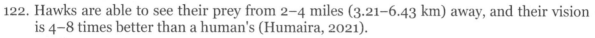

134. Lizards are able to detach their tails to get away from predators or when they are in great distress.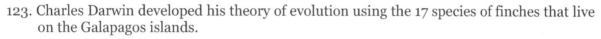

135. There are some species of geckos that don't have legs, but they aren't snakes.

136. Unlike most reptiles, alligators spend two years looking after their babies (Rudy, 2022).

137. Chameleons can rotate their eyes 360° and are able to focus them in opposite directions while also changing into any color they detect in their surroundings.

138. One of the main differences between alligators and crocodiles is that crocodiles are able to live in saltwater (Rudy, 2022).

139. Basilisk lizards, or *Jesus Christ Lizards* are able to run on water for short periods of time.

140. Komodo dragons, the largest lizard in the world that are native to Indonesia, have venom glands that cause blood to stop clotting when they bite something.

141. Nano-chameleons are the world's smallest reptiles, and they can fit on the tip of your finger (Shawna, 2022).

142. Reptiles' scaly, dry skin helps them avoid drying out and allows them to live away from water.

143. In the American South, some view alligator meat as a healthy alternative to farm-raised meats.

144. Gecko feet aren't actually sticky; they're really covered in invisible hairs that grip to surfaces.

145. Gila monsters consume all the calories they need for a year in three or four large meals.

Amphibians

146. Amphibian comes from a Greek word that means *both kinds of life.*

147. There are over a thousand different species of frog in Brazil alone (Butler, 2019).

148. Amphibian skin is permeable, which means they need to stay wet to survive (Strauss, 2018).

149. Frogs use their eyeballs to swallow their food by rolling them back in their heads to push the food down.

150. Mucus is what makes amphibians slimy and what keeps them wet.

151. The housefly-sized Paedophryne amauensis is the current smallest known amphibian.

152. All salamanders have poisonous skin.

153. There are over 5,000 different species of frog (Schmidt, 2021).

154. Some frogs are able to freeze themselves solid in winter.

155. Goliath frogs can weigh up to 7 lbs—3 kg—which is the same weight as a newborn baby (*5 Fun Frog Facts*, 2023).

156. Cane toads are toxic at all stages of life and poison all who touch them.

157. Salamanders have been known to engage in cannibalism when the other salamander is smaller than them.

158. Chinese Giant salamanders that weigh 66 lbs—30 kg—are the world's largest amphibians (BBC Wildlife Magazine, 2023).

159. Axolotls are able to regenerate their limbs when they are wounded regardless of the site of injury.

160. Amphibians are creatures between evolutionary periods and, in millions of years, they may fully move onto land.

161. American bullfrogs can jump the highest at 21.5 ft—6.5 m—in a single jump (Critter Squad, 2023).

162. After Disney released *The Princess and the Frog* in 2010, there was a rise in young children getting salmonella after kissing frogs.

Mammals

163. Mammals are the most adaptive animal group on Earth, and that applies to humans too (National Geographic, 2015).

164. There are 6,495 different species of mammals spread across all the oceans and every continent (Burgin et al., 2018).

165. After the dinosaurs, the Cenozoic era began, or the era of the mammal, and we're still in it today.

166. The platypus and four different species of echidnas are the only mammals that lay eggs (Davis, 2022).

167. Over 300 types of fruits depend on bats for pollination, like bananas or mangoes (3 Awesome Facts, 2018).

168. When bears hibernate, they can go 100 days without drinking, passing waste, or eating (Bachman, 2023).

169. You would be able to hear a howler monkey from up to 3 miles away (Schreiber, 2023).

170. Sloths move so slowly that algae are able to grow on their fun and become a type of camouflage.

171. Giraffes are the tallest animals on Earth at 18 ft—5.5 m—tall, which is about the height of 3 humans (National Geographic, 2016a).

172. The phrase *you're never more than 6 ft—1.8 m—from a rat* is untrue in the modern world, though there are as many rats as people on Earth (Pritchard, 2012).

173. Male platypuses have a venomous gland behind their foot that would be lethal if you touched it.

174. African elephants are the largest land mammal, weighing 13,227 lbs—6,000 kg—which is 3 times heavier than a car (*Top 10 Facts About Elephants* , 2022).

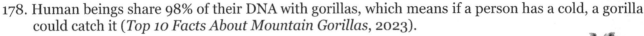

175. Though flying squirrels can glide, bats are the only mammals that can fly (*13 Awesome Facts*, 2018).

176. Every zebra has a unique pattern of stripes, and this may be how they recognize each other (National Geographic, 2017a).

177. Polar bear fur is translucent, and it only looks brilliantly white because the snow is reflecting onto it.

178. Human beings share 98% of their DNA with gorillas, which means if a person has a cold, a gorilla could catch it (*Top 10 Facts About Mountain Gorillas*, 2023).

179. Rhinoceroses have a poor sense of vision and are not able to see a motionless person standing 98 ft—30 m—away (*Top 10 Facts About Rhinos*, 2023).

180. Crystal the Capuchin Monkey has been in 30 films and has a box office gross of $2.5 billion (*Crystal the Monkey*, 2023).

181. Giraffes have long blue tongues that can reach lengths of 20 in.—53cm (National Geographic, 2016a).

182. The saying *an elephant never forgets* is not untrue, as the part of the brain that stores memory is the biggest in elephants (*Top 10 Facts About Elephants*, 2022).

183. During World War II, a regiment in Poland adopted a brown bear cub as a morale booster.

184. The teeth of mice grow at a rate of 0.01 in.—0.03 cm—a day for their entire lives (Ehrlich, 2023a).

185. Horses' ancient ancestors were the size of golden retrievers, and they looked more like small goats.

186. Beavers naturally help to control the flow of water by ensuring banks do not overflow.

187. Like farm pigs, warthogs roll themselves in mud to protect themselves from the sun and clean themselves.

188. It's a myth that there are *Alpha wolves*; this behavior only appeared in captivity when provoked by researchers (Pappas, 2023).

189. Binturongs or bearcats are mammals native to South Asia that naturally smell like popcorn.

190. Quokkas are known as the world's happiest animals because it appears they have permanent smiles on their faces.

191. Every day, an anteater can eat up to 30,000 ants (*Giant Anteater*, 2023).

192. Foxes are able to retract their claws like cats, and they are the only member of the dog family able to do this (*25 Amazing Facts About Foxes*, 2023).

193. Reindeer is the only species of deer where the males and females both grow antlers.

194. At 2,790 ft—850 m—the beaver's dam in Wood Buffalo National Park in Alberta, Canada is the largest in the world (*World's Largest Beaver Dam*, 2022).

Buildings, Castles, and Megacities Architecture

Castles

196. The word *castle* comes from the Latin word for *fortress* because that's what castles mainly were.

197. On average, it would have taken 10 years to build a castle and would have cost £200,000,000—$2.5 million—in today's money if it was made of stone (Wishart, 2017).

198. Malbork Castle in Poland is thought to be the largest castle, but Windsor Castle in the United Kingdom is the largest but still inhabited castle.

199. Some castles have even made it to the screen, such as the Neuschwanstein Castle in Germany, which inspired the Disney Castle, or Alnwick Castle in the United Kingdom, where some of Harry Potter was filmed.

Mega Cities

200. A *megacity* is "any city with more than 10 million inhabitants," such as New York, Tokyo, or Mexico City. There are 33 megacities as of 2023, but there will likely be 47 by 2050 (Dyvik, 2023a).

201. Currently, Tokyo is the largest megacity on Earth with a population of 37 million, but by 2100, it will be Lagos in Nigeria, as its population has already grown tenfold in the past 50 years (Iberdrola, 2023).

202. Other megacities are Delhi, India, Sao Paulo, Brazil, Mumbai, India, Dhaka, Bangladesh, and Karachi, Pakistan.

203. The three largest public transportation systems in New York City, Shanghai, and Beijing are all housed in megacities (Mammadzade, 2019).

204. Tokyo has the busiest of these public transportation systems, and Shinjuku station is known as the most crowded station, with almost 3 million commuters using it every day (Steen, 2022).

205. Sixty percent of the world lives in a megacity, so if you're reading this, you're more likely than not to live in one! (*Megacities*, 2023)

206. Almost 70% of carbon dioxide emissions come from the world's megacities; however, cities like Chicago have worked to offset this by creating a street tree planting program (City of Chicago, 2023).

207. New York City's population of 20 million is supported by an army of 14,000 licensed taxi cabs (*Yellow Cab*, 2023).

208. Mumbai's Dabbawalas deliver approximately 200,000 lunchboxes each day with remarkable accuracy, and there is only an error in every 16 million transactions (Rathi, 2017).

209. In São Paulo, Brazil, helicopters are symbols of wealth for the rich, so the city is home to the largest fleet of helicopters on Earth (*The Capital of São Paulo*, 2022).

210. Manila's traffic costs the Filipino government $70 million a day because of increased transportation costs, fuel expenditures, and lost hours (Shiga, 2021).

211. In 2010, Beijing, China, experienced a traffic jam that lasted 12 days and stretched over 62 m—100 km (*The Longest Traffic*, 2023).

Hotels

212. Hotels began as rest stops for travelers because getting places used to take a lot longer. Often, it was just a room in someone's house or even the outhouse.

213. In Ancient Rome, hotels grew into places the wealthy would go just to relax, such as the House of Sallust in Pompeii.

214. Nishiyama Onsen Keiunkan Hot Springs Inn in Japan is the oldest hotel on earth you can still stay at. It's been in the same family for 1300 years (*Koshu Nishiyama*, 2023).

215. The First World Hotel in Pahang, Malaysia, is the world's largest hotel, with 7,3511 rooms and a variety of shopping opportunities (Tymann, 2023).

216. You can stay at the Stanley Hotel, Colorado, from Stephen King's horror film *The Shining*, and it is considered one of the most haunted hotels on Earth.

217. Necker Island, a private island hotel in the British Virgin Islands, is the most expensive evening stay at $113,000 a night (Braswell, 2023).

218. The Ice Hotel in Lapland, Sweden, is entirely made of ice sculptures by international artists, and guests have to sleep in thermal clothes on beds made of ice.

219. Manta Resort in Pemba Island, Tanzania, is an underwater hotel that offers guests views of coral reefs and tropical marine life.

220. Jules' Undersea Lodge, located in Key Largo, Florida, is the only hotel you can reach by scuba diving, and you need to dive 21 ft—6 m—to reach it (*Jules' Undersea Lodge*, 2023).

221. Giraffe Manor in Nairobi, Kenya, is a unique hotel because you'd be staying with the giraffes that roam the property.

222. Palacio de Sal is a hotel in the Bolivian salt flats that is entirely made of salt.

223. Deep Sleep, an underground hotel in Snowdonia, Wales, is the deepest hotel in the world at 1,375 ft—419 m—underground (World's Deepest Hotel, 2023).

224. The Dog Bark Park Inn is a hotel in Idaho that is shaped like a giant beagle, and you enter your room through its stomach.

Greek and Roman Architecture

225. Many Greek and Roman buildings still stand today, in part because of their craftsmanship. Most of what has been left behind are temples and public buildings, which you can still visit today.

226. In Greece, the Parthenon still stands, and throughout its history, it has been a temple for Athena, a Christian church, a mosque, and now a museum open to all.

227. When it was created, the Parthenon was filled with color, but the English Victorians decided the decorated statues were improper, so that's why we have the white marble.

228. Throughout Europe, you can see Roman buildings, and some things, such as the Roman aqueducts, were built on top of them to be used in the modern world.

229. Roman roads are also still in use, such as one that connects London to York in the United Kingdom.

230. The Colosseum could fit up to 80,000 spectators, which is the same amount as the Old Trafford football stadium in the United Kingdom (24 *Mind-Blowing*, 2021).

231. Ancient Rome had 500 m—800 km—of aqueducts supplying the city with water, and it was one of the most sophisticated systems in the ancient world (Appleton, 2022).

232. The Roman arch is thought to be the foundation of modern architecture because it helps to distribute weight.

233. Domes were also a huge advancement for architecture as they were the most efficient type of building. They allow for excellent acoustics, and heat is able to be evenly distributed through them.

234. The famous Dome of the Rock, a holy site in Jerusalem, is one of the first Islamic sites to ever be completed, and the dome is entirely covered in gold leaf.

235. You would think the world's most expensive building would be a private luxury, but it's the Masjid Al-Haram in Saudi Arabia, at $100 billion, where Muslims *hajj* (Renner, 2022).

Plants, Trees

236. Plants can be found on every continent, including Antarctica, and there are more than 320,000 species of plants on Earth (Hodgson, 2020). Without them, there would be no oxygen to breathe, so we must take care of our green protectors.

237. Humans consume 150–200 different plant species, though only 30 plant species provide 90% of all nutrition (FAO Regional Office for Asia and the Pacific, 2023).

Trees

238. There are an estimated 3 trillion trees on Earth, and these are necessary for oxygen production (Kilgore, 2022).

239. Trees evolving 300 million years ago was a turning point for the Earth as it allowed more species to live on land because there was shelter and food for them (McLendon, 2022).

240. The largest trees on Earth are the sequoias, which grow on the North West Pacific Coast in Sequoia National Park in California.

241. Methuselah, a Great Basin Bristlecone Pine, is the oldest tree still alive; it began to grow while the pyramids were being built in Ancient Egypt. Its location is kept under wraps so no harm is done to the tree.

242. Trees can use an underground network of fungi to communicate with each other about threats such as insects so the trees can fortify their natural defenses.

243. At half an inch—1.6 cm—the dwarf willow that lives in Arctic environments is the world's smallest tree (Potter, 2023).

244. The rainbow eucalyptus in Papua New Guinea has barks that shed in uneven strips, leaving behind a rainbow design on the tree.

245. Surprisingly, 58% of all tree species only grow in one country; Brazil, Colombia, and Indonesia have the highest amount of these single-country, or endemic, tree species (McLendon, 2022).

246. The average tree is made up of 99% dead cells, with the living parts being the phloem, the roots, and the leaves (Crazy Critters, 2019).

247. A typical mature tree can provide enough wood to make up to 170,100 pencils (Hodgson, 2020).

248. The art of bonsai originated 5,000 years ago in China, which evidences human appreciation for cultivation at an early period (*Bonsai*, 2022).

Flowers and Plants

249. With its peachy scent and soft pink color, the Sweet Juliet Rose is the most expensive flower on Earth, as it sold for £5 million (Deepa, 2023).

250. Common edible flowers are cornflowers, honeysuckle, pansies, and roses; you can put them in teas or as garnishes on salad.

251. The Victorians used flowers as a type of language. For example, a bouquet of baby's breath, red carnations, and red roses could be a declaration of undying love and devotion said in secrecy. Flowers can hear and respond to the buzzing of bees by producing more nectar to attract pollinators.

252. Sunflowers move throughout the day to follow the sun. If you have some in your backyard, try setting up a time-lapse camera so you can see it for yourself!

253. Roses are the most popular flower, with over 1 billion produced globally, possibly because of their scent, beauty, and ability to symbolize so many things (Chelsea Flower Show, 2019).

254. Tulips were so popular in the 1600s that their bulbs were worth more than gold, and their market crashed the Dutch economy.

255. There are an estimated 400,000 different flowering species on Earth, which includes a wide variety of blooms (Thorne, 2002).

256. A total of 167 crocuses are needed to produce only 1 g of saffron, making it one of the most expensive spices on Earth (Skinner & Parker, 2020).

257. Seventy-five percent of all plants require pollinators like hummingbirds, bees, or butterflies to spread their seeds (Pollinator Partnership, 2023).

258. Carnivorous plants, such as the Venus Fly Trap, have devised a system of counting so that they are not tricked by false alarms. [1]

259. An insect needs to brush up against the trap twice to be caught in it. It's important not to set off Venus Fly Traps unless you're a bug because then the plant cannot do what it's meant to do!

260. Plants are able to fight, such as the Giant Water Lily, which grows with large spiked leaves that crush all the other plants competing for sunlight.

261. Phytoplankton, the microscopic plants that cover the sea, create 50% of the world's supply of oxygen (NASA Earth Observatory, 2016).

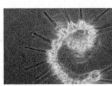

---

[1] a

262. The smell of fresh-cut grass is actually a distress signal from the plant. So the next time you're mowing your lawn, just know that fresh scent is really a screaming plant.

263. Ginkgo plants are the oldest on Earth, with the species originating 250 million years ago (Crazy Critters, 2019).

264. The Giant Montane Pitcher Plant has been known to devour small mammals amongst the other creatures unfortunate enough to fall into it.

265. Though humans use caffeine to stay awake, caffeine evolved in coffee plants as a natural insecticide.

Flying Objects

Early Flight

267. Humans have always dreamed of flight: In the ancient Greek myth of Icarus, a man and his son escape a tower using flying machines before the son falls to his death.

268. In 400 B.C.E., kites were invented in China, and soon, humans used them to attempt to fly. This technology inspired parachutes and paragliders.

269. Leonardo Da Vinci created around 500 sketches of flying machines, but his dream had a sad end as he killed a servant by making them fly a prototype.

270. The first science fiction story in English, *The Man in the Moone*, features a man creating a contraption powered by 10 geese to fly himself to the moon.

271. The first flight of humans was in 1783 using an early version of the hot air balloon, and it was viewed by the likes of Benjamin Franklin and John Addams in Paris.

272. Lagâri Hasan Çelebi, an Ottoman aviator, is thought to be one of the earliest people to take flight as he strapped a rocket to himself in the 17th century and supposedly lived.

Airships

273. Airships fly by filling a balloon with a gas lighter than the atmosphere, normally using 245 ft^3—6.9 m^3—of helium, which is equal to almost 5,000 party balloons (Neer, 2000).

274. During the first airship flight of 1785 over the English Channel, inventors Jean-Pierre Blanchard and Dr. John Jeffries had to strip their clothes to lessen their weight to avoid falling into the water.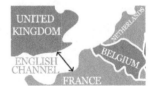

275. During World War I, of Germany's 115 Zeppelin airships, 53 were lost, and 24 others were ruined beyond repair (Castlelow, 2017).

276. Hydrogen stopped being used in airships after the Hindenburg disaster of 1937 which killed 36 passengers when it docked in New Jersey (History.com Editors, 201 8c).

277. The first event coverage filmed by a Goodyear blimp was the 1955 *Rose Bowl*, and it was mainly an ad for their rubber business.

278. In 1919, the first transatlantic flight in an airship took place, and it was a whopping 108 hours, which is almost 6 times as long as our modern longest flight! (Science and Technology, 2023)

Planes

279. In 1903, the first airplane flight of the Wright Brothers only lasted 12 seconds (1903 Wright Flyer, 2023a).

280. Airplanes fly by pushing air down with the wings and using the *lift* of the air to stay in the sky.

281. At 2,301.81 mph—3,704 km/h—the Virgin Galactic plane *Unity* is the fastest plane and it is able to leave the Earth's atmosphere temporarily (Cutmore, 2023).

282. The Christmas bullet airplane of 1919 was meant to have wings that flapped like a bird, but the wings fell off each time the plane tried to take off.

283. Since it debuted in 1967, the Boeing 737 has sold 11,500 units making it the most-produced plane in history and probably the plane you've ridden on (Mickeviciute, 2023).

284. The Saudi Arabian Crown Prince's private jet, complete with a concert hall, is the most expensive private plane owned valued at $500 million (Private Jet Charter Team, 2023).

285. In the average Boeing 747, there are 6 million parts and 40,000 rivets on just one wing! (Bowers, 1997)

286. With no fatal accidents in any of the 380 planes since their introduction in 1993, the Airbus A340 is the safest commercial plane (Singh, 2022).

287. In World War II, the Messerschmitt Me 163 Komet was a rocket propelled fighter that could fly and climb fast, but its fuel only lasted 3 minutes. The fuel was so dangerous that it exploded upon contact with clothing (Dowling, 2014).

288. The Solar Impulse 2 is a solar-powered aircraft that completed a circumnavigation of the Earth in 2016, traveling 25,000 m around the world. It relied entirely on solar energy for power (Wei-Haas, 2018).

289. At any given time, there are 5,400 flights in the sky, with over 10 million passenger flights scheduled each year (*Air Traffic by the Numbers*, 2022).

290. In 1947, Chuck Yeager became the first person to fly faster than the speed of sound at a speed of 700 m—1,126 km—per hour and an altitude of 43,000 ft—13,106 m (Enriquez, 2022).

291. The Antonov AN-225 Mriya was the largest aircraft carrier in the world and was able to carry 250 t of weight, which can be other smaller planes or helicopters (Antonov AN-225 Mriya, 2023).

292. U-2 spy planes can cruise at an altitude of 70,000 ft—21,000 m—with a weight of 3,000 lbs—1,350 kg—making them ideal for covert operations (Augustyn, 2018).

Warplanes

293. Costing the United States Air Force $2.1 billion, the Northrop Grumman B-2 Spirit is the most expensive plane produced, and it takes $135,000/hr to operate (Thomson, 2019).

294. Throughout World War II, the United States produced the most planes with 297,000 airc raft, and in 1941, produced more planes than Japan did during the entire war (Burns, 2007).

295. During *The Blitz*, Germany dropped around 3,000 bombs on England for 57 nights, which is a rate of 52 bombs per day (*The Blitz Around Britain*, 2018).

296. With roughly 5,217 active aircraft, the United States Air Force is the largest on Earth, with a price tag of $181.1 billion (*Largest Air Forces*, 2021).

297. Around 378,613 planes were destroyed over the course of World War II, with the Soviets losing the most at 106,000 (*World War II Aircraft Losses*, 2023).

298. The Fi 156 Storch was a warplane so light it was able to take off at 200 ft—60 m—and land in as little as 66 ft—20 m (*Fieseler Fi 156D-1*, 2023).

299. F-22 warplanes are able to climb 62,000 ft—18,897 m—per minute, which makes them ideal for close combat scenarios (Lenkov, 2022).

Hot Air Balloons

300. Hot air balloons use the scientific principle *hot air rises* to fly by heating air in a balloon with a flame that can be used to control the craft's altitude.

301. At 68,986 ft—21,026 m—Dr. Vijaypat Singhania set the record for the highest hot air balloon flight at twice the height commercial airlines fly (Bailey, 2015).

302. Richard Branson and Per Lindstrand were the first people to cross the Atlantic in a hot air balloon in 1987, completing the journey in 33 hours (Albuquerque International Balloon Festival, 2023).

303. In 2013, 433 hot air balloons took off from the French-Lorraine Mondial Air Balloon Gathering, making it the largest take-off in history (Bailey, 2015).

304. For over $5 million, you can purchase a hot air balloon trip over Mt. Everest in what is the most expensive hot air balloon voyage (Bailey, 2015).

305. In 1935, the hot air balloon Explorer II set a world record for altitude at 72,395 ft—22,066 m (*Cabin, "Explorer II"*, 2023).

Dinosaurs

306. Paleontologists are currently discovering new dinosaur species at a rate of 45 per year (Greshko, 2022).

Triassic and Jurassic

307. Though dinosaurs appeared in the Triassic period 251 million years ago, they would not dominate until the Jurassic period.

308. The biggest dinosaur of this period was Lessemsaurus at around 32 ft—10 m—and 7716 lbs—3500 kg—but this was still 4 times smaller than the T-Rex (*Lessemsaurus Dinosaur*, 2023).

309. One of the larger dinosaurs of this period, the ichthyosaur, is mistaken for a prehistoric dolphin, but it was just a reptile that evolved like a dolphin.

310. Plesiosaurus is what people imagine the Loch Ness Monster to be, but it was only about 9 ft—3 m—long and not much bigger than a person (Scotese, 2011).

311. Pangea hadn't broken up yet, which means our seven continents were one large landmass, and the climate for these dinosaurs was mostly desert.

312. The only reptile that survived the Triassic period to the modern day is the mighty turtle.

313. Most dinosaurs in *Jurassic Park* really come from the Cretaceous period, not the Jurassic.

314. Ledumahadi Mafube was the largest land animal in this period, weighing 24,000 lbs—10,886 kg—which is about 2 elephants (Boy Scouts of America, 2018).

315. Brachiosaurus grew to be 80 ft—24 m—long and was about as tall as a four-story building (Hilfrank, 2014b).

316. Allosaurus was an early relative of the T-Rex, but it had strong arms to grip its prey instead of the T-Rex's puny hands.

317. Though around the size of a school bus, 30 ft—9 m—long, Stegosaurus' brain was the size of a plum (Stegosaurus, 2014).

318. While human beings have 33 vertebrae, Diplodocus had over 100 vertebrae just in its neck and tail (*7 Interesting Facts About Diplodocus*, 2023).

319. Running as fast as a car cruises through a neighborhood, Allosaurus was able to run 21 mph—33 kph (Hilfrank, 2014a).

320. Pterosaurs, a flying dinosaur, ranged from the size of a fighter plane at 40 ft—12 m—to the size of a small bird (Monastersky, 2009).

321. Stegosaurus could live to be 75–100 years old (Griffin, 2022).

Cretaceous

322. Titanosaurian Argentinosaurus is thought to be the largest dinosaur from this period at 80 t, though that may be challenged by the potential Puertasaurus Reuili at 100 t (*Which Were the Biggest Dinosaurs*, 2009).

323. The most famous dinosaur from this period, the Tyrannosaurus, Rex had 50–60 banana-sized teeth and bit off 220 lbs—100 kg—of meat at a time (National Geographic Kids, 2018e).

324. Triceratops is thought to have used its horns for males to fight for the attention of the females.

325. Velociraptors were about the size of turkeys, and they could run at the speed of a car, 25 mph—40 kph (Hendry, 2013).

326. The tooth of an Iguanodon was one of the first dinosaur fossils ever identified in 1822.

327. T-Rex's lived about 28 years, and we know this because we can date their teeth like the rings of a tree.

328. Triceratops fossils are some of the most expensive, with one specimen being purchased for $1 million (Bryan, 2021).

329. In rare cases, dinosaur fossils have preserved soft tissues, such as skin and even blood vessels, which could be 75 million years old.

330. The most expensive fossil around is that of Stan, an almost entirely complete T-Rex, which sold for $31.8 million at auction (Hunt, 2022).

331. Spinosaurus' bony back frill would have been used to let other dinosaurs know that coming close meant a fight.

332. The name *Tyrannosaurus Rex* in Latin translates to *tyrant lizard king*.

333. On Triceratops, the shortest horn was made from keratin, which is the same thing your nails are made of.

334. The asteroid that brought the end of the dinosaurs was 6 miles—9.6 km—long, which would take you 15 minutes to drive (*Asteroid Impact*, 2022).

335. Today, the only remaining relatives of the dinosaurs are birds, alligators, and crocodiles.

336. The dinosaurs were only around for 4% of Earth's history, which is about 57 minutes of a 24-hour day (University of Kansas, 2023).

337. A sparrow-sized raptor created the smallest dinosaur footprints ever found at only 0.5 in.—1 cm—big (Irving, 2018).

Things That Go

Cars

339. In 1886, Mercedes-Benz created the first automobile, the *Motorwagen*, which had three wheels and looked more like a bicycle.

340. The roughly 1 billion cars on Earth produce 4.6 billion mt of carbon dioxide a year, making them the 4th largest polluting force (*Greenhouse Gas Emissions*, 2022).

341. At $28 million, the Rolls Royce Boat Tail is the most expensive car money can buy, and it even comes with a champagne fridge (Perez, 2022).

342. In 2021, there were 278,063,737 personal and commercial cars registered in the United States alone (Munson, 2021).

343. If the computer inside your car was printed out, the code on it would stretch out for 100 miles—160.9 km (*15 Random Car Facts*, 2023).

344. For its safety features and price, the Toyota Corolla is the best-selling car of all time, having sold 45 million cars since 1966 when it was unveiled (Poland, 2021).

345. *New* car smell is caused by the combination of chemicals, adhesives, and plastics used on the interior of a car when it is manufactured.

346. When it debuted in 1908, the Ford Model T was $825, which would cost you $18,000 today, and it took 12 hours to assemble one (*15 Random Car Facts*, 2023).

347. Irvin Gordon set the record for highest mileage on a personal vehicle at over 3 million m, which is equivalent to going around the world 120 times (Poland, 2021).

348. Faster than most rollercoasters, the Koenigsegg Jesko Absolut is the car for a speed demon with a top speed of 330 mph—531 kph (Teague, 2023).

349. In 1896, Walter Arnold was the first person to be given a speeding ticket for driving a whopping 8 mph—12.8 kph (Poland, 2021).

350. The average car has around 30,000 parts, and it takes 4,800 welds to ensure the correct parts are where they need to be (*How Many Parts*, 2023).

351. Between 1966 and 2017, fuel efficiency has risen from 13.5 mpg—5.7 kml—to 22.3mpg—9.8 kml—in 2017 (Sivak, 2019).

Motorcycles

352. The MTT Y2K is the fastest bike made today, with a speed of 273 mph—439 kph—and because of this, only 5 are made a year (Bradley, 2023).

353. The Honda Super Cub is the most-produced motorcycle in history as of 2014, when cumulative worldwide production reached 87 million units in March 2014. It has been sold in more than 160 countries (Honda, 2014).

354. Dipayan Choudhury performed the longest backward motorcycle ride in 2014 at 125 m—202 km. Don't try that at home! (Padway, 2018)

355. The Petroleum Reitwagen was the first gas-powered motorcycle created in 1885, but the first steam-powered bike was used in 1869.

356. At $100,000, the Ducati Superleggera V4 is both the most expensive and exclusive motorbike you can buy because only 500 were produced (Stein, 2023).

357. Riding 2,116.5 m—3,406.17 km—Carl Reese set the record for longest 24-hour ride in 2017 to raise awareness for veterans (Padway, 2018).

358. Stunt performer Alex Harvill's 425 ft—129.5 m—high jump in 2012 is the highest to date, though performing another stunt, Harvill lost his life 9 years later (Sokol, 2022).

359. Weighing 5.22 t, the Panzerbike is the heaviest bike ever made, and it had to be powered by the same engine that powered German World War II tanks (Padway, 2018).

360. Around 600 million motorcycles are on the road today, with India riding 200 million of those bikes (Riders Share, 2023).

361. Though good for thrill seekers, motorcycles are also one of the more dangerous vehicles, as motorcyclists are 28 times more likely to be in a fatal crash than other drivers (Bieber, 2023).

Trucks

362. Weighing more than 50 elephants, the *Beast of Belarus*, at 360 t, is the largest truck manufactured (Lewis, 2022b).

363. The word *truck* comes from the 17th-century term for the wheels used to carry cannons into battle.

364. Hummer EV Pickups are the most expensive pickup trucks on the market, costing $108,300, and they're able to go from 0 to 60 mph—0 to 96.5 kph—in 3 seconds (Kennedy, 2023).

365. Monster truck drivers will do an average of $10,000 of damage to their vehicles during a show, which has to be repaired by the next performance (Pevos, 2018).

366. Currently, there are 15.5 million trucks used by the American shipping industry, and the number is expected to grow by 21% over the next few years (Top 10 Interesting Facts about Trucks, 2019).

367. With a towing capacity of 40,000 lbs—18,143 kg—the Ford F-250 would be able to pull the weight of 2.5 T-Rexes (Smith, 2023).

368. There are 3.5 million shipping truck drivers in the United States, and with a salary of $90,000 a year, it's not a bad job! (Kopf Logistics Group, 2021)

369. Each monster truck tire costs up to $2,600, and on average, they are taller than the average person (Pevos, 2018).

370. Trucks typically drive over 100,000 mi—160,934.4 km—a year, and they provide 70% of the household products in the United States (*7 Trucking Facts*, 2022).

371. Every year, the monster truck show Monster Jam crushes 3,000 cars, and sometimes buses or planes are also used (Meinert, 2023).

372. In 2020, the record for the world's longest truck convoy was set in Cairo, Egypt, with a chain of 480 trucks (*Largest Parade of Trucks*, 2020).

373. The BelAZ 75710 is the biggest haul truck in the world, and it is able to tow 450 t, which is around 64 elephants! (*Off-Highway Trucks*, 2023)

Rivers, Lakes, Waterfalls

River

375. The Nile River is the longest in the world at 4,160 m—6,695 km—and it flows through 11 different countries (Saunders, 2023).

376. On the other hand, the Roe River in Montana is the smallest at 200 ft—60 m—which is about as long as a hockey rink (Maki, 2019).

377. The Amazon River is home to many iconic fish species, like piranhas and electric eels, and also one of the world's largest freshwater fish, the arapaima.

378. Caño Cristales in Columbia is known as the River of Five Colors because its aquatic plants turn the river into a liquid rainbow.

379. Connecting cities such as Nanjing and Shanghai, the Yangtze River is the busiest river, with 2.93 billion t of cargo shipped on it a year (Xinhua, 2020).

380. The Amazon River, the second-largest river in the world, discharges 28 million gal of water into the Atlantic each year and houses 2,400 different species of fish (Amazon Aid, 2023).

381. Discovered near the mouth of the Nile, the ancient city of Thonis-Heracleion was once a major port city and now is a treasure trove of artifacts.

382. Martin Strel, a 67-year-old Slovenian swimmer, has set multiple records by swimming the lengths of the Amazon, Mississippi, and Yangtze rivers.

Lakes

383. Lake Baikal in Siberia is the world's deepest lake at 5,000 ft—1524 m—and it holds 20% of the world's freshwater (Water Science School, 1999).

384. The Earth has 117 million lakes, but 90 million of them aren't enough to even cover 2 football fields (Oskin, 2014).

385. Though Finland has the nickname *Land of One Thousand Lakes*, there are actually over 187,000 lakes in the country (HOBO, 2023).

386. Located in the Andes Mountains, Lake Titicaca is the highest navigable lake on Earth, with an elevation of 12,500 ft—3,810 m—and an area of 3,200 sq m—8,300 sq km (Encyclopaedia Britannica Editor, 2023).

387. Lynne Cox was the first person to swim Lake Titicaca, which is colder than Arctic waters and leaves swimmers with mysterious bites.

388. Vicki Keith was the first person to swim all over the Great Lakes in 1988, and now she runs a swimming group for disabled children.

389. In 1937, 16-year-old Marilyn Bell became the first person to swim Lake Ontario, covering a distance of 40 m—64 km—in close to 21 hours (*Marilyn Bell*, 2022).

Waterfalls

390. The roar from Victoria Falls in Zimbabwe is so loud it can be heard 25 m—40 km—away; that's like a whole town over! (*Victoria Falls*, 2013)

391. Angel Falls in Venezuela is the tallest waterfall at 3,212 ft—979 m. That's 3 times the height of the Empire State Building (Maya & Michael, 2017).

392. Every second, 3,160 t of water go over Niagara Falls, which is enough to fill a little over three Olympic-sized swimming pools (Niagara Falls USA, 2023).

Mountains and Volcanoes

Mountains

394. Of the world's highest mountains, 30 are in the Himalayas, including Mt. Everest, which is 29,035 ft—8,850 m—tall (National Geographic, 2018c).

395. Eighty percent of the world's freshwater comes from the ice on mountains, and you've probably drank some with brands like Arrowhead (Water Science School, 1993).

396. The United Nations made December 11th International Mountain Day to make sure we keep protecting these environments.

397. Mount Denali, or Mount McKinley, is the tallest mountain in the United States at 20,310 ft—6,190 m—but it is also the coldest place on Earth at its peak (Whitman, 2023).

398. Only 500 people have been able to complete the 7 summits, which is climbing the highest mountain on each continent (Dawson, 2022).

399. The Himalayas were formed when the Eurasian and Indian tectonic plates collided, and today the plates are still pushing together, so the Himalayas are slowly growing.

Volcanoes

400. The Pacific *Ring of Fire* is home to 75% of all active volcanoes in the world; it stretches from Chile to Alaska, then over to the Pacific Islands (National Geographic, 2023b).

401. Yellowstone's geyser is actually a volcano that could go off at any time, and it would cover the entire United States in ash. Luckily, that's unlikely.

402. Around 350 million people live within the danger zone of a volcano, that's 1 in 20 people (National Geographic Kids, 2018f).

403. Right now, 20 volcanoes are erupting as you're reading this. Many have constantly flowing lava, like in Volcanoes National Park in Hawaii (Cain, 2016).

404. Manua Loa in Hawaii is the world's tallest volcano at 13,679 ft—4,169 m—but if it were measured from the base of the seafloor it would be taller than Mt. Everest (*Mauna Loa*, 2023).

405. At 22,569 ft—6,879 m—the Nevados Ojos del Salado is the tallest volcano in the world (Global Volcanism Program, 2023).

Rainforests

406. Though tropical rainforests only cover 3% of the planet, they are home to more than half of the plants and animals on Earth (9 Rainforest *Facts*, 2019).

407. Surprisingly, 99% of these species have yet to be studied, and many scientists think they could have the key to fighting diseases like cancer. One in particular, the Lapacho, is already used to fight cancer (1 Facts, 2016).

408. We lose an area of rainforest as big as 40 football fields every minute because of deforestation (9 *Rainforest* Facts, 2019).

409. One in four people depend on a rainforest for their livelihood, whether that be for food or income. Maybe you or your parents are some of them! (*9 Rainforest Facts*, 2019)

410. The Amazon rainforest is so big that if it were made a country, it would be the ninth largest in the world.

411. Many of the things we eat, like cocoa, mangoes, bananas, and coffee, come from the rainforest, but also a lot of medicines we use.

412. Scientists estimate that there are 16,000 different species of trees and around 400 billion individual trees in the Amazon, which is 50 times the number of people on Earth (*Top Facts About the Amazon* , 2023f).

413. Tropical rainforests are some of the oldest ecosystems on Earth. Most dinosaurs would have lived in a tropical rainforest.

414. Five thousand languages are spoken by the different peoples who live in rainforests with 839 of those being in Papua New Guinea alone (*Rainforests Explained*, 2023).

415. The Amazon is often called the *lungs of the earth* because it absorbs 1/4 of all the carbon emitted on Earth (National Geographic, 2023a).

416. Between 17 and 20% of the Amazon has been destroyed in the past 50 years due to deforestation (Roy, 2023).

Deserts

417. Deserts aren't just hot places; the term technically means any place that receives less than 10 in.—25 cm—of rain a year, so there are polar deserts (Nunez, 2019).

418. The Antarctic Polar Desert is the largest on Earth at 5.5 million sq m—14.2 million sq km—which is almost twice as big as the Sahara (Ryan, 2023).

419. Some parts of the Atacama desert in Chile have never had any rain over its 40 million-year existence.

420. With a population density of 80 people per 0.5 m—1 km—the Thar desert is home to more people than any other desert on Earth (Wikramanayake, 2023).

421. A new great wall is being created in China, but this time made of plants to encircle the Gobi desert and prevent dangerous sandstorms.

422. Dust storms in the Sahara are powerful enough to carry sand to the United Kingdom and coat cars.

423. Las Vegas is the most populated desert city with a population of 646,790 people who each, on average, use 222 gal—849 l—of water a day (Renner, 2021).

424. Only 20% of the world's deserts are covered by sand; many are made of mountains, ice, or barren rock (Bryan, 2023).

425. The Sahara desert is the largest hot desert on Earth, and it covers a size equal to China at 571,661,496 m—9.2 km (WPS, 2023).

426. It's thought that millions of years ago, the Sahara was underwater, which gives its sand a soft texture and is why fossils of sea life have been found in it.

427. The Carcross Desert in Canada is the smallest in the world at 1 sq m—1.6 sq km—which is the size of the city center of London (Zerkel, 2020).

428. On average, 12.3 million tourists visit the Sahara every year, with most of them coming from Europe (Naji, 2019).

429. There are only 33 deserts in the world, and of these, 19 are hot deserts (Admin, 2021).

430. Deserts are not the result of climate change; however, *desertification*, which refers to "fertile or green land becoming desert," is a result of human activity.

431. The Gobi desert in Mongolia is the site of many dinosaur fossils, and it was where the first dinosaur egg fossils were discovered.

Desert Animals

432. Over 3,000 different species call the deserts home, and many are nocturnal to avoid the hotter temperatures during the day (Daly, 2019).

433. To get something to drink, the Namibian desert beetle can harvest water out of the fog in the air with its wings.

434. Made famous by the Looney Tunes, roadrunners can run 26 mph—42 kph—but they don't make the *meep meep* noise (Birdfact, 2022).

435. Camels don't store water in their humps but instead are able to drink large amounts of water in single trips, and they are adapted for dehydration.

436. The meerkats of Southern Africa's deserts are not as friendly as their little smiles make them seem, and they are easily able to kill snakes that threaten them.

437. To avoid the heat, the Mojave desert tortoise is known to spend 95% of its life hiding in cool rock burrows (Gopherus agassizii, 2023).

438. Kangaroo rats native to the southwestern United States are able to jump up to 9 ft—2.75 m—which is almost as tall as a building (*Kangaroo Rat Fact Sheet*, 2023).

439. Though some species of desert tarantulas can be as big as dinner plates, none of them have a venom that poses a serious threat to humans.

440. Camels don't really spit when they're upset; really, it's more like they're vomiting onto the offending creature to make them go away.

441. Horned lizards, which live in the western United States, are able to shoot a stream of blood from their eyelids to deter predators.

442. Native to North Africa and the Arabian Desert, fennec foxes are the smallest foxes on Earth, and they use their big ears to get rid of body heat.

Desert Plants

443. Some cactus species can go two years without water, but the indoor varieties often need to be watered more, so keep an eye on your prickly friends.

444. Mesquite trees have roots of up to 80 ft—24 m—which is as long as a tennis court, so they can reach all the water nearby (Mackenzie, 2019).

445. Joshua trees from the southwestern American deserts are thought to be named for the biblical figure Joshua because they hold their arms out to pray.

446. *Pereskia cacti* were the first plants 20 million years ago to store water within themselves, which became an important adaptation for all plants (Mackenzie, 2019).

447. Every few years, the Atacama desert erupts in a carpet of purple flowers after the El Nino storms, and in 2022, this event qualified it as a protected national park.

DNA

449. DNA stands for deoxyribonucleic acid, and it's a polymer composed of two polynucleotide chains that coil around each other to form a double helix. It's like an instruction manual you have built into you!

450. Friedrich Meischer was the first person to isolate and see DNA in 1869.

451. The DNA in our bodies would stretch out 10 billion miles, which is from Earth to Pluto and back if it were uncoiled (Ng, 2015).

452. In a single cell, the DNA stretched out would be over 6.5 ft—2 m—long (Desai, 2022).

453. Rosalind Franklin discovered the DNA double-helix in 1953, but due to her sudden death, the three men on the project took credit for her work.

454. All human beings share 99.9% of the same DNA, and that 0.1% is what makes us look different from one another (*10 Amazing DNA Facts*, 2022).

455. About five to eight percent of our DNA is not human; instead, it comes from viruses that have infected us throughout human history (*10 Amazing DNA Facts*, 2022).

456. We share around 60% of our DNA with the common banana (Classes for Curious Minds, 2019).

457. With just a little bit of spit, there are companies all over the world that can identify all of the DNA in your body.

458. DNA forensic evidence can identify a person with just a strand of hair and can be used years after the crime is committed.

459. Because of our DNA's finite ability to be reproduced, human age could only ever get up to a max of 125 years (Petsko, 2019).

460. It takes about eight hours for a cell to completely copy all the DNA within it when the cell divides (Protein Data Bank in Europe, 2021).

461. Over 10 million strands of DNA could fit within a single inch—2.54 cm.

462. As all animals evolve, including us, we lose parts of our DNA that we no longer need.

463. It cost $2.7 billion and took 13 years to map out the human genome (Mullin, 2022).

464. Typing out the human genome at a rate of 60 words per minute for 8 hours every day would take you around 50 years (Helmenstine, 2020).

465. The only cells in your body that do not contain DNA are red blood cells, and mammals are the only animals that have this trait.

466. It is possible for an animal, including humans, to be a chimera, which means having two DNA profiles.

Genes

467. Only 3% of DNA is responsible for our genetics, but scientists are currently discovering what the other 97% does (Press Office, 2001).

468. Chromosomes are the packaging DNA comes in because, without them, DNA would be too big to fit into a cell.

469. There are an estimated 30,000 genes in human DNA, which were mapped as part of the Human Genome Project (National Human Genome Research Institute, 2020a).

470. There are 46 chromosomes in the human body, and in most cases, there are only 2 of them that control your sex at birth (*Chromosome Information*, 2023).

471. Genes were discovered because of the experiments German monk Gregor Mendel did on pea plants in the 1800s.

472. Some people have a genetic mutation that means they only have to sleep around four hours a night to feel completely rested (Pflanzer, 2016).

473. Things such as musical ability or intelligence are not genetic, but aggression likely is.

474. If cilantro tastes like soap to you, it's because of a variation in one of your genes found in a small portion of the population.

475. Only 12% of women have a genetic mutation that gives them super*vision* or the ability to see more colors than most people (Walcott, 2015).

476. Mutations in your genes occur a thousand times a day because of exposure to sunlight or copying errors, but most are harmless.

477. Some people have a genetic mutation that allows them to grow their muscles larger than average, like real-life superheroes!

478. Before genes were discovered, scientists thought you could inherit acquired traits, like if your dad is strong, you'd be strong.

479. The *sports gene*, which is often found in runners, is a mutation that lets you run faster and makes your reactions quicker.

Fishery

481. Between 970 and 2,700 billion wild fish were caught between 2007 and 2016. So, each person on Earth would be given 121 billion to 337 billion fish over 9 years (Igini, 2022a).

482. Fish fossils found in the stomachs of people and dogs show that the first fishermen lived 500,000 years ago.

483. Trawlers catch fish like halibut or lobster using a net with weights on the bottom to grab everything on the sea floor.

484. Per capita, Japanese people consume the most fish on average, with each person eating 14 large fish's worth of meat a year (Asturpesca, 2023).

485. If you want to know where the fish you're eating is from, check the FAO number, which will tell you what zone of the world it was caught in.

486. Tuna is the most common seafood of choice, and it is 85% of all of the finfish caught in the wild (Atuna, 2023).

487. Half of all fish are caught by the top 7 producing countries, with China catching 15% of all fish (Igini, 2022a).

488. Ancient Egypt is thought to be where fishing lines, nets, and spears developed.

489. The seine nets herd fish into the net and are most commonly used to catch fish at the surface or on beaches.

490. At \$3,600 a pound—0.45 kg—bluefin tuna is the most expensive fish on earth, and it's commonly used in luxury sushi (Lyons, 2023).

491. Atlantic bluefin tuna, the fish in your sandwiches, is on the endangered animal list as their population has shrunk by 50% since 1970 (Igni, 2022a).

492. Gillnets are long sheets of netting used in open water and have a higher risk of catching animals like dolphins or turtles who get caught in them.

493. In 2020, the Food and Agriculture Organization estimated that 38.98 million people are employed in fisheries worldwide (Cassidy, 2022).

494. At 472 ft—144 m—the Atlantic Dawn is the biggest fishing vessel on Earth, and it is banned from the waters around Africa because of its danger to the ecosystem (Atlantic Dawn, 2012).

495. The 4.56 million fishing vessels deployed throughout the world catch 50% of all the fish people consume (Cassidy, 2022).

496. *Dredges* are cages that are dragged along the seafloor in the hopes of catching shellfish like clams or scallops.

497. Fish farming only became common 50 years ago, but now it accounts for 50% of the fish we consume a year (Ritchie, 2019).

498. Sannakji is a dish from Korea where an octopus is cut up while alive, so when it is served, the legs and suckers are still moving.

499. If overfishing does not slow down, by 2048, almost all of the edible fish in the ocean will be gone (Igni, 2022a).

500. The pink color in farm-raised salmon, which accounts for 70% of all salmon, is dyed to seem more appetizing (Pomranz, 2017).

Sport Fishing

501. Mac Daddy's Million Dollar Lure is the most expensive lure ever used, valued at a million dollars and covered in gold (Young, 2022). w

502. At 2,664 lbs—1,208 kg—Great White Shark is the largest fish ever caught, and a porpoise was used as bait by the lucky fisherman (*10 Interesting Facts About Fishing*, 2023).

503. Together, sport fishermen spend \$45 billion a year on the assorted gear and permits necessary for fishing (Young, 2022).

504. Fly-fishing, the practice of using a fly or small insect to sit on top of the water as bait, is the most popular type of sport fishing.

505. Some sport fishermen believe it is good luck to kiss their catches before releasing them back into the wild.

506. At 270 casts an hour, Brent Olgers set the record for the most consecutive catches in a 24-hour period at 6,501 (*List of Fishing Facts*, 2023).

507. The oldest book on fishing ever discovered was written by a medieval nun in 1496 called *A Treatyse of Fysshynge Wyth an Angle*.

508. Every year, it is estimated that 30,000–50,000 fish derbies occur around the United States, and they can last up to 10 hours! (Bass Angler, 2022)

509. It's considered bad luck to bring your fishing rod inside with you before going on a fishing trip.

510. Largemouth Bass are the most popular game fish in the United States, and that's where the Bass Pro Shop gets its name (Young, 2022).

511. With 40 million participants, sport fishing is the fourth most popular sport in the United States (Editorial Staff, 2016).

Oceans and Islands

Oceans

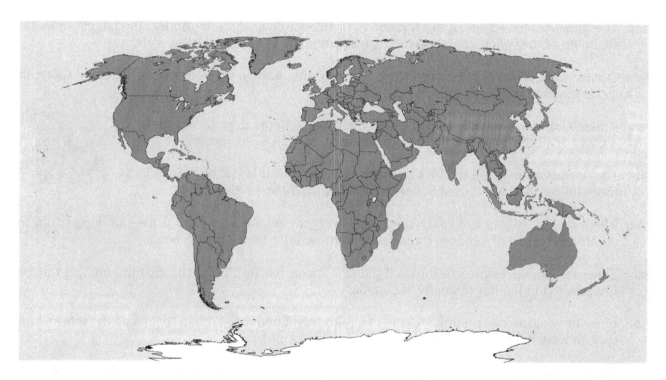

512. Around 96.5% of the world's water is in the Earth's oceans, and they cover 70% of the Earth, making us a water world (Admin, 2017).

513. Tsunamis can move 500 mph—804 kph—through the ocean; that's one wave you want to avoid surfing! (Catrona, 2018)

514. *Pacific Ocean* means *peaceful sea* in Latin, but the largest ocean on Earth is more often known for its tsunamis and extreme storms.

515. Currently, there are 228,450 known species in the ocean, but because the ocean is only 5% explored, there could be millions more (Doyle, 2015).

516. Because of the over three million shipwrecks and other items lost to the sea, it's estimated there are more artifacts on the ocean floor than in all the world's museums combined (Catrona, 2018).

517. The Great Barrier Reef in Australia is the world's largest living structure at 1,615 m—2,600 km— of organisms, which can be seen from space (Admin, 2017).

518. More people have been to the moon than the Marianas Trench, which is the deepest point on Earth at 1,580 m—2,550 km (Catrona, 2018).

519. At the ocean's deepest points, lakes made of water are saltier and denser than the surrounding ocean form, and these lakes even have waves.

520. At its widest point of the stretch between Indonesia and Columbia, the Pacific is five times wider than the moon (Catron, 2018).

521. Antarctic Bottom Water is the coldest water on Earth, but its temperature is no longer constant because it has risen over the past few years due to climate change.

522. The Mid-Oceanic Range in the Atlantic is 10 times longer than the Andes, the largest mountain chain out of the water, at 40,390 m—65,001 km—long (Catrona, 2018).

523. Ocean water looks blue because the water can only absorb the red end of the color spectrum, leaving behind the blues and greens.

524. Though coral reefs only cover 0.1% of the ocean's floor, they are home to a quarter of all the creatures that live in the ocean (Puffin Team, 2023).

525. The Arctic Ocean is the smallest of the five oceans, but it is still one and a half times bigger than the United States (*Where Is the Highest Tide?*, 2019).

526. There are 20 million t of gold, enough for everyone on Earth to have 8 lbs—3.6 kg—within the oceans, but much of it is deep underwater or too small to see (Okafor, 2022).

527. Tides are caused by the gravitational pull the moon has on the Earth, with the highest tides on Earth found in the Bay of Fundy in Canada.

528. Close to 750,000 m—1.2 million km—of cables travel under the ocean to give us the internet and they all were manually installed by divers (Satariano, 2019).

529. Light is only able to be seen through 330 ft—100 m—of water, so this means that most of the oceans, and by extension, Earth, live in total darkness (Okafor, 2022).

530. The sea level is rising 0.1 in.—3.4 mm—a year, which may seem small, but for the communities on the coasts, this amount of water is already destroying homes (Okafor, 2022).

531. Deep sea vents can reach temperatures of 700371°C—which is 7 times higher than the hottest temperature on Earth's surface (Smith, 2023).

Islands

532. Greenland is considered the world's largest island, and it would be Australia, but Australia is considered a continent.

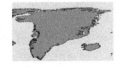

533. With 141.4 million residents, Java, an island in Indonesia, is the most populated in the world with twice the population of Great Britain (*Most Populated Island*, 2023).

534. Just Enough Room Island is the smallest inhabited island in the world and it's just enough room for a single occupied house.

535. Ellis Island in New York was expanded by artificial means using the dirt being excavated to build the New York City subway.

536. In 1972, an American millionaire tried to establish the *Republic of Minerva* near the Tonga islands, but his republic was promptly destroyed by the Tongan people.

537. Like many islands, 80% of the life found in Madagascar is only found there because the islands become evolutionary isolated (Ducksters, 2019).

538. With over 500,000 tourists last year, Bermuda is the most popular island to visit in the Caribbean because of how easy it is to get to from the United States (Morton, 2023).

539. Over its 13,000 volcano-made islands, Indonesia is the most volcanically active place on Earth, with 6 of the world's most active volcanoes (Dobson, 2021).

540. Tristan da Cunha is the most remote island in the world, nearly 2,000 m—3,218 km—from South Africa, and only 10 boats travel there a year (Sowden, 2013).

541. Because of its cold climate and sparse vegetation, Devon Island is the largest uninhabited island on Earth, and NASA uses it to test its Mars rovers.

542. Borneo, the third largest island, is shared by Indonesia, Malaysia, and Brunei because of the borders left behind by the British and Dutch colonists.

Money

History of Money

544. The ancient Chinese first used paper money in the first century, 500 years before it was used in Europe.

545. Parmesan cheese was used in the Middle Ages for currency as well as loan collateral because it is always valued.

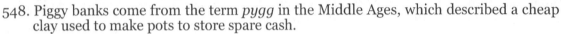

546. First introduced by King Henry VIII in 1489, the pound sterling is the oldest currency on Earth (*10 Fun Facts About Money*, 2022).

547. Cowrie shells, whale teeth, and beans are all things that have been used for currency throughout history. ww

548. Piggy banks come from the term *pygg* in the Middle Ages, which described a cheap clay used to make pots to store spare cash.

Modern Luxury

549. With a net worth of $230.5 billion, Elon Musk is the richest person alive as of 2023 (Forbes, 2023b).

550. If you can't become a CEO, the best-paying job in the world is a general surgeon with a salary of $292,317 a year (Gurmukhani, 2022).

551. With a net worth of 520 million, Mariah Carey spends $100,000 every time she travels to send exotic flowers to herself (Hoffower, 2020).

552. The ancient Romans used coins as propaganda; for example, after Caesar was assassinated, Brutus minted coins proclaiming him the new leader.

553. After World War I, the value of German money was so low that Germans would use bills to wallpaper their houses as it cost less than real materials.

554. Technically, Buckingham Palace is the most expensive house on Earth, valued at $4.9 billion, and you can visit for £16.50—£33 (Darling, 2021).

555. Steve Cohen, a hedge fund billionaire, purchased a 14 ft—4.2 m— preserved tiger shark in 2004; think what kind of house you could buy with that! (Lisa, 2019)

556. The Centurion card created by American Express is a credit card so exclusive that you have to be invited to apply for it.

Economies

557. Luxembourg has the highest GDP per capita of $135,700, which makes its citizens the richest on average (Wisevoter, 2023).

558. The United States has a GDP of 20.89 trillion, which makes it the highest-producing country on Earth (*Top 15 Countries by GDP*, 2022).

559. North Korea produces $45 million worth of counterfeit money every year, making it the largest producer of fake money (Dulin, 2018).

560. Nauru, a small Pacific Island nation, has the lowest GDP on Earth at $133.2 million (Wisevoter, 2023).

561. With 8,000 mt of gold, the United States has the largest reserve of gold, and this is twice the amount of gold Germany has (Statista Research Department, 2023).

562. Peru holds 98,000 mt of silver in its reserves and is third in the world in silver production (Pistilli, 2021).

563. The American Federal Reserve is missing two-thirds of the $100 bills that it has printed.

564. In the United States, it costs ¢2 (two cents) to make ¢1 because of the cost of copper, so the country is debating discontinuing the small coins (*10 Fun Facts About Money*, 2022).

565. In 2008, when Buenos Aires had a shortage of change, shop owners would give customers change with candy.

566. Only 8% of the world's money is cash; the rest of it is made up of electronic transfers, which are based on the holdings of banks (Lovitch, 2022).

567. There are over 1.6 million ATMs on Earth, and they are on every continent; even Antarctica penguins are big spenders! (Dulin, 2018)

568. The Palau islands created silver dollars with a vial of holy water in them to commemorate the 150th anniversary of Mary's apparition in the country.

569. In the United States, the average American has $56 of loose change lying around (Dulin, 2018).

570. The late Queen Elizabeth II is the most common face on international currency, appearing on 100 different coins and banknotes.

571. With a GDP per capita of $308, Burundi in East Africa has the poorest citizens on average in the world (Rao, 2023).

572. It is estimated that the trackable amount of money on earth is $30.7 trillion, but the number could be as high as $70 trillion (*How Much Money*, 2023).

573. While Sir Isaac Newton is most famous for discovering gravity, the pride of his career was catching counterfeiters at the Royal Mint.

Enormous Weather

Hurricanes

574. Hurricane winds can reach speeds close to 200 mph—320 kph—which is only 24 mph—40 kph—less than the fastest roller coaster on earth (Admin NG, 2016).

575. Typhoon Tip is the largest hurricane on record, with a size of 1,379 mi—2,220 km—wide, which is the size of the United States (Admin NG, 2016).

576. So far, 35 Atlantic hurricanes have reached category 5 status in the past 100 years, and 5 of those hurricanes have made landfall in the United States (Lord, 2022).

577. Before 1979, all hurricanes were named for women, but now the World Meteorological Association alternates between male and female names for each storm.

578. The Great Hurricane of 1780 is the deadliest in history, with 22,000 deaths amidst the Revolutionary War (Opfer & Gleim, 2013).

579. Hurricane Katrina was the costliest hurricane in United States history, with damages equalling $161 billion, and some consider it the most destructive (Opfer & Gleim, 2013).

Tornadoes

580. In 1989, the deadliest single tornado ever recorded hit Bangladesh, killing 1,300 people and destroying 20 villages (National Geographic Kids, 2017a).

581. Tornadoes can reach speeds up to 298 mph—480 kph—which makes them the fastest winds on Earth (National Geographic Kids, 2017a).

582. The Tri-State Tornado in 1925 is the largest in history, with a width of almost 1 m and over 174 m—280 km—travelled (Hirschlag, 2023).

583. There are over 200 tornadoes a year from west Texas to North Dakota in a region more commonly known as Tornado Alley.

584. Tornadoes are most common in the United States, and Texas experiences the most with an average of 120 a year, that's multiple storms a day over the tornado season (National Geographic Staff, 2019).

585. The 2011 tornado outbreak was the largest in history, with a total of 350 tornadoes over a single month and $12 billion in property damages (Hirschlag, 2023).

Storms

586. There are 16 million thunderstorms a year on Earth, with 2,000 occurring as you are reading this (Donegan, 2020).

587. Overfarming in 1930s Midwestern America caused Black Sunday, the largest sandstorm in history, and was part of a series of years with heavy sandstorms called the Dust Bowl.

588. An average thunderstorm lasts about 30 minutes and is 15 m—24 km—long, which would take you about 5 hours to walk (Donegan, 2020).

589. The largest hailstone ever recorded was 7.4 in.—18.8 cm—tall and 9.3 in.—23.6 cm—wide, which is the size of your typical dinner plate (Korosec, 2019).

590. Recently, in 2021, Texas experienced the most extreme snowstorm in history, with around 3 and 8 in.—7.6 and 20.3 cm—of snow that shut off power in the state (Grabianowski et al., 2022).

591. Around 25 million lightning strikes occur a year, but these strikes only kill around 26 people a year, so if you stay inside during a storm, you'll be fine (Donegan, 2020).

592. The 2014 thunderstorm in India was the most powerful recorded at 1.3 billion V, which was 10 times more powerful than the previous largest storm (Čirjak, 2020).

Fires

593. The Siberian Taiga Fires in 2003 were the largest wildfires in history, burning 55 million ac of forest and reaching over 4 countries (Igini, 2022b).

594. Humans cause 89% of wildfires, so Smoky the Bear is right when he says that only humans can prevent them (10 Wildfire Facts, 2023).

595. On average, a wildfire can move at 14 mph—22.5 kph—but can move faster depending on the terrain and wind (*10 Wildfire Facts*, 2023).

596. *Black Saturday* in 2009 was the deadliest wildfire in history, killing 173 people in Australia and destroying 2,000 homes (Agence France-Presse, 2023).

597. Wildfires are necessary for the health of forests because they help some trees spread their seeds or get rid of diseases, but these wildfires need to be controlled.

598. There are over 100,000 wildfires in the United States a year, and they burn around 4–5 million ac of land annually (National Geographic, 2022b).

Floods

599. Typically, flood waters are 10 ft—3 m—to 20 ft—6 m—high, but in 1841, the Indus Valley Floods reached a height of 100 ft—30m (Andrews, 2017).

600. Wetlands save the United States 30 $billion in flood damages because they act as natural barriers, but they are one of the most endangered ecosystems (*10 Facts About Flooding*, 2016).

601. Around 54 million people were impacted by floods in 2022, and because of climate change, the population affected by floods will rise 24% over the next few years (Burgueño Salas, 2023).

602. In 1919, molasses rather than water flooded the city of Boston at 35 mph—56 kph—killing 21 people and injuring 150 (Sohn, 2019).

603. Only 6 in.—15 cm—of floodwater is needed to knock you off your feet, and 2 ft—0.6m—is enough to pull a car away (Eden, 2023).

604. Flooding is the most common death from a natural disaster after heat because flash floods can carry disease or destroy houses within minutes.

Amazing Technologies

Phones

606. All iPhones in advertisements display 9:41 a.m. as the time because that is when Steve Jobs announced the first iPhone.

607. For over $5 million, you can buy an iPhone plated with gold and encrusted with diamonds and own the most expensive phone (Shukla, 2023).

608. In 2021, the average person spent 5 hours on their phone, with people worldwide spending 3.8 trillion hours with the glowing box (RingCentral Team, 2022).

609. Almost 90% of Americans own cell phones, and 85% of these are smartphones (Mobile Fact Sheet, 2021).

610. When you use a touchscreen, you're dragging around an electric current around a computer to make selections.

611. Antonio Meucci, not Alexander Graham Bell, was the inventor of the phone, but he was not recognized until 2002.

612. In 2002, an American company tried to market a cell phone for dogs priced at $500, but it did not catch on (Meltzer, 2013).

613. Twice the size of a penny, the Zanco Tiny T2 is the smallest functional cell phone if you're looking to travel light.

Computers

614. Ada Lovelace is considered the inventor of the computer because, in the mid-1800s, she created the concept of the algorithm.

615. The Frontier supercomputer in Oak Ridge National Laboratory is the fastest on Earth and is twice as fast as the Japanese supercomputer in second place (These Are the Top 5 Fastest, 2023).

616. Sometimes, we shout at our computers when we're frustrated, but shouting and sound vibrations can slow your computer down.

617. Though now defunct, the most expensive computer ever built was the Semi-Automatic Ground Environment System (SAGE) at $8 billion (Lyons, 2022).

618. If the human brain were a computer, it would be the most powerful on Earth, with 3580 TB of memory (Editorial Staff, 2021).

619. Modern computers are 100,000 times more powerful than the computer that sent humanity to the Moon (Anderson, 2023).

620. Nowadays, a 1-GB hard drive weighs less than 1 g, but the first one gig hard drive weighed the same as a refrigerator (Victoria, 2022).

Internet, Tech Industry

621. In 2023, the internet hit 5.3 billion users, which is a 60% increase from usage in the 1990s (*5 Facts About the Internet*, 2023).

622. Surprisingly, 90% of the internet and its data have been created between 2016 and 2018 (Marr, 2018).

623. Google receives 1.2 trillion search requests a year, which works out to 40,000 Google searches every second (Victoria, 2022).

624. With 3.03 million users, Facebook is the most popular social media site, and it has held this title for multiple years (Lua, 2023).

625. To do a basic Google search, 1,000 computers in Google headquarters create results in 0.2 seconds (Victoria, 2022).

626. CAPTCHA, or the robot test, stands for *Completely Automated Public Turing Test to Tell Computer and Humans Apart.*

627. Almost 92% of internet users use a social media site daily, with TikTok being the fastest-growing site in 2023 (*5 Facts About the Internet*, 2023).

628. In 2021, 500 hours of video were uploaded to YouTube every minute (Minaev, 2021).

629. The United States tech industry makes over $1.8 trillion a year (Beckman, 2023).

630. Many tech companies test their products in New Zealand because it is more isolated, so news of failure cannot spread as quickly.

631. Dyson, the company that makes vacuums, has introduced noise-cancelling headphones that also filter the air around you.

632. In 2023, the company AromaJoin introduced the Aroma Player, which allows you to smell the things you see on screen (Ehrhardt et al., 2023).

633. It took the radio 38 years to reach 50 million people, but the iPod took only 3 years to reach the same milestone (Gabriel, 2019).

634. Nose Metal has introduced a pillow that can adjust itself as you sleep to get you the best rest possible.

635. Like something out of a spy film, the Lumus AR Lenses will give you access to the internet in your glasses.

636. Are you ever home alone with no toilet paper in arm's reach? Charmin invented a robot that brings toilet paper to you in 2020.

Amazing Places

North America

638. With 39.6 million visitors annually, the Las Vegas Strip is the most popular tourist attraction, with its 30 casinos and indoor amusement parks (Hammel, 2023).

639. Having opened in 1904, the New York City subway is the oldest in the world, and with 424 stations, it's also the largest underground rail (*51 Fun & Interesting*, 2023).

640. There's a time capsule that was buried underneath the Hollywood Walk of Fame in 1990, which has a Barbie, Michael Jackson's gloves, and a MASH script to be opened in 2060.

South America

641. Though Machu Picchu sits 7,000 ft—2,133 m—up into the Andes Mountains in Peru, it's thought that no wheels were used to transport the 50 lbs—22.6 kg—stones that make up the city (Murphy, 2010).

642. During the rainy season, the salt flats of Bolivia become a large mirror, and walking on it feels like you're walking through the sky.

643. In Colombia, you can find the Valle de Cocora, which has the largest palm trees on Earth at close to 200 ft—61 m—which is as tall as 11 giraffes (Morton, 2019).

Europe

644. Venice is known for its unique canals, but because of climate change, it is sinking at a rate of 0.07 in.—2 mm—a year, and eventually, we won't be able to visit it anymore (Royal Museums Greenwich, 2023).

645. The different sides of the Matterhorn perfectly face different cardinal directions—south and west toward Italy and north and east to Switzerland.

646. There is a legend that after St. Basil's Cathedral was completed in Moscow, Russia, Ivan the Terrible had the architect blinded so he could never create anything like it again.

647. The dome that sits on top of the cathedral in Florence, Italy, is the largest in the world, and it alone took 16 years to build (Asia London Palomba, 2023).

648. For most of Mont St. Michel's history, the tiny monastery town was only accessible during low tide, and this allowed it to never be invaded.

649. The Eiffel Tower in Paris was originally built in 1889 just to be a gateway into the World's Fair, but its popularity with tourists made it a French landmark.

650. Founded in 1827, the London Zoo is the oldest public zoo on earth; before it opened, zoos were only for the wealthy or scientists.

651. The Tower of Pisa was never straight; almost immediately after its construction, the tower began to sink into the marshy ground.

652. The entire Greek island of Santorini is volcanic rock, so the beaches are made of volcanic ash and basalt stone, which color the sand black.

Asia

653. To preserve the beauty of the Forbidden City in Beijing, China, ancient architects built the roofs to be too sloped and slippery for birds to be able to land on them.

654. The pink palace of sandstone Hawa Mahal in India has 953 windows that ensure the wind always flows through the palace and allow women to see out into the city (Akshatha, 2018).

655. India's most famous tomb, the Taj Mahal, would cost $115 million to build in modern money, and it took 17 years to build (Kiddle, 2023).

656. It's a myth that you can see the Great Wall of China from space, but at 1,500–5,000 miles—2,414–8,046 km—long, it's rightly a wonder of the world (Mason, 2019).

657. If you visit the Grand Palace in Thailand, you have to make sure your shoulders and knees are covered and that you're wearing white or black to honor the late king.

658. Women weren't allowed to climb Mount Fuji until 1872 because it was believed their beauty would make the jealous goddess inside it cause a volcanic eruption.

659. Hong Kong has the highest number of skyscrapers in the world, at 8,000, which is twice as many as New York City (Kaur, 2023).

660. Kyoto is home to 3,000 different temples and shrines for the Shinto faith, and the city is known for being the spiritual heart of Japan (Enjoy Travel, 2023).

Middle East

661. Petra in Jordan is thought to be one of the oldest cities in the world, with a record of its founding going back to 321 B.C.E, but only 15% has been able to be explored (Zutshi, 2023).

662. The Gate of Hell in Turkmenistan is a pit that has been on fire since a Soviet oil rig fell into it 50 years ago and has resisted all efforts to be extinguished.

663. At 2,716 ft—827 m—the Burj Khalifa in Dubai is the tallest building in the world and is almost 3 times taller than the Empire State Building (McCarthy & Hood, 2022).

Australia and the Pacific

664. Over one million glass tiles cover the Sydney Opera House, which is big enough to house seven planes (*Interesting Facts About Sydney*, 2023).

665. Vaadhoo Island in the Maldives has a sea of stars caused by the glowing plankton that lives off its coasts.

666. Shark Bay in Australia has the highest amount of stromatolite fossils in the world, and the salt that comes from its saline pools is the purest money can buy.

The Arctic

667. Of the half a million visitors who go to Iceland every year, 80% visit the Blue Lagoon to enjoy the bathwater-like hot springs with healing properties (*Facts About the Blue Lagoon*, 2015).

668. Around 1,000 t of ice are used to build the annual Ice Hotel in Sweden, which is enough ice to make 700 million snowballs (*Icehotel Facts*, 2019).

Our Brilliant Bodies

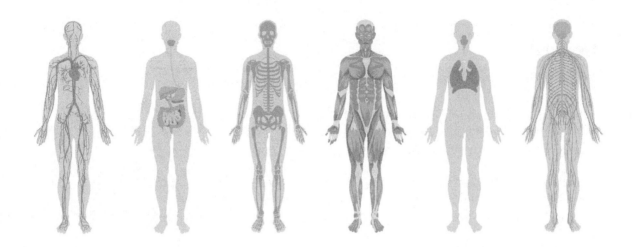

669. The amount of blood cells in your body could go around the Earth four times (National Geographic, 2016b).

670. In an average lifespan, hearts beat around 3 billion times (National Geographic, 2016b).

671. There are 21 different species of humans, and archaeologists are discovering new ones (Vinopal, 2023).

672. It's too dull for human eyes to detect, but human beings glow in the dark.

673. Our eyes stop growing past three months, which is why babies' eyes seem so big on their tiny heads (Tappity, 2023).

674. No other species on earth blushes like humans can so enjoy your rosy cheeks!

675. Eight percent of the average person's body weight is their blood (National Geographic, 2016b).

676. You're not able to swallow and breathe at the same time, which is why you sometimes choke on water when you drink too fast.

677. When you wake up in the morning, you are about 0.03 in.—1 cm—taller because, at night, the cartilage between your bones has stretched out (Dr. Chris and Dr. Xand, 2023).

678. Your stomach acid is strong enough to dissolve metal, but you shouldn't be testing that.

679. We produce enough spit in our lives to fill 5 bathtubs; that's 40,000 l! (Dr. Chris and Dr. Xand, 2023)

680. Hearts are the strongest muscles in the body because they pump up to 2,500 gal of blood a day (NectarSleep Editorial Team, 2019).

681. Our appendixes aren't useless; they house necessary bacteria essential for digestion.

682. Blood isn't red because of the iron in it but because of how much air that particular blood cell is holding.

683. The water in our bodies is 1 part salt to 100 parts water, which is 1/3 of the saltiness of the sea (Tappity, 2023).

684. There are 206 bones in the human body, and 27 of them are in the human hand alone (Bones, 2012).

685. The human jaw has a bite force of around 200 lbs—90.7 kg—which is around that of a snapping turtle (Vinopal, 2023).

686. Women blink 19 times a minute, while men only blink 11 times a minute (Vinopal, 2023).

687. Humans have the same amount of hair on them as chimpanzees, but much of our hair is too thin to be noticed.

688. Yawning is thought to be the brain's way of cooling itself down.

689. Because atoms are never able to be permanently destroyed, all of the atoms inside you are recycled from the universe.

690. Green eyes are only found in two percent of people, so if you have them, count yourself unique!

691. Skin is the body's largest organ, and it makes up 15% of your body weight (Fish, 2021).

692. On average, your nose can produce up to a cup of mucus a day.

693. There are between 2–5 million sweat glands on the body, but they are collected on your brow, feet, and armpits (Osborne, 2021).

694. You tend to favor one nostril even if you're not trying—one nostril tends to be breathing in 75% of your total air (Tappity, 2023).

695. Itching is our bodies' way of protecting us from things like parasites, insects, and diseases they could spread.

696. Pinky fingers, though small, make up for 50% of our hand's grip strength and are mighty (Ng, 2015)!

697. We know all fingerprints are unique, but your tongue also has a print special to you.

698. Between 2,100 and 2,400 gal of air are breathed in by your lungs every day, which is enough to fill 700–800 balloons (National Geographic, 2017b).

699. Fingertips wrinkle in water as the outer layer of skin absorbs water, which then helps you to grip things underwater.

Ships

History of Ships

701. In 1900, when the Prinzessin Victoria Luise set off from Hamburg, it was the first cruise ship to set sail.

702. The ships Columbus arrived in the Americas in, the Pinta and the Nina, only had crews of 30 and were as big as an average bus.

703. Ships were so important to the Vikings that they were cremated in their boats in elaborate ceremonies.

704. The word *quarantine* comes from the Italian word for *forty* because ships had to wait forty days in port if they were infected by the plague.

705. Sails were invented by the Ancient Egyptians for their cargo ships that moved supplies down the Nile.

706. *Feeling blue* is an expression that comes from sailing and is used to refer to the blue flags sailors would raise when their captains died.

707. The Pesse canoe, which is housed in a museum in the Netherlands, is the oldest ship that has been found, dating back to 8040 B.C.E.

708. In 1620, the famous Mayflower journey took 66 days, which was the average journey across the Atlantic (*Mayflower*, 2023).

709. Ferdinand Magellan is thought to be the first person to circumnavigate the globe, but it was actually his crew as Magellan was killed along the way.

710. In 1975, the Edmund Fitzgerald, a cargo ship, became the largest shipwreck in history, with all of its 29 crew members lost (MI News Network, 2022).

711. Steamships were invented in 1794, and by the mid-1800s, they were able to cross the Atlantic in 15 days.

712. Ancient Polynesians crossed thousands of miles of open water in only canoes to find their societies, which led to their reputation as the best sailors.

713. The Japanese Navy had the largest submarine on record, and it was a submerged aircraft carrier able to carry up to 3 folded planes.

Modern Ships

714. At 1,504 ft—458.45 m—the supertanker, the Seawise Giant, is the largest ship ever built, its length equal to the Empire State Building (McFadden, 2020).

715. Laura Dekker became the youngest person to sail around the world at the age of 16 during a journey that took 518 days (*15 Facts About Boats*, 2023).

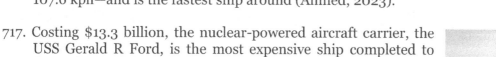

716. Faster than a metro train, the Francisco is a catamaran able to go 66 mph—107.6 kph—and is the fastest ship around (Ahmed, 2023).

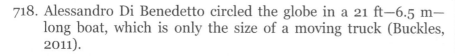

717. Costing $13.3 billion, the nuclear-powered aircraft carrier, the USS Gerald R Ford, is the most expensive ship completed to date (Tiwari, 2022).

718. Alessandro Di Benedetto circled the globe in a 21 ft—6.5 m—long boat, which is only the size of a moving truck (Buckles, 2011).

719. The 6-masted schooner "The Wyoming" is the largest wooden ship ever built at 450 ft—140m—long, which is the size of 10 fishing boats (Ahmed, 2023).

720. Ships have a lifetime of 20–30 years, while sailboats have around 30–40 years before they break apart (Boater's Insurance, 2021).

721. Eight ships have gotten stuck in the Suez Canal over its century-and-a-half-long history, with the most recent being the Ever Given in 2021.

722. Owned by Malaysia's richest man, the History Supreme is the most expensive yacht on Earth, costing $4.8 billion with a Tyrannosaurus Rex skeleton on board (Nast, 2022).

723. With over 150 different ghosts, the Queen Mary, permanently docked in Long Beach, California, is thought to be the most haunted ship you can visit (Mambra, 2018).

724. Around 50,000 merchant ships are crossing the ocean at any given moment, and most of the things you use, like your clothes or food, come by ship (Baraniuk, 2016).

725. The Dover Strait in the English Channel is the busiest shipping lane on Earth, with over 500 ships passing through the strait daily (Seaway, 2022).

Cruise Ships

726. Royal Caribbean's Oasis-class ships are the biggest passenger ships at 1,181 ft—360 m—long and have amenities like waterparks and theatres on board (World's Largest Cruise, 2023).

727. Every week, the larger cruise ships go through 20,000 ice cream cones and the average tourist on the ship gains a pound—0.45 kg—a day (*37 Interesting Cruise*, 2021).

728. Because of superstition, many cruise ships do not have a deck 13, and Italian cruise ships don't have a deck 17 for the same reason.

729. At $70,539 per person, a cruise on the Seven Seas Splendour from Spain to France is the most expensive ticket around (Pellegrino, 2022).

730. Now, swimming pools are regular sights on cruise ships, but in 1912, the Titanic became the first ship to have a swimming pool.

731. Cruise ships dump around 1 billion gal of sewage into the ocean a year, making them one of the world's biggest polluters.

732. In 2019, 20.4 million people went on cruises, with Royal Caribbean being the most popular cruise line (Statista Research Department, 2019)

Farming

733. Over 2/3 of all freshwater on Earth is used for agriculture, with a single cow using 44 gal—170 l— a day (Envirotech, 2021).

734. The world's largest farm, Mudanjiang City Mega Farm in China, covers 22.5 million ac and is about the size of Portugal (Gonzalez, 2023).

735. Pigs are thought to have an intelligence level equal to that of a three-year-old child.

736. Cows have a memory of three years, and they are capable of making friends, which is why they get sad when separated from the herd.

737. Organic farming is two and a half times more labor-intensive than conventional farming, but it is also ten times more profitable.

738. Almost 38% of the Earth's surface is used for farming, with 1/3 of that being used for cropland and the other 2/3 for grazing pastures (*Land Use in Agriculture*, 2020).

739. Wheat is the most common crop on Earth, followed by rice, corn, and bananas.

740. About 30% of the food grown in the United States is never sold because it is *ugly*, even though it is fine to eat (Farmhands, 2020).

741. There are more than 6,000 different kinds of apples grown around the world, with China and the United States leading production (Sharma, 2021).

742. The world's best employees, bees, contribute $15 billion worth of crops to the global economy every year through pollination (Bhutto, 2020).

743. An extraordinary corn crop in the 1970s is what led American President Richard Nixon to approve corn syrup and why it's in everything you eat in the United States.

744. Chickens can remember up to 100 different faces.

745. There are over 1 billion cattle on Earth, with cows outnumbering people in Uruguay 3 to 1 (Van Niekerk, 2023).

746. The average American farmer produces enough food for 165 people, which is around 3 times as much as they produced in 1970 (Sharma, 2021).

747. Contrary to the belief of seven percent of American adults, brown cows do not produce chocolate milk (Bentoli, 2017).

748. Sheep only produce 7–10 lbs—3.17–4.5 kg—of wool a year, which is just enough to make one sweater (2017).

749. Almost 1/4 of the world's population works in agriculture, which is down 44% from 1991 due to new technology (Farmhands, 2020).

750. Feeding 22% of the global population, China has more farmland than any other country, and 23% of all rice comes from China (*Top 10 Agricultural*, 2020).

751. By 2050, farmers will need to be producing 70% more food to be able to feed the growing population (Sharma, 2021).

752. It's a myth that GMOs, or genetically modified organisms, are bad for you—most of the crops we eat are GMOs because their wild varieties are not suitable to eat.

753. The word *farm* comes from the old French term *to rent or lease*, as early medieval farmers could not own their lands.

Farming History

754. When agriculture began over 11,400 years ago, it's thought the first thing ever grown was the seedless fig in Jericho (Shaw, 2007).

755. The world's first farms were in Ancient Mesopotamia, or modern-day Iraq, where river water made the earth very fertile.

756. Using selective breeding, ancient Mesoamerican farmers took 0.74 in.—19 mm—ears of ancient inedible corn and made it into the 7.4 in.—190 mm—corn on the cob we love today (Plumer, 2014b).

757. Irrigation was first used in 6000 B.C.E in Ancient Egypt and Mesopotamia and is considered the most important development in farming history.

758. Without human domestication 7,000 years ago, bananas would be green tough fruits mainly made of seeds.

Farming Technology

759. Developed in Israel, an apple-picking robot is able to mimic the gentleness of human harvesting, and it picks apples 10 times faster than the average person.

760. Cow milking robots are able to milk 60–90 units of cows a day compared to the human's 22 units of cow milking a day (*Robotic Milking*, 2023).

761. In San Carlos, California, the world's first automated farm uses robots to monitor crop growth as well as harvest the plants.

762. A tractor the same weight as the space shuttle, the *Big Bud*, was discontinued in 1977 because the company producing its 8 ft—2.4 m—tires went out of business (Nichols, 2023).

763. The *Vegebot* created by Cambridge scientists is able to give a thumbs up or down to determine the quality of lettuce.

Poisons in Nature

765. Poisonous things make you sick when you eat them, while venomous things will hurt you if they bite you.

766. You can normally tell an animal is poisonous because it is brightly colored, which is nature's *Not a snack!* sign.

Poisonous Plants

767. Over 100,000 exposures to poisonous plants are reported every year in the United States, and luckily, most of these are nonfatal (Froberg et al., 2007).

768. Belladonna, or deadly nightshade, is the world's most poisonous plant, and only 10 berries are enough to kill an adult.

769. Lily of the Valley is a plant that symbolizes love and even has been used in Kate Middleton's bouquet, but if the seeds are ingested, it can be fatal.

770. Hemlock water-dropwort causes facial muscles to spasm when eaten, leaving a creepy smile on the victim's face.

771. Rosary peas are used in jewelry because it's thought the poisons in them will kill the bad spirits that try to attack you.

772. Using a cosmetic made of belladonna, lead, and arsenic, Giuanemialia Tofana was able to poison 600 men over 20 years in 17th-century Rome (Toomer, 2020).

773. One of the most common poisonous plants is the stinging nettle, but when cooked, the leaves can be made into a salad.

774. Castor oil is used in many home remedies, but the seeds of the plant can be toxic, especially to children.

775. Overconsumption of yellow dock can cause severe nausea, but it is also used to treat anemia.

776. The poisons in the Pacific Yew Tree have been used to treat cancer by using the same toxins that make people sick to kill cancer cells.

777. Nightshade may be poisonous, but it has been used since the Middle Ages to dilate eyes, both for cosmetic and medical reasons.

778. If you come into contact with poison ivy, you can use rubbing alcohol to remove the poison from your skin.

779. Rather than renounce his beliefs, Socrates famously poisoned himself with a drink made of hemlock.

780. Foxglove is a purple-belled plant that is used in heart medicine, but if you take too much, it would likely cause a heart attack.

781. The famous red-capped mushrooms of storybooks are not so fantastical as they can cause comas and seizures.

782. Death cap mushrooms cause the most deaths a year because they resemble common edible mushroom varieties and taste nice.

Dangerous Foods and Poisonous Animals

783. Pufferfish, when improperly cooked, is 1,200 times more deadly than cyanide, which makes it the most poisonous animal on earth (*The Most Poisonous Animals*, 2023).

784. From Southeast Asia and Australia, the *Cerbera odollam* is a fruit responsible for a death a week in Kerala, India (Williams, 2022).

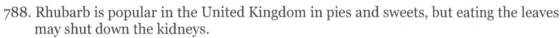

785. A popular item in Japanese sushi, sea urchin, should be carefully consumed as some species when eaten will cause extreme sickness.

786. *Jamaican vomiting sickness* is caused by ingesting the ackee fruit, and it was known to kill 50 people in 2001 (Kantor, 2020).

787. Cashews must be cooked before they can be eaten because they have a poison in them that can cause intense stomach pain.

788. Rhubarb is popular in the United Kingdom in pies and sweets, but eating the leaves may shut down the kidneys.

789. Cyanide is found in apple seeds, but most dangerously almonds, as 50 bitter almonds have enough cyanide in them to be fatal (Chaouali et al., 2013).

790. Poisonous dart frogs have enough toxin in their skin to kill 10 grown men, and it's thought they get their poison from the insects they eat (National Geographic Kids, 2014b).

791. Greenland sharks have a type of antifreeze in their blood so they can survive in the Arctic and this antifreeze makes them deadly to eat.

792. Five birds are known to be poisonous, but the hooded pitohui was the first discovered as it tasted odd and made peoples' hands numb to handle it (Hoare, 2022).

793. If you're ever at a dinner party and they serve polar bear, know that eating the liver has enough vitamin A in it to kill 52 adults.

794. Monarch butterflies have developed poisons to protect themselves from predators, and pink lady butterflies mock their colors to benefit from this as well.

Stupendous Science

Chemistry

795. Each time you crack a glow stick, you're setting off a chemical reaction where dye mixes with a phosphorescent molecule.

796. Around 70% of all matter in the universe is made of hydrogen, and when helium is added, this number rises to 99% (Siegel, 2020).

797. Because ice is the less dense form of water, 1 in.—2.54 cm—of rain is the same amount of water as 10 in.—25.4 cm—of snow (Puiu, 2016).

798. Since the 1950s, around 20 man-made atoms have been synthesized, but most of them do not last more than a few seconds.

799. Helium changes your voice because sound travels two to three times faster through the lighter element than oxygen (*100 Fun Chemistry Facts*, 2019).

800. Francium is the most expensive naturally occurring element at a few billion for 100 g because it decays so quickly (Helmenstine, 2019).

801. Though we need to breathe oxygen, 78% of Earth's atmosphere is made from nitrogen (Atmosphere, 2023).

802. Dmitry Mendeleev did not set out to create the period table; instead, he was hoping to make a cheat sheet for an exam.

803. Tri-cyclic acetone peroxide is the most unstable chemical substance, as it only takes being brushed up against it for it to explode.

804. Glass is a substance in between phases of matter because it flows at an imperceivably slow pace, making it an amorphous solid.

805. Mercury and bromine are the only elements that are liquid at room temperature, but they are very toxic, so just appreciate them from afar.

806. Plutonium is considered the world's most dangerous natural element because not only is it used in nuclear bombs, but it is also the most radioactive. In addition, it is carcinogenic.

807. Metals were the first elements discovered as ancient humans were able to isolate them and mix them to create stronger bonds called alloys.

Physics

808. Light is the fastest thing in the universe, with a speed of 983,571,056 ft—299,792,458 m—per second (5 Interesting Facts About Physics, 2023).

809. If the nucleus of an atom was a basketball, the closest electrons would be golf balls 2 miles—3.21 km—away (Fenker, 2023).

810. Weight is the measurement of how strong the force of gravity is on you, and your mass is how much matter you contain.

811. All of the visible matter in the universe only makes up two percent of its mass, so most of the universe is occupied by *dark matter* (Chivers, 2010).

812. In summer, the Eiffel Tower is 5.9 in.—15 cm—taller because the metal expands in heat (Fifty Physics, 2020).

813. According to Einstein's theory of relativity, everything moves slower than light, so if you were able to move faster than light, you could be faster than time.

Amazing Inventions and Discoveries

814. The first telegraph message ever sent was in 1844, and Samuel Morse, its creator, wrote: *What hath God wrought!*

815. Percy Spencer accidentally invented the microwave while doing experiments on radar and realizing his chocolate bar had melted.

816. Around 600 years before the European printing press, the ancient Chinese were printing religious texts, schoolbooks, and etiquette guides with the printing press.

817. Marie Curie was the first woman to win the Nobel Prize for her work with radioactivity, but this ground-breaking research took her life in 1934.

818. Thomas Edison electrocuted an elephant with an AC electrical current to make it seem dangerous in an effort to promote DC currents.

819. In 1878, the first moving picture ever made was an 11-frame clip of a horse running.

820. Escalators were originally designed as a ride for Coney Island in 1895, and that may be why it's sometimes fun just to go up and down them.

821. Édouard-Léon Scott recorded the first sound, a shaky version of "Au Clair de la Lune" in 1857, but he was trying to gather a written transcript of the song.

822. Millennia before Benjamin Franklin's shocking experiment, Thales of Miletus was the first person to notice the effects of magnetism and static electricity.

823. In 1925, the first television broadcasts were of King George VI's coronation.

824. Alfred Nobel put all his money into the Nobel Prize after an accident involving his invention, dynamite, killed his brother.

825. Nuclear fission was first discovered in 1938, and while it brought us renewable nuclear energy, it also brought the atomic bomb.

Medicine and Disease

History of Disease

826. A doctor in Ohio in the 1830s claimed that ketchup had medicinal value, and it was sold as a pill.

827. In the 19th century, milk was used as a substitute for blood in transfusions.

828. Until the 19th century, Europeans would eat Egyptian mummies to cure common ailments like headaches.

829. The Black Death killed a third of Medieval Europe's population, and in today's numbers, that same third is 24 million people (History.com Editors, 2010b).

830. Pliny the Elder recommended powdered female pig poop for pregnant women in Ancient Rome.

831. In the early 1900s, people believed radiation was good for you, so they would wear radioactive pendants and use antiaging radioactive cosmetics.

832. In 1518, a dancing plague spread around a small French town where people danced until death, and it claimed 400 lives (Andrews, 2018b).

833. Until the 1800s, people did not wash their hands in hospitals, and it was even thought washing your hands was bad for you.

834. Cigarettes used to be prescribed as a medicine for asthma in the 1800s by companies like Kellogg's.

835. Mercury, a very dangerous and toxic chemical, was once thought to be the secret of immortality.

836. People in ancient Egypt used moldy bread to heal cuts, which actually worked because of fungus' ability to kill bacteria.

837. Before people knew arsenic was a poison, it was used to treat malaria and diabetes and was used for makeup.

838. People used to believe that cancer was a hungry animal in the body, so they would press dead small animals on the afflicted person to appease the cancer.

839. Before germ theory, the common belief was that a *miasma* came up through the ground from cemeteries and made people sick.

840. The cesarean section, or C-section, was named after Julius Caesar because he is rumored to be the first person born through the procedure.

841. In Ancient Mesopotamia, diseases were diagnosed not on people but on the body parts of their sacrificed animals.

842. Penicillin was invented by accident in 1928 when Dr. Alexander Fleming went off on vacation and came back to find that mold in his petri dish stopped bacteria from growing.

843. Ancient people used to drill holes in their heads to relieve headaches and migraines.

844. Louis Pasteur proved germs existed by showing how food went rotten because of bacteria.

845. Rats were actually not the carriers of the Black Death; it was the fleas that attached themselves to the rats.

846. Glasses were thought to have been invented between 1268 and 1300, and the first pair were magnifying glasses attached by a hinge (*When Were Eyeglasses Invented*, 2022).

847. Vaccines were discovered in 1796 when scientists realized girls who had been infected with less dangerous cowpox did not get smallpox.

848. Some believe the hysteria of the Salem Witch Trials was caused by a fungal infection spread by grain that had gone off.

Modern Disease

849. After 3,000 years of being the deadliest disease on Earth, in 1980, smallpox became the first disease to be completely eradicated.

850. Leeches are still used in modern medicine, specifically after plastic surgery procedures.

851. Currently, heart disease is the leading cause of death in the world, killing 17.9 million people a year (*The Top 10 Causes*, 2020).

852. Almost 400,000 people die from the common flu every year, and the swine flu in 2009 was the last influenza epidemic (Dattani & Spooner, 2022).

853. In 2009, Coke was sued by the Center for Disease Control for pretending Vitamin Water is healthy—in fact, it's just 33 g of sugar water.

854. The first successful heart transplant was performed in 1967 in South Africa by Christiaan Barnard.

855. When insulin was discovered in 1923, the patent was sold for $1 so that everyone would be able to afford it.

856. A deficiency in Ribose-5-Phosphate Isomerase (RPI) is the rarest disease on Earth, but the last time it was diagnosed was in 1984 (*Top 10 Rare Diseases*, 2023).

Treasures

Historical Treasures

857. In 1848, the California Gold Rush began after gold was found near San Francisco, and throughout the rush, over $2 billion of gold were found in the region (History.com Editors, 2010a).

858. Ancient Egypt's most famous treasure, the tomb of King Tut, held roughly $3 million worth of gold (*Inside King Tut's*, 2023).

859. The search for the Holy Grail is one of the longest ongoing treasure hunts, having begun in Medieval England, though no such artifact has ever been found.

860. El Dorado, the city of gold, was the most famous treasure hunt of the 17th century, and though no single city was ever found, the Spaniards were able to send over 100 t of gold to Europe for the monarchy.

861. The Ark of the Covenant is supposedly in Ethiopia; however, it lies in a room where only the guardian of the ark is allowed to see it, and it has never been studied properly.

862. An ancient wonder of the world, the massive ivory and gold-plated statue of Athena was thought to have been stolen by the Romans, but it was never found.

863. The Titanic is the most valuable shipwreck treasure, with over $300 million worth of lost diamonds and items that fetch millions at auctions (*5 Most Interesting Shipwreck*, 2023).

864. Tomb raiding has been a common problem in Egypt, first with the British, who stole most of Egypt's artifacts in the 1800s, and then in the modern era as trinkets are sold online.

865. In 1907, the Crown Jewels were stolen from Ireland, and though there were many suspects, the thieves nor the jewels have ever been found.

866. Though Atlantis is a myth, the sunken city of Heracleion off the coast of Egypt is a unique treasure with thousands of coins and jewels as well as insight into ancient life.

867. The Amber Room, with its walls covered in jewels, was the pride of the Romanov family, but in World War II, it was supposedly stolen by the Nazis and has never been seen again.

Modern Treasure Hunts

868. Forrest Fenn's treasure of $1–$3 billion has yet to be found, even though Fenn himself created a series of clues to help the public find it (History Channel, 2023).

869. In the aftermath of the Russian Revolution, 8 of the 52 Russian Faberge Eggs have gone missing, with the most recent one found in 2007 (History Channel, 2023).

870. Though not a shiny treasure, the Dead Sea Scrolls are one of the most valuable because they contain the history of the Bible, and many are thought still undiscovered.

871. A 150-year-old mystery, the Beale Ciphers are a series of 3 clues that would lead a person to a treasure in the Virginia hills.

872. If found, the Lemminkainen Hoard in Finland will be the most valuable buried treasure ever found at over $20 billion (The Sun, 2021).

873. At the end of World War II, the Nazis were rumored to have hidden their stolen gold in Lake Tolpitz in Austria, but nothing has ever been found.

874. Blackbeard's treasure is one of the last pirate treasures to remain undiscovered as the ship was found, but the hoard was not.

All that Glitters

875. At $200–250 million, the Hope Diamond is the single most expensive piece of jewelry that was originally made by King Louis XIV in 1668 (*Top Ten Most Expensive*, 2023).

876. Like the Disney movie, a real treasure planet exists that is entirely made of diamond, but it's millions of light years away from Earth.

877. The Star of Asia is a 330-carat sapphire that is famous for the perfect star, which naturally blooms from the stone.

878. At a value of £3–5 billion, the British Crown Jewels are the most valuable royal jewels on earth, and you can see them in the Tower of London (Finnis, 2023).

879. With $62 billion, the most valuable fictional treasure trove is that of the dragon Smaug from *The Hobbit* (Acuna, 2012).

880. Tiffany's most famous piece, the Tiffany Yellow Diamond, has only been worn by two women in history, one being Audrey Hepburn in *Breakfast at Tiffany's*.

881. Sapphires are thought to be the favorite jewel of the British Royal Family as they've been worn by everyone from Queen Victoria to Princess Diana and symbolize royalty.

882. La Peregrina pearl is the most symmetrical pearl in the world, and it was most famously worn by Elizabeth Taylor, who was gifted it by her husband.

883. The Koh-i-Noor diamond was presented to Queen Victoria as a symbol of her conquest of India, but it had historically adorned the royalty of Southeast Asia.

Cursed Treasures

884. The area around the Lost Dutchman mine is said to be cursed, as many who have gone looking for the wealth of gold have gone missing.

885. The Black Orlov Diamond is famous not only for being beautiful but also for the curse it seems to have on it, as three of its owners have died while owning it.

886. Though the most expensive jewel, the Hope Diamond is also thought to be cursed as misfortune follows it, but maybe bad luck just follows the rich (Woodward, 2023).

887. The cursed Aztec gold from *Pirates of the Caribbean* has its roots in the wealth stolen from Montezuma because it only brought death and misfortune to the Spaniards.

The Wonderful, Peculiar History

Ancient Egypt

888. Mummy bandages would stretch out 0.9 m—1.6 kg—if they were rolled out, which would take you about 20 minutes to walk (Kuroski, 2017b).

889. Some Egyptologists believe that King Tut was killed by a hippopotamus bite because he was buried with a caved-in chest.

890. Archaeologists have found toilets in some Egyptian tombs; maybe they needed a poop before heading to the afterlife.

891. Rather than soft feathers, the Egyptians used slaps of stone with an indentation in them to sleep on.

892. Slaves would be covered with honey to attract flies for their wealthy masters.

893. Ancient Egyptians were able to figure out the world was round using the shadows of their obelisks.

894. Toothpaste was invented in Ancient Egypt and was made of salt, pepper, and iris flowers.

Ancient Greece and Rome

895. The Greeks believed red-headed people were secretly vampires due to their sensitivity to sunlight and paler-than-average skin.

896. For the Greeks, a unibrow was a symbol of intelligence and beauty.

897. Professional mourners were women who followed after funeral parties wailing, and the more of them there were, the more powerful a person was.

898. Some Greeks would not eat fava beans because they believed that they held the souls of the dead inside them.

899. Doctors would taste people's bodily fluids so that they could diagnose them with their ailment.

900. History's first influencers were triumphant Roman gladiators, who were hired to promote merchant's products when they won.

901. The emperor Caligula was considered to be insane, and once, he went to war against the sea itself.

902. A slave boy had to follow Julius Caesar around and say, "*Memento mori*," which means "Remember you are mortal."

903. Charioteers would drink a concoction of goat dung in vinegar as a sports drink in the middle of their races.

904. At Roman dinner parties, it was common to see foods like dormice and flamingo.

905. Romans used to use stale urine as toothpaste because of the ammonia in it.

Medieval World

906. A pig was executed by hanging in France for the crime of killing a child in 1386 after a murder trial.

907. Men wore long pointed shoes because the length of a man's shoes was thought to show how wealthy and powerful he was.

908. Medieval women would pluck their hairlines to have the biggest forehead possible, which was considered beautiful.

909. In the Middle Ages, people thought eating with silverware was sacrilegious because God gave humans hands to eat with.

910. Gossiping women were forced to wear a *Scold's Bridle*, which was a metal cage that prevented them from further gossiping.

911. During the Great Schism of the Christian church from 1378 to 1417, there were three different popes fighting for control of the church (Oakley, 2023).

912. William the Conqueror's body was so bloated when he died that his body broke out of the coffin before he was laid into the ground.

Kings and Queens

913. During King Henry VIII's reign, he employed *grooms of the stool*, whose job was to wipe his bottom when he used the toilet.

914. The British Royal family's original family name was German, so they eventually changed it during World War I to *Windsor* to sound more British.

915. Mansa Musa, the medieval king of the Mali Empire, is thought to be the richest man who has ever lived with a wealth so large it's unquantifiable (Mohamud, 2019).

916. One in two hundred men is a direct descendant of the Mongol leader Genghis Khan (Khan, 2022).

917. Marie Antoinette once wore an elaborate hairdo that had a reaction of a naval battle made of hair on it.

918. In 1795, Napoleon Bonaparte published a romance novel that bombed on the market and was disliked by critics.

919. After her husband died in 1861, Queen Victoria continued to mourn and wear black for the rest of her life.

Life-Saving Survival Facts

Things to Avoid

920. In a flood, never swim in flood water, especially if it is moving, because there could be electric wires exposed, which puts you at threat of electrocution.

921. It's a myth that you can eat what an animal does; you really should not eat anything you forage unless you're absolutely sure it's safe.

922. You'll know food has gone bad if there's mold, an odor, the texture feels off, or the meat is slimy.

923. Most kinds of cactus will make you ill if you try to drink the water from them, so you'll be better off finding water elsewhere.

924. Peeing on a jellyfish sting is a myth; instead, remove the tentacles and then use rubbing alcohol or vinegar if medical help is not around.

925. It's good to avoid exposed places like hills if you pick a camping spot; instead, try to find places naturally sheltered by trees or rocks because you will benefit from natural protection.

Adventuring Tips

926. You should always make sure three people know where you are whenever you go somewhere in case one can't be reached or something happens to them.

927. The universal signal number for distress is three, so always call out or blow a whistle three times to signal you need help (Miller, 2014).

928. If it begins to get dark when you're lost in nature, stay where you are until it gets light because it's more likely you'll get more lost if you move.

929. If you don't have bottled water, boil water for at least one minute, then pass it through a filter, like a cloth, so that it's safe to drink (*Emergency Disinfection*, 2015).

930. When you're not sure where you are, stay where you are and look for a landmark you may have passed before to reorientate yourself.

931. A person can survive without water for three to five days, so it's better to be sure your water is safe to drink rather than chance it when you don't need to.

932. If someone has frostbite, don't rub them or put them into warm water as this could cause more damage; instead, slowly heat them up with blankets.

933. Rather than just using a big coat for the cold, it's better to layer thinner pieces of clothing to stay warm because the warmth gets trapped between the layers.

934. Hypothermia tends to develop at 30–50°F (-1–10°C) and symptoms are shaking limbs and unclear thinking (Miller, 2014).

935. Once you find a source of water, head upstream as it will be cleaner at the source, and you'll likely find a higher point to see where you are.

936. Before going out on an outdoor excursion, make sure you have a compass, enough food for what you plan to do, and appropriate clothing for the weather.

937. If you don't have matches, the easiest way to start a fire will be using glasses or a magnifying glass and concentrating the beam on a dry brush.

938. Whenever an object penetrates your skin, keep it in until you can find medical help because otherwise, you will lose more blood.

939. The sun rises in the east and sets in the west no matter where you are, which makes it the most dependable navigation trick.

940. While dehydration is dangerous, drinking too much water can also overload your system and cause you to pass out.

941. When you find yourself lost in the woods, you need to locate water and shelter before thinking of things like food.

Protecting Yourself

942. In case someone tries to restrain you, tense up your muscles while they tie the restraints so when you relax, the ties will be loose.

943. When you don't have bug spray, lavender or citronella are the best ways to repel mosquitos, and you should move away from standing water.

944. For most wild animals, the trick to avoid them attacking you is to back away slowly—if you run, it may trigger their predatory instinct.

945. If you see a shark, defend yourself with anything you can and aim for the nose, eyes, or gills before exiting the water as fast as possible.

946. You cannot suck the venom of a snake bite; instead, you should try to hold the affected limb below heart level and apply pressure.

947. When camping in bear country, always make sure you have bear spray with you and never keep any food or trash around your campsite.

948. It may feel mean, but if you see an animal in danger, always leave it be because it could be diseased, or rescuing it could put you or others in danger.

949. Toss rocks into rivers to see how deep they are and ensure the river is not moving faster than your jogging pace if you want to cross.

950. When you're bleeding, make sure to apply pressure to the wound with gauze or clean fabric until the bleeding stops.

Oil, Gas, Rocks, Minerals, Jewels

Oil

951. Venezuela has the largest oil reserves in the world, with 298.35 billion BBL, which is 9 times the amount of oil in the United States (*11 Facts About Oil*, 2015). w

952. Ancient societies used oil for things like medicine or sealant, which has continued today as oil is what we make plastic from.

953. Oil has been referred to as *Texas Tea* and *Black Gold* because of the Texas oil boom in the 1800s, which made the Rockefeller fortune.

954. At 1.85 billion BBL per day, the United States is the highest consumer of oil, using enough to fill the tanks of 100 million cars (*11 Facts About Oil*, 2015).

955. Ghawar Field in Saudi Arabia is the largest oil field in the world, producing 5 billion BBL of oil a day and covering an area the size of London (*Top 12 Interesting Oil Facts*, 2023).

956. The price of oil crashed in the 1870s because demand was lower than production, so oil was cheaper than water in many regions of the United States.

Gas

957. The smell of rotten eggs isn't natural with gas; companies added the smell so it would be easier to find leaks.

958. Animals, including humans, produce methane as well because of bacteria in our guts, with cows passing the most gas at 231 billion lbs—100 billion kg—a year (*Agriculture and Aquaculture*, 2021).

959. The Middle East has the largest amount of natural gas reserves in the world, with 2,686 trillion cu ft of natural gas, which is 42% of all natural gas on Earth (Turgeon & Morse, 2023).

960. Natural gas produces 25–30% less carbon dioxide than oil and 50% less than coal, making it one of the more environmentally friendly energy sources (Statoil Contributor, 2015).

961. As soon as 500 B.C.E., the ancient Chinese built bamboo pipelines for natural gas and used it to heat water.

962. Over 72 million people rely on natural gas every day, and it's used to power 11 million cars worldwide (Pro Gas Admin, 2022).

Rocks and Minerals

963. Most of the Earth's surface is made of granite, like the countertops, while the ocean floor is made of a volcanic rock called basalt.

964. Metamorphic rocks, or rocks that come from volcanoes, are the hardest on Earth, with quartzite taking the lead due to its high volume of mineral quartz.

965. Talc is the softest rock on Earth, and it has been used to make sculptures, but more recently, it's been used to make talcum powder for babies.

966. Mount Augustus in Western Australia is thought to be the largest piece of singular rock on Earth at 2,352 ft—717 m—tall, which is a little over twice the height of the Eiffel Tower (M, 2023).

967. Currently, bedrock in northeastern Canada is considered the oldest rock on Earth at 4.3 billion years old, and the Earth is only 4.5 billion years old (Steenblik Hwang, 2023).

968. Hematite is a type of magnetic rock that you may have seen made into bracelets that stick together without any clasps.

969. Pumice is a type of rock that can float because of the little holes in it, and you may have seen it used for a pedicure in a nail salon.

970. Based on all the technology and amenities that the average American uses, they need 40,630 lbs—18,428 kg—of minerals per year (*Minerals*, 2023).

971. There are 100 minerals common on Earth; however, there have been 5,300 different kinds of minerals identified (GeologyIn Staff, 2023).

972. Bridgmanite is the most common mineral on Earth, making up 38% of the planet's volume, but you'll probably never see it because it's in the mantle (Bressan, 2016).

973. Kyawthuite, a dark orange crystal, is the rarest mineral, as only one specimen has ever been found in the Mogok region of Myanmar.

974. At $25,000 per oz—28 g—rhodium is the most expensive mineral because of its use in cars, airplanes, and electronics (Mat, 2023).

975. Diamonds are the hardest minerals on Earth, and they can't be shattered, only chipped or scratched.

Jewels

976. The Ancient Greeks believed amethyst helped you resist intoxication, which is why the word amethyst means *not drunk*.

977. At $3.93 million per carat, blue diamonds are the most expensive jewels on Earth, and they have been worn by royalty, like Queen Victoria (Editorial Team, 2023).

978. Under sunlight, Alexandrite is green, and under artificial light, it turns red, which is why people use the phrase *emerald by day, ruby by night* about it.

979. Based on a story from the Exodus, the 12 different gemstones that were worn by an Israelite leader became associated with the zodiac, and thus birthstones were born.

980. No surprise, diamonds are the most popular jewel used in jewelry, and they're closely followed by sapphires and rubies.

981. Because amber is made of the fossilized sap of ancient trees, it is the softest gem and also the birthstone of November.

Insects

983. There are 200 million bugs for every person, making them the most abundant species on Earth (Okafor, 2022b).

Beetles and Ants

984. A ladybug or ladybird beetle will eat up to 5,000 insects in its lifetime. Not only are they pretty, but they also protect your garden! (NG Admin, 2018)

985. In Japan, Stag Beetles, with their prominent horns, are a popular household pet.

986. Dung beetles can push over a thousand times their weight, which is like a person trying to pull six buses (NG Admin, 2018).

987. Titan beetles are the largest insect on Earth at 6.6 in.—16 cm—long, which is about as long as a paper note in any currency. Luckily, they only live in the Amazon! (Nelson, 2022)

988. Red Cochineal Beetles have been used to dye food, cosmetics, and clothing red for centuries and even now.

989. Some people think ladybugs or ladybirds are good luck, and their number of spots means how many years of luck you'll have.

990. Cockroaches can live up to a week without their heads attached.

991. Because they are sold as pets, stag beetles are the most expensive insect to buy; they cost around $89,000 (Singh, 2022).

992. Every year, termites cost up to $30 billion in property damage in the United States (Orkin, 2023).

993. Leafcutter ants grow a fungus garden inside their nest so they can feed the colony.

994. People are outnumbered by ants 1.4 million to 1, and there are about 10 quadrillion ants on Earth right now (Marketing Team, 2021).

995. Bullet ants have the most painful sting as it is said their bite feels like walking over hot charcoal.

996. In Argentina, an ant nest was found that was 3,700 miles—5,954 km—wide, which is further than the distance from California to New York! (National Geographic Kids, 2016d)

997. Driver ants have jaws so strong that people indigenous to the Congo have historically used them to sew wounds.

Flying Insects

998. Every firefly has a different light pattern because they use them to attract mates.

999. To attract a mate, male stoneflies do push-ups until a female is impressed, not too different from humans!

1000. Fruit flies were the first living things sent to space, though because of their lifespan, the flies that saw the moon were different than the ones that left Earth.

1001. Bees are considered the most intelligent insects because they can make decisions and plan ahead.

1002. Only 24 hours after a fruit fly lays its eggs do they hatch and begin feeding on rotting food.

1003. When gathering food, a bee may fly up to 6 m in a day (Smithsonian, 2023b).

1004. Adult female mayflies have the shortest lifespan on Earth of at most five minutes, during which they have to find a mate and lay their eggs (Cofresi, 1999).

Butterflies, Moths and Creepy Crawlies

1005. Queen Alexandra's birdwing is the largest butterfly on Earth at 9 in.—25 cm—which is about as big as an adult's foot (Rothery, 2023).

1006. Butterflies were named for one butterfly species, the male Brimstone butterfly because it has yellow-colored wings.

1007. Moths navigate using the moon; this is why they are attracted to man-made light, which gets them lost.

1008. Some moths and caterpillars look like bird poo to avoid predators, like the Chinese Character caterpillar.

1009. Around 2,000 silkworms are needed to produce just one pound of silk; that's why it's so expensive (Smithsonian, 2023). Praying mantises are able to jump with extreme precision in a way that resembles many cats.

1010. The witchetty grub is the most popular insect food in the world; it's either served raw or barbecued in Australia.

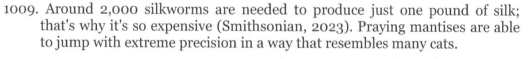

1011. Some praying mantises have been known to prey on hummingbirds; you gotta have ambition!

1012. There are thousands of mites that live on the skin of human beings and feed on our dead skin cells (Stromberg, 2014).

Pirates

1013. The golden age of piracy is thought to be from the late 1600s to the early 1700s, and it's when pirates like Calico Jack and Anne Bonney were active.

1014. Eyepatches were worn to help pirates' eyes adjust to the dark below decks more quickly, not because they all were missing eyes.

1015. Parrots were kept on pirate ships less as pets and more to be sold to zoos and wealthy people in Europe.

1016. The pirate accent, words like *matey* or *arr*, come from the 1950 movie *Treasure Island* and not from how real pirates talked.

1017. Pirates didn't make people walk the plank; normally, they just tied them up and threw them overboard.

1018. Earrings were worn by pirates to prevent seasickness, as part of dress codes, or as a souvenir from their travels.

1019. Rather than treasure maps, pirates were more interested in stealing sailing charts, which told them where merchant ships would be.

1020. Pirate captains were elected by the crew, and if they had failed to do their jobs well, they could have been voted out.

1021. Buried pirate treasure is a myth; most pirates immediately burned the money they stole in the different port towns.

1022. Each pirate ship had a different flag that symbolized the captain, but the common symbols like skulls and hourglasses were meant to reference a pirate's short life.

1023. Legends of the Kraken may have been based on giant squid sightings, though giant squids only reach lengths of 43 ft—13m.

1024. Pirates were often hired by governments to act as a navy, like the privateers Queen Elizabeth I hired to fight the Spanish.

1025. Pirates have existed as long as people have been using boats to move goods, and even Julius Caesar was kidnapped by pirates once.

1026. During the golden age of piracy, there were over 5,000 pirates active in the Caribbean alone (Royal Museums Greenwich, 2022a).

1027. Piracy became an attractive career option because working on merchant vessels or for the army paid less, and pirates in newspapers seemed glamorous.

1028. The Caribbean was the popular pirate hangout because law was less established in European colonies, and trade was booming in the region.

1029. If a pirate ship was threatened, the captain would change their clothes so that they could blend into the crew and not be captured.

1030. Whistling on a boat was thought to be bad luck because it was competing with the wind.

1031. Pirate ships were not large; they had to be small so they could quickly escape and navigate difficult waters.

1032. Pirate tattoos were often slave branding, as many pirates were escaped slaves or indentured servants.

Famous Pirates

1033. The world's most successful pirate was a woman named Ching Shih, who commanded an armada of 1,800 ships (Liles, 2023).

1034. Blackbeard set his beard on fire by weaving hemp into it, and the trick was used to intimidate prisoners.

1035. Captain Kidd claimed to have buried some of his treasure, but since nothing has ever been discovered, it may have been one last trick before he was hanged.

1036. Black Sam Bellamy, or the *Robin Hood of the Sea*, was the richest pirate with a fortune of $120 million (Landrigan, 2014).

1037. To make sure he never *forgot who he was*, Blackbeard once shot at a member of his own crew.

1038. Captain Kidd helped to found a church in Georgetown and had a reserved pew for himself and his family.

1039. Calico Jack is credited with popularizing the *Jolly Roger*, or the skull and crossbones flag.

1040. Though it was considered bad luck for women to be on pirate ships, Anne Bonney and Mary Read became two of the most prominent pirates of their era.

1041. In 2011, Blackbeard's ship, the Queen Anne's Revenge, was found off the coast of North Carolina mostly intact.

1042. At the peak of her career, Ching Shih was so powerful that the Chinese government had to pay her to stop piracy, which she accepted.

1043. Jack Sparrow is thought to be based on both Calico Jack and John Ward, both of whom were known for their daring.

National Parks

America's National Parks

1044. National parks have been referred to as *America's best idea* by historian Wallace Stegner because the country introduced the world to the concept.

1045. In Yosemite National Park in California, you can find three of the ten tallest waterfalls in the world (Dierickx, 2015).

1046. The only state in the United States that does not have a national park is Delaware, while California has the most at nine.

1047. The Great Smoky Mountains are the most popular national park on Earth, with 12 million visitors annually, and it's one of the United States' last temperate rainforests (Hafer, 2023).

1048. If you put all of the United States national parks together, you would get a land total of 84 million ac, which is bigger than all of the United Kingdom (Myers, 2016).

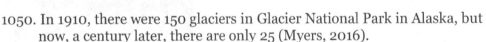

1049. Yellowstone National Park was the world's first in 1872, and after it was founded, the idea caught on to nations all over the world.

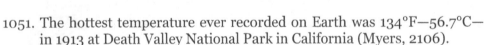

1050. In 1910, there were 150 glaciers in Glacier National Park in Alaska, but now, a century later, there are only 25 (Myers, 2016).

1051. The hottest temperature ever recorded on Earth was 134°F—56.7°C—in 1913 at Death Valley National Park in California (Myers, 2106).

1052. In the early 1900s, garbage would be left in piles around Yellowstone so tourists could see bears, but after many attacks, bear-proofed food canisters became mandatory.

1053. Arches National Park in Utah has the highest density of naturally occurring arches with 120 m—193 km—of 2,000 arches, that's 16 arches a mile—1.6 km (Gates, 2021).

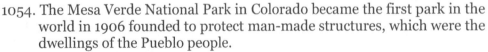

1054. The Mesa Verde National Park in Colorado became the first park in the world in 1906 founded to protect man-made structures, which were the dwellings of the Pueblo people.

1055. The acidity and heat of Yellowstone's hot springs and geysers would be able to dissolve a human body in one day.

1056. In Great Sands National Park in Colorado, the sand dunes *sing* as the wind flows over the grains of sand.

1057. The Ahwahnee Hotel in Yosemite National Park is a luxury hotel with views of the park, and its guests have been President Kennedy and the Kinging and Queen of England.

1058. Mammoth Cave National Park is considered the most haunted natural wonder on Earth, with over 150 paranormal events and ghost sightings (Moss, 2019).

1059. In the United States, there are 247 threatened or endangered species that are protected within the national parks (Dierickx, 2015).

1060. It would take you a little less than a year of constant walking to explore the 18,000 miles—28,968 km—of hiking trails in the American national parks (Dierickx, 2015).

1061. Supai Village in the base of the Grand Canyon is the most remote place in the United States, and they still have their mail delivered by pack mule.

1062. Scenes on Tatooine in the first two Star Wars films were filmed in Death Valley; however, the park now cannot allow filming because it could endanger the wildlife.

National Parks Around the World

1063. Northeast Greenland National Park is the largest in the world at 375,000 sq mile —972,000 km² —which makes it 77 times bigger than Yellowstone (Lesso, 2023).

1064. Moyenne, an island in the Seychelles, is the world's smallest national park at 24 ac, which is the size of an American football field (Ham, 2022).

1065. There are 8 billion visitors to the world's 550 national parks every year, which generates $600 billion of revenue from tourism (*World's Protected Natural Areas*, 2015).

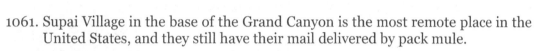

1066. Salonga National Park is only accessible by the Congo River and is the densest area of rainforest on the African continent.

1067. The Great Barrier Reef National Park in Australia is the largest area of protected ocean at 133,000 sq m—344,468 km2—which is the same area as Japan (Kai, 2023).

1068. Serengeti National Park in Tanzania is home to the Great Migration, where millions of herbivores like wildebeests or zebras search for new feeding grounds.

1069. Komodo National Park in Indonesia was founded in 1980 to protect the Komodo Dragon, and it is the only place on earth where you can see the lizard.

1070. Nowell's Limestone Moss is a type of moss only found in the Yorkshire Dales National Park in the north of England.

1071. Waterton-Glacier International Peace Park was founded in 1932 as the world's first peace park, as it covers land across the United States and Canada border.

1072. Kruger National Park in South Africa is the oldest in the country and also the largest national park in Africa, with the park taking up about the size of Belgium.

1073. Cabo de Hornos National Park in Chile is the most southern national park on earth as it lies within the Chilean Antarctic province, near the last inhabited city of the south.

1074. The Aboriginal people have been living in Kakadu National Park in Australia for 65,000 years, and they are the oldest living culture on earth.

Weapons

1075. Humans' first weapons were stones and clubs, which were followed by axes, and later knives and swords when metalworking was developed.

Guns

1076. Gunpowder was invented by the Chinese as early as the 1st century and was originally used just for entertainment.

1077. The pistol used to kill Billy the Kid in 1881 cost a collector $6.03 million, making it the priciest gun sold to date (Metesh, 2023).

1078. In the 10th century, the Chinese fire lance, an arrow propelled by gunpowder, was created as an early version of a gun.

1079. The McMillan Tac-50 sniper rifle has made the longest on-target shot in history with an 11,614 ft—3,540 m—range, which is 30 football fields (Maccar, 2021).

1080. At 1,000,000 bullets a minute, the Metal Storm is the fastest-firing machine gun, but it has never been used in combat (Young, 2023).

1081. Machine guns were used for the first time in the Boer War in 1899 after their invention in 1884 by Hiram Maxim.

Swords, Arrows and Historical Weapons

1082. A 5,000-year-old sword found in Turkey was proven to be the oldest sword ever discovered, and it's made of bronze.

1083. Made in 1850, a 0.2 in.—7 mm—pocketknife from Sheffield is the smallest knife on earth, with the weapon no bigger than a penny (Lawson, 2023).

1084. *Le Petit* protector rings were guns attached to rings that were advertised to women in the 19th century as a means to protect themselves.

1085. Before swords were able to be mass-produced, they were status symbols in the Middle Ages, and many would be highly decorated to wear as accessories.

1086. The *urumi* from India is known as one of the world's deadliest swords because it is both a whip and a sword with multiple blades.

1087. Using a katana, the best medieval Japanese samurai were known to strike an opponent down with one strike.

1088. The German Zweihänder, Japanese Ōdachi, and the Scottish Claymore all tie as the longest swords used in history with a length of 6.6 ft—2 m (*Longest Sword*, 2023).

1089. Though King Arthur's sword in the stone is just a legend, a sword found stuck into a slab of stone in Tuscany has been a site of pilgrimage for centuries.

1090. The Mughal ruler Tipu Sultan's gold-adorned sword is the most expensive sword ever sold, bringing in $17.3 million at auction (Cambal, 2023).

1091. Lightsabers are years away from being developed because lasers aren't able to stay in a single beam, and plasma is too hot to be held by a person.

1092. In 1971, Harry Drake set the record for the furthest an arrow has been shot at a little over a mile (Cooke, 2021).Historical Weapons

1093. At 188 t, the Panzer VIII Maus tank made by the Germans in the 1940s is the biggest ever created, with a weight twice that of a space shuttle.

1094. A *Pear of Anguish* may seem like a silly name for a weapon, but this tool was put inside peoples' mouths in the 16th century to widen them.

1095. *Man catchers* were spiked, hooped weapons used up until the 18th century that were able to grab armored men off horses.

1096. The Panjandrum was a weapon invented for World War II that was a machine gun on a turning wheel, but it always lost control in tests.

1097. Despite the name, the medieval Spanish Tickler was no laughing matter, as the hooks were meant to rip people apart.

1098. Like something out of a cartoon, a curved gun was invented by the Nazis to shoot around corners, but it failed because bullets go too fast to turn.

1099. We may not think of shields as weapons, but in Ancient Rome, the tortoise-shaped shield formation made soldiers formidable in battle.

1100. Rather than stretching them, the Scavenger's daughter was a medieval weapon that compressed a person's body.

1101. Not for fun and games, aerial darts used in World War I were like sharp knives dropped onto enemy troops.

1102. In a failed World War II experiment, the United States once tried to attach bombs to bats so they would roost, and then the bomb could be detonated.

1103. Greek fire, one of the most famous ancient weapons, was a green fire able to burn on water, making it deadly, but we still have not discovered the formula.

1104. With 153 emeralds and 9 diamonds, the Gem of the Orient, created by Buster Warenski is both the fanciest and most expensive knife ever made (Oishya, 2017).

1105. All fire axes need to be red so that all at the scene of the emergency can identify them.

Population

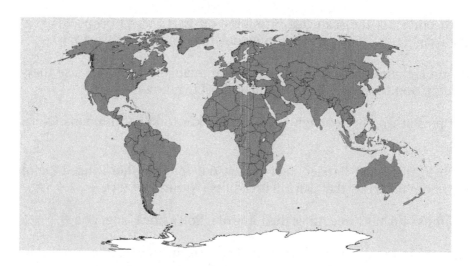

1106. There are roughly 8 billion people on Earth right now, with China and India making up 18% of that, with populations of 1.2 billion each (*Population*, 2022).

1107. Since 1950, the population has grown by 5.5 billion, but the United Nations now predicts that the population growth will begin to slow (Population, 2022).

1108. Europe is the most densely populated continent on Earth, with Monaco being the most crowded country with 25 people per half a mile—0.8 km (Regional Information Centre for Western Europe, 2022).

1109. Greenland is the least densely populated place on Earth, with a whopping 0.14 people per half a mile—0.8 km (Global Data, 2023).

1110. World Population Day is July 11th, and in 2023, the theme was allowing the female population to take their place in the world.

1111. More than half of the world's population lives in cities, and the United Nations predicts people will continue to flock to cities for work.

1112. In New Zealand, there are more sheep than people; they outnumber the human residents five to one (Badgamia, 2023).

1113. Vatican City is technically the least populated country, with a total of 510 permanent inhabitants (Dyvik, 2023c).

1114. Residents of New York City are the most linguistically diverse as 800 different languages are spoken (*The World's Most Linguistically Diverse*, 2018).

1115. As of 2022, Armenia was the country with the highest ratio of women, with women being 55% of the total population (Dyvik, 2023b).

Dangerous Animals

1117. The Nile crocodile has the strongest bite force on Earth at 5,000 psi. That's close to the weight of 2 small cars chomping down on you (Spanner, 2023).

1118. Mosquitos are technically the most dangerous animals on Earth because they kill around 725,000 people a year due to malaria (Ling, 2023).

1119. The golden poison frog has enough toxin on its skin to kill 10 humans (Nazario, 2023).

1120. If you swim in the Great Barrier Reef, watch out for the Blue Ringed Octopus, which has venom in its bite that can kill 26 adults (Nazario, 2023).

1121. A hippopotamus bite has three times the force of a lion's bite (Ling, 2023).

1122. Wolves are common villains in fairy tales because, in the Middle Ages, death by wolves was a common fear until they were hunted to near extinction.

1123. Komodo dragons are the world's largest lizards, and they have killed 4 people over the last 33 years with their powerful venomous bites (Nazario, 2023).

1124. Like domestic cats, a lion's claws are retractable, but these nails are 1.5 in.—4 cm—long, which is about half your finger (Scheffer, 2019).

1125. The *Jaws Effect* is a scientific term for the human fear of shark attacks, which was mainly encouraged by the film *Jaws*.

1126. Saw Scaled Vipers are the most dangerous snakes based on human attack rate, which is particularly high because of their territorial aggression.

1127. Pufferfish aren't dangerous by themselves, but when they are incorrectly prepared as a part of a Japanese delicacy, they can cause death through food poisoning.

1128. Pythons are able to swallow human beings whole, such as one in Indonesia, which was cut open to reveal a missing woman inside.

1129. Box jellyfish, almost invisible floating bags, are responsible for 20–40 deaths in the Philippines each year (Nazario, 2023).

1130. Cape Buffalos are known as *Black Death* because when they are wounded or hunted, the herd turns into a mob that moves at 35 mph—56 kph (Nazario, 2023).

1131. Almost 99% of all rabies cases come from pet dogs, which makes them the fourth most dangerous animal (Gallagher, 2022).

1132. Though they have a cute image, when a hippo is territorially threatened, it can match the running speed of a human and gore them with its massive teeth.

1133. For 3 years in the mid-1700s, a *beast* killed over 100 people in rural France. Historians believe it was possibly a wolf or an escaped zoo lion.

1134. Around 96% of bear attacks involve brown bears, which means 24 of 25 bear attacks will have involved a brown bear (Gallagher, 2022).

1135. Occasionally, a string of tiger attacks will be linked to one predatory and aggressive tiger.

1136. If you encounter a black bear, make lots of noise; if it's a brown bear, stay quiet and low, and if it's a polar bear, it was nice to know you.

1137. The teeth of a moray eel are backward in its jaw so that it can hold onto prey more easily.

1138. African Elephants have the largest teeth of any animal, as their tusks are actually long incisors.

1139. If you're looking for shells on the sea floor, watch out for the cone snail, whose venom can paralyze and kill you.

1140. Cheetahs are the fastest land animals and can reach speeds up to 69 mph—112 kph—which is the speed of a car on a motorway (National Geographic Kids, 2018a).

1141. The Cassowary, a bird from Australia, has been known to break into peoples' homes, and they are able to disembowel humans with their claws.

1142. Leopard Seals are some of the apex predators of the polar region, and they have been known to drag humans underwater and drown them.

1143. On average, hippos are the most dangerous animals on the African continent, as they kill twice as many people as lions.

1144. The only animals known to prey on humans are crocodiles, lions, tigers, and komodo dragons.

1145. Human fears of things like spiders may be evolutionary traits designed to protect us that our ancestors have passed down.

1146. Most of the world's dangerous animals only attack humans when they enter their territory, when they are protecting their young, or as a natural response of the animal. For these creatures, humans are the most dangerous animals because of environmental destruction, poaching, and hunting.

Weird Sea Creatures

1147. The punch of the peacock mantis shrimp is strong enough to break an aquarium tank.

1148. Mudskippers are fish that can walk on land with their front fins, and like amphibians, they would drown if they spent all day in the water, so they sun themselves on rocks.

1149. You can see all the internal organs of a sea cucumber in the Pacific, which is aptly named the Pink See-Through Fantasia.

1150. Red handfish have fins that look like hands, and they use these to crawl along the bottom of the sea floor.

1151. Frilled sharks are living fossils as they emerged 80 million years ago and swim less like modern sharks but slither like the ancient Ichthyosaur.

1152. Giant larvaceans, which are only 4 in.—10 cm—build themselves mucus palaces, inside which they stay safe from predators (*Discover 9*, 2022).

1153. Mimic octopuses can pretend to be other sea creatures like crabs or eels to find prey.

1154. The immortal jellyfish can reproduce from itself when it *dies*, making the same animal able to exist forever unless it's eaten.

1155. Giant squids do exist, and on average, they are half the size of blue whales at 43 ft—13 m—long, but we only see them when they wash up on shorelines (Shapely, 2015).

1156. When anglerfish mate, the male latches onto the female and is slowly absorbed into her before his purpose is fulfilled and he dies.

1157. Giant tube worms are some of the only creatures that do not use the sun in any way for their energy; instead, they feed off bacteria near volcanic vents.

1158. Jellyfish have survived five mass extinctions and have done so without a brain, a heart, or bones—they pack light.

1159. Hagfish don't have jaws, so instead, they burrow into whale carcasses with their worm-like bodies.

1160. Blobfish only look like sacks of fat with faces when they are brought to the surface because they normally live at the bottom of the ocean.

1161. The gulper eel's mouth is 11 times the size of its body which it uses to swallow large prey or crustaceans whole (Terra, 2023).

1162. Stubby squids have massive eyes that almost look like googly eyes or painted-on designs, but they're big because they live so deep in the ocean.

1163. Goblin sharks can extend their jaw out of their face to catch prey.

1164. Dumbo octopuses are called that because they flap big ears on the sides of their heads to swim, like the famous circus elephant.

1165. A catfish's entire body is covered in taste buds.

1166. Coelacanths, fish who lived with the dinosaurs, were thought to be extinct until 1938, when they were discovered off the coast of South Africa.

1167. Lungfish can live out of the water for several years by creating themselves a mucus cocoon in wet sand.

1168. In a minute, Atlantic hagfish are able to produce enough slime to fill a standard bucket.

1169. There are some theories that Amelia Earhart was never found because coconut crabs entirely devoured her corpse.

1170. Dinner plate jellyfish are some of the only jellyfish who actively hunt for prey instead of waiting for it to come to them.

1171. Sunfish do not have tails and instead, they float around to bask in the sun at the surface of the water.

1172. In Ancient Rome, lampreys were used as a form of torture when someone would be thrown into a pit of them and have their blood sucked from their body.

1173. Triggerfish have teeth that are oddly similar to human teeth.

1174. Whiplash squids float along the bottom of the ocean and use what looks like two long legs to balance themselves.

1175. Throughout history, oarfish have inspired stories of sea serpents because they can be 56 ft—17 m—long, which is about the length of a bowling lane (Nelson, 2023).

1176. Glass squids are transparent, so they can avoid casting shadows, which would attract predators.

1177. The fangtooth fish may have a terrifying name and two rows of razor-sharp teeth, but it's only the size of a grapefruit.

Brain, Sense & Detection

1178. The Ancient Greeks thought the brain was unimportant and that its purpose was to ensure the heart stayed warm.

1179. Information in the brain travels at 268 mph—431 kph. That's as fast as a Bugatti sports car (11 Fun Facts, 2019).

1180. The human brain is the only thing that has named itself; don't think about that one too long!

1181. It's a myth that humans only use 10% of the brain; in fact, we use all of it all the time, even when we sleep (Wells, 2017).

1182. True multitasking is impossible; we are switching between two activities at a fast rate, but this is often not successful.

1183. For numbers, short-term memory lasts about seven seconds, while for letters, it lasts for nine; give it a try! (Burket, 2019)

1184. The brain itself cannot feel pain. When you have a headache, it comes from other nerves telling the brain something is wrong.

1185. Your brain has an average of 12,000–60,000 thoughts a day and most are repetitive or negative thoughts (Burket, 2019).

1186. Forgetting is a part of healthy brain function because it allows your brain to adapt to the world around you and store only the most important things.

1187. Our brains have 100,000 miles—160,934 km—of blood vessels, which could encircle the earth 4 times (*Amazing Facts You Didn't Know*, 2020).

1188. Researchers think humans have around 400 smell receptors in their noses, which can detect over 40 billion odor-carrying compounds (Parry, 2023).

1189. Human beings can tell the difference between pure scents and the combinations of 1 trillion different things.

1190. Your iris, or the colored part of your eye, is a muscle that can change the size of the pupil when needed.

1191. On average, people blink 15–20 times a minute. Bet you're thinking of blinking right now! (Hersh, 2020)

1192. Humans have around 8,000 taste buds, though this number does decrease throughout our lifetime to around 5,000 in later years (Hammond, 2017).

1193. The human brain uses 20% of the output from the taste buds and 80% of the output from smell to determine how a food tastes (Gravinaet al., 2013).

1194. Our ears contain the smallest bones in our bodies—the malleus, the incus, and the stapes.

1195. You may have heard your ears keep growing as you age, but really, it's that the cartilage in them breaks down over time.

Meteors

1197. Meteors are chunks of rock that orbit the sun and are sometimes called shooting stars because when they burn up in Earth's atmosphere, they create a streak of light.

1198. The word meteor comes from the 15th-century French term for *an atmospheric phenomenon.*

1199. Wishing on these falling stars comes from the Greek astronomer Ptolemy, who thought they meant the gods were peeking down onto the Earth.

1200. In ancient times, meteors were thought to be signs from the heavens, such as the meteor shower in the third century C.E., which made people think the sky cried for St. Lawrence.

1201. NASA has estimated that 48.5 t of meteor dust fall onto Earth a year, which is like an entire sandy beach falling on Earth (Dobrijevic, 2021).

1202. The Nomenclature Committee of the Meteoritical Society asks that you donate a certain amount of any meteorite you find, and then you can sell or keep the rest.

1203. A study in 1985 found that a meteor will hit a person once every 180 years, so the odds are you won't get smacked with a space rock (Hartson, 2013).

1204. The International Space Station is at risk of being hit by 100,000 meteors, so it is covered with an inch of Kevlar, the material for bulletproof vests, to protect it (Temescu, 2006).

1205. Around 95% of all meteors are made of chondrites, which are minerals that were created when the sun was born (NASA, 2018).

1206. Most meteors are 50 miles—80 km—to 75 miles—120 km—away from Earth, but when our atmosphere is only 6,000 m—9,656 km—that's not too far! (Kalomiris, 2022)

1207. The Tunguska event in Siberia, a mysterious explosion with the force of a nuclear bomb that leveled 500,000 ac of forest, was thought to be caused by a meteor (Choi, 2008).

1208. Because Martian meteorites are rare, only 34 exist on Earth, and they can go for $500 for 0.02 lb—1 g (Temescu, 2006).

1209. In 1833, the brightest meteor shower on record occurred as thousands of meteors shone in the night sky; normally, only 100 meteors would fall in a shower.

1210. Most meteors come from the Asteroid Belt, which is a stretch of 1.1 and 1.9 million asteroids between Mars and Jupiter (*What Are Meteorites?*, 2020).

1211. In the 17th century, it was thought meteors fell out of thunderstorms, so they were called thunderstones.

1212. Between 10 and 50 meteors fall on Earth every day, but most are too small for any of us to notice (Kjørstad, 2022).

1213. Meteors can be different colors depending on what metal makes them up; for example, calcium burns purple, and iron burns yellow.

1214. Though the Hoba meteor weighs 60 t, or the same as 30 grand pianos, it did not leave a crater, which made scientists think it fell slowly (Kalomiris, 2022).

1215. Fireballs are meteors that burn brighter than Venus; they can be heard 30 m—48 km—away, and you can see them during the day (Dobrijevic, 2021).

1216. The Brenham Meteorite Main Mass is the most expensive meteor ever bought at auction, bringing in around $1.2 million (Daley, 2016).

1217. On average, the tail of a meteor can only last a few seconds, though some can last a few minutes.

1218. Thousands of meteors are on sale online or at auctions, but in South Africa, it is illegal to sell meteors.

1219. Meteors are able to travel 44 m—71 km—a second, which is almost 300 times faster than a jet (Evers, 2023b).

1220. While many meteors reach the ground each year, scientists only recover five or six a year to study (The Planets, 2014).

Meteor Showers

1221. If you want to view a meteor shower, it's best on a moonless night, and you should check your local meteorological society to see when the next one is.

1222. There are 20 different main meteor showers, and they occur throughout the year at predictable times (Space for Kids, 2017).

1223. Meteor showers occur when the Earth passes through the orbit of a comet, and the dust falls through the Earth's atmosphere.

1224. The Leonid meteor shower, which occurs every 33 years, is the brightest meteor shower, and the next one will be in 2028 (Dobrijevic, 2021).

1225. Almost 2 billion years ago, Vredefort Crater had impacted with a radius of 118 m—190 km—and at 18 m—28 km—larger than the meteor that killed the dinosaurs, it was the biggest on Earth (line, 2013).

1226. The Yarrabubba Crater in Western Australia is the oldest meteor crash site at 2.2 billion years old, and it may have been what allowed the planet to warm up (BBC, 2020).

1227. There are 70 impact craters on Earth with a size of 3.7 m—6 km—which is the length of 54 football fields (Blakemore, 2015).

Toilets

We Used to Do What?

1228. The Ancient Minoans were the first to dump their waste into their local bodies of water, so they also invented sewers.

1229. In medieval castles, clothes were stored in chamber pots or toilets because it was thought the smell would keep away pests.

1230. Ancient Rome's sewers were so big that fully loaded wagons could have fit into them if they chose to.

1231. While China had some kind of toilet paper by 1393, normally rice paper, it took the West until 1857 to use toilet paper.

1232. You would have been able to break into a castle through the toilet hole, but it would be dirty work!

1233. People in the Middle Ages didn't actually throw their poop out the window; they buried it in deep pits.

1234. However, when they needed to empty the liquid in chamber pots, they would say, "Gardez l'eau," which is where *loo* comes from.

1235. Before Febreeze, people would stuff pomegranates full of cloves to be an air freshener.

1236. Toilets did not change for much of human history; from 500 B.C.E to the late 1800s, most people used a hole in the ground.

1237. In the Victorian era, toilets were also pieces of artwork and would be decorated with gold or Japanese-inspired paintings.

1238. Going to the toilet in ancient Rome was a social experience as there were no dividers, and everyone faced each other.

1239. Until the 20th century, public restrooms were mainly for men, but for department stores, ladies' washrooms had to be created.

1240. In ancient China and Japan, human waste was collected and then sold as manure for farmers.

1241. Toilets got the nickname *the throne* because, in castles, only rulers had access to the small rooms.

1242. After the creation of a modern sewage system in 1865, deaths from cholera and typhoid dropped significantly in London.

All Hail the Porcelain Throne

1243. The first flush toilet was invented in 1596 for Queen Elizabeth, but it didn't catch on until 1851.

1244. In the United States, using the phrase *the john* for the toilet is a reference to this inventor, John Harrington.

1245. A 2,400-thousand-year-old toilet was found in Xi'an, China, with early flush technology.

1246. There is a $19 million toilet on the International Space Station, making it the most expensive in the world (Shah, 2007).

1247. World Toilet Day is on the 19th of November, and it is a project by the United Nations to increase global sanitation.

1248. The average person spends 73 hours per year pooping, which becomes 240 days of their lifespan pooping! (How Much of Your Life, 2020)

1249. Toilets use 5–7 gal of water to flush, but there are low-flush toilets out there that use as little as 1 gal (Toilet, 2017).

1250. The first cubicle in a public toilet is the least used, which also means it's often the cleanest!

1251. Haewoojae is a toilet-themed park in South Korea where you can find a toilet museum and toilet sculptures.

1252. The word *toilet* comes from the French word for *cloth*, and it was originally associated with the upper classes.

1253. In Texas, there are toilets made of two-way glass, so you can see everyone going past, but they can't see you.

1254. Nowadays, we're used to porcelain toilets, but until the 1900s, most toilets were made out of wood.

1255. Almost 60% of the world, that's 4.5 billion people, do not have access to a flushing toilet today (Ferguson, 2019).

1256. The world's largest toilet is at the Children's Museum in Indiana, where you can take pictures with the whole family.

1257. Most people think the world's most luxurious public toilet is in Paris because it has stained glass and mahogany paneling, but it does cost €2 to use.

1258. The most expensive toilet paper is made of 22-karat gold, and it costs over $1 million! (Achiam, 2016)

Parasites and Microbes

Parasites

1260. Between 800 and 1.2 billion people are currently infected with roundworm, but only 15% of them have symptoms (Gallagher, 2022).

1261. Tapeworms are associated with up to 70% of epilepsy cases (Gallagher, 2022).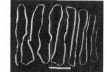

1262. These are some hard-core dieters who encourage purposely injecting tapeworms as a way to lose weight, which could kill you.

1263. There are between 75,000 and 300,000 species of parasites, and it's impossible to know the exact amount because of how microscopic they are (Williamson, 2023).

1264. Ticks can consume up to 100 times their body weight in blood (Campbell et al., 2010).

1265. Cordyceps from *The Last of Us* is a real parasitic fungus that possesses insects and forces them to do their bidding; luckily, it only infects insects so far.

1266. The tongue-eating louse is a type of parasite that eats and replaces a fish's tongue until the fish dies.

1267. Around 2 billion people on Earth are currently infected with some kind of parasite (*3 Surprising Facts*, 2016).

1268. Mistletoe isn't just for kissing under; it's a parasitic plant that takes nutrients from its host tree.

1269. The most common survival strategy in the wild is parasitism because it uses low energy and is high reward.

1270. Ectoparasitoid wasps are the real-life xenomorphs from *Alien* because they lay their eggs in a host bug, which then hatches through its chest, killing it.

1271. The horsehair worm can grow up to 1 ft—0.3 m—long, and it takes control of bugs' bodies and forces them to drown themselves (Young, 2020).

1272. When snails eat flatworms, the parasite's eggs are laid in the snail's eyes, and when they hatch, the eyes explode.

1273. Malaria is the most common parasitic disease as it is spread by mosquitos, and there are currently 247 million cases on Earth (T*he Top 10 Causes*, 2020).

1274. Cuckoos are a type of parasitic bird that lays the eggs of their young into other birds nests, and when the cuckoo hatches, it pushes all other chicks out of the nest.

1275. The longest parasite on Earth is a worm that lives in Sperm Whales and can grow to be 90 ft—27.4 m—long (Hall, 2021).

Microbes

1276. Microbes were the first creatures to evolve half a billion years ago in the ocean.

1277. There are 39 trillion microbes in the human body, with most of these being in the human gut (Looi, 2020).

1278. Humans did not see microbes until 1674, when the microscope was invented, because almost all microbes are invisible to the human eye.

1279. It's a possibility that jet lag may be caused by the microbes in our gut being out of sync with the rest of our body due to the changed sleep schedule.

1280. The microbes in your body outnumber the genes in your DNA one hundred to one (30 Mind-Blowing, 2021).

1281. When put together, the microbes in your body weigh up to 3 lbs—1.3 kg (Cowan, 2023).

1282. No two people have the exact same sets of microbes.

1283. There are over a trillion different species of microbes, which would make them the most diverse organism on Earth (Looi, 2020).

1284. The *Thiomargarita namibiensis,* or the sulfur pearl of Namibia, is the only microbe you can see with the naked eye.

1285. There are more bacteria in a single person's mouth than people on all of Earth (*30 Mind-Blowing,* 2021).

1286. Most microbes have yet to be identified: In one scoop of ocean water, there were over a million never-before-seen species (Rice, 2008).

1287. The bacteria *Deinococcus radiodurans* feeds on radioactivity, so it is being considered a way to clean up nuclear waste.

1288. Every person emits a unique microbial cloud that could be used to identify them.

1289. There are at least 1,200 types of microbes in your mouth, and while some cause things like bad breath or tooth decay, others protect you from disease (Vedantu, 2023).

1290. One drop of water can contain up to 50 million microbes (Vedantu, 2023).

Sleep

1292. Almost 12% of people dream entirely black and white, but before the invention of the color television, more people dreamt in black and white (Murzyn, 2008).

1293. On average, humans spend a third of their lifetimes asleep, though this greatly depends on their age (Wurr, 2011).

1294. In 1963, Randy Gardner set the record for the longest time without sleep at 11 days and 25 minutes (Conlon, 2023).

1295. Only 15% percent of the population sleepwalks, and it's a myth you can't wake a sleepwalker. You should if they're in danger (*Quick Dose*, 2022).

1296. The brain has nightmares when it is experiencing higher levels of stress or anxiety, and emotions in nightmares aren't fear but more often guilt or confusion.

1297. It's a myth that you swallow spiders in your sleep; in reality, a spider would run away from you if it bumped into you in the night.

1298. As mammals, we are the only animals who can delay sleep, which may be an adaption to human schedules.

1299. It should take 10–15 minutes to fall asleep. If it takes longer, it's best to do a relaxing activity, no phone, until you feel drowsy (Feather & Black, 2020).

1300. Our sense of smell does not work as well when we are asleep; this partially is why we need fire alarms.

1301. Falling into the void is the most common dream, followed by being chased (*The 10 Most Common Dreams*, 2023).

Sharks, Whales, Dolphins, Turtles

Sharks

1303. Sharks are the only fish that have eyelids, which means they're not dead-eyed.

1304. Rather than scales, sharks are covered in dermal denticles, which are more like teeth. This is why shark skin is rough.

1305. Though we imagine sharks as fearsome, the plankton-eating whale shark is the largest, which also makes it the biggest fish.

1306. Great White Sharks are fearsome at 20 ft—6 m—long, but they're still 3 times smaller than their dinosaur ancestor, the Megalodon (Smithsonian, 2022).

1307. Unlike most fish, sharks do not have bones and have skeletons of cartilage, which is what your nose is made of.

1308. Sharks go through around 30,000 teeth in their lifetimes because they never stop growing new ones; the dentist's bill must be huge! (*10 Things You Didn't Know*, 2023)

1309. There is an electrical sensor on the tips of sharks' noses, which gives them a *sixth sense* to be able to feel creatures moving in the water.

1310. Dwarf Lantern sharks are the smallest species of shark, and they're only about as long as a phone.

Whales

1311. Blue whales are not only the biggest whales but also the biggest animal on Earth, weighing 200 t; that's a bit less than 100 elephants (*Blue Whale*, 2023).

1312. Humpback whales do not eat for half of the year while they're in their tropical breeding grounds and only feed when they migrate to the Antarctic.

1313. Sperm whales have the largest brains on Earth; it's five times the size of a human's (Mackenzie, 2023).

1314. The tails of humpback whales are as unique as human fingerprints and are how scientists identify them.

1315. Dwarf Sperm whales are the smallest species of whale at 9 ft—2.8 m—which is about the length of a car (*Dwarf Sperm Whale*, 2022).

1316. Some whales have multiple stomachs, such as the Baird's whale, which has 13 stomachs it uses to digest deep-water squid (Koch-Schick, 2022).

1317. Sperm whales can dive up to 6,561 ft—2,000 m—which is a little over a mile underwater (How Deep Can a Whale Dive?, 2023).

1318. Unfortunately, 6 out of the 13 great whale species are endangered (Blue Whale, 2023).

Dolphins

1319. Orcas, or killer whales, are the largest dolphin at 23 ft—7 m—and they are top of the global ocean food chain (Schmidt, 2020).

1320. Dolphins are known to play with pufferfish-like balls and even ingest some of their toxins for fun.

1321. All dolphin species use a series of clicks, whistles, and chips to communicate. They're so vocal some scientists have tried to teach them to speak.

1322. When hunting, some dolphins use a tactic called *fish-whacking*, where they smack fish with their tails to stun them.

1323. Dolphins are second in intelligence only to humans and are able to recognize their reflections in the mirror (*20 Fun Dolphin*, 2019).

1324. Like bats and whales, dolphins use echolocation to locate prey, which is when sound waves bounce off objects in space.

1325. There is evidence that dolphins give each other names as each member of the pod has a distinctive whistle the others use.

1326. Every two hours, dolphins shed their outer layer of skin to help them swim faster (Croteau, 2022).

Turtles

1327. Turtles don't have teeth, but instead, they use a beak to grab onto food, which is made of the same keratin your hair is made of.

1328. Only 1 in 1,000 marine turtle babies make it to adulthood due to threats such as pollution and predators (*Top 10 Facts About Marine Turtles*, 2023).

1329. It's a myth that a turtle can come out of its shell—a turtle's shell is part of its skeleton.

1330. Snapping turtles bite with a force of 209 N, which is enough pressure to break your bone (Forest Preserve District Willcounty, 2021).

1331. Sea turtles cry to get rid of excess salt in their bodies, not because they're sad.

1332. The Mary River turtle collects moss and grass on its head while living in the water that resembles hair, so it's often called the *punk rock turtle*.

1333. Of the 356 species of turtle, 161 are endangered, which means every 4 out of 10 turtles is endangered (Heimbuch, 2020b).

Robots

1335. The word *robot* comes from the Czech word for forced worker; let's hope the robots never realize that!

1336. Leonardo Da Vinci, of Mona Lisa fame, created one of the first designs for a humanoid robot in 1495 that could sit up and move its head.

1337. Before modern robots, there were automatons—moving machines that ran on water, clockwork, or air instead of computers or electricity.

1338. The first programmable robot wasn't invented until 1954, and its design laid the groundwork for the automation of certain jobs.

1339. Sophia the robot received Saudi Arabian citizenship in 2017, which makes her the first robot to have a nationality.

1340. Almost 45% of all the world's robots are produced in Japan, and the Japanese use their robots to staff hotels and restaurants (*Japan Advanced Manufacturing*, 2023).

1341. South Korea employs the most robots on earth at 631 robots per 10,000 employees. Do you want to work with a robot? (McCarthy, 2018)

1342. Robots are used in space exploration, and the Mars rover Curiosity used to sing "Happy Birthday" to itself millions of miles from Earth.

1343. Robotics and artificial intelligence are related, but two different things—robots are more about the ability to do tasks.

1344. The robot apocalypse is a long way off; today, most robots can only perform programmed tasks, and AI is still in the early stages.

Art & Artists

1346. Frida Kahlo's work was declared part of Mexico's cultural heritage, which is why it is rare to see her pieces on display elsewhere.

1347. It took Michelangelo four years to paint the ceiling of the Sistine Chapel, but when it was finished, his spine was permanently disfigured.

1348. The smallest painting on Earth is the Mona Lisa, painted on half the width of a human hair, or the *Mini Lisa* (York, 2013).

1349. There are 500 identified plant species and around 190 different flowers within the *Birth of Venus* by Botticelli (Burke, 2022).

1350. Pablo Picasso was once accused of stealing the Mona Lisa because he accidentally bought other artwork stolen from the Louvre in the same heist.

1351. For the first four decades of the Olympics, it was possible to win medals in music, architecture, sculpture, painting, and literature.

1352. The most expensive painting as of today is the Salvator Mundi by Leonardo da Vinci which was bought for $450 million at auction (DiMarco, 2023).

1353. Sir Isaac Newton invented the color wheel in 1706 by refracting white light into its six colors.

1354. Salvador Dali's famous melted clocks were inspired by his watching Camembert cheese melt in the sun.

1355. Vincent Van Gogh averaged a painting a day and produced nearly 900 works of art over his lifetime (Department of European Paintings, 2019).

Sports

1356. Only 200 of the 8,000 sports played worldwide have international recognition (Sportspodium, 2017).

1357. In 1971, golf was the first sport played on the moon by astronaut Alan Shepard.

1358. Barry Bonds currently holds the record for most home runs at 762,48 more than Babe Ruth (*MLB Baseball Career*, 2023).

1359. Running is the oldest Olympic sport, and at the first Olympics, there were three feet races of varying lengths.

1360. The longest boxing fight in history lasted 7 hours and 19 minutes over 110 rounds in 1893 (Boxing News Staff, 2021).

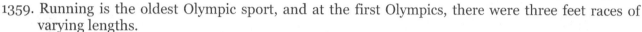

1361. Christiano Ronaldo holds the record for most goals in a career at 834 goals in 1,160 games as of 2023, and his career isn't over yet!

1362. The Portuguese football star is also the best-paid athlete, as he earns $136 million a year (*The World's Highest-Paid*, 2023).

1363. Michael Phelps holds the record for most Olympic medals won at 28 for his accomplishments in swimming (*Top Olympic*, 2010).

1364. Women were allowed to compete in the Olympics for the first time in 1900, but only in tennis.

1365. Football—soccer—is the most popular sport on Earth, with 3.5 billion fans, and it is followed by cricket with 2.5 billion fans (Shvili, 2020).

1366. After 2028, Paris, London, Athens, and Los Angeles will be tied for hosting the Olympics the most times at three times apiece (Wood, 2010).

1367. If you're looking into getting into horseback riding, just know that equestrian is the most expensive popular sport.

1368. Tom Brady has the record for most touchdowns in NFL history, with 649 over his career (National Football League, 2023).

1369. Tennis players run an average of 3 miles—4.8 km—in a single match, which is impressive given a court is only 78 ft—23.77 m—by 36 ft—10.97 m (*Tennis Court Dimensions*, 2020).

1370. The fastest volleyball serve on record was 84 mph—135.6 kph—which is as fast as a speeding car (Leon Demolishes VNL, 2021).

1371. At 38,652 points, LeBron James holds the record for most baskets scored throughout an NBA career (Merrell, 2023).

1372. Tug of war was an Olympic sport from 1900–1920, with Britain winning the most medals in the event.

1373. The longest match of cricket in history was 14 days long, as was played between England and South Africa in 1939 (Sherifi, 2021).

1374. Hockey pucks have to be frozen before they are used in games so that there is less resistance on the ice.

1375. The fastest knockout in boxing history happened in 10.5 seconds when Al Couture punched Ralph Walton in 1946 (Lee, 2012).

1376. Running and wrestling are thought to be the oldest sports in human history because both require no equipment.

1377. Live pigeon shooting was a sport at the Olympics only once in 1900 and, due to its violence, was discontinued.

1378. To keep himself cool, Babe Ruth would wear a piece of cabbage under his hat and change it every two innings.

1379. A racehorse must win the Preakness Stakes, the Kentucky Derby, and the Belmont Stakes to be awarded the triple crown.

1380. Nolan Ryan was the first MBL player to ever pitch a baseball over 100 mph—160kph (Liles, 2021).

1381. Polo is known as the *sport of kings* because of the amount of royalty who play the sport.

1382. Diamondbacks player Randy Johnson once threw a fastball that exploded an unfortunate bird on impact.

1383. With 116 lanes, the Inazawa Bowling Centre in Japan is the largest bowling alley in the world.

1384. Jesse Owens broke 4 world records in track and field in 45 minutes at the Berlin Olympics in 1936.

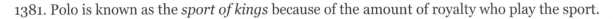

1385. Baseballs used in the MLB only have a lifetime of 5–7 pitches (Lee, 2012).

1386. In 1457, golf was banned from England because it distracted the population from practicing archery.

Crazy Beliefs in the Past

1388. The Ancient Greeks believed sneezing was a sign from the gods, and sneezing before an important task was a good omen.

1389. People thought the fast speeds of trains would drive passengers insane because humans had never gone that fast before.

1390. The witching hour, when evil forces would walk the Earth, was thought to be between midnight and 1 a.m.

1391. In the Middle Ages, people believed there was a plant from the region of Mongolia that grew lambs called the *Lamb of Tartary*.

1392. Alchemists in the 17th–18th centuries thought they could turn lead into gold and even create an immortality cure.

1393. Turkeys were worshipped as gods by the Maya and played important roles in their ceremonial rites.

1394. The 19th-century Europeans believed that a person's skull size had something to do with their intelligence.

1395. People could be accused of being witches if they were too sarcastic or didn't hear a question.

1396. Male Vikings believed mathematics was a type of magic, so women were put in charge of household finances.

1397. Two school-age girls were able to convince the world in 1917 that fairies were real using photographs of paper fairies.

1398. The ancient Chinese believed the world was created after an ancient giant died and his body became the Earth.

1399. Sailors mistook manatees for mermaids with their clubbed tails, but you'd think it would be hard to not see that whiskered face!

1400. The Mayans believed the world was going to end on December 12, 2012, but luckily they were wrong about that one.

1401. Dolphins were thought to be people cursed to live in the sea for their misdeeds by the ancient Greeks.

1402. The Aztecs thought they needed to practice human sacrifice so that the sun would be fed and continue to rise.

1403. A drink of crushed snails and sugar was thought to relieve a sore throat in the Middle Ages.

1404. Pope Gregory IX thought that black cats were vessels of Satan so he put out an order for their extermination.

1405. Before the 17th century, medieval people thought children were born evil, which is why Jesus is always painted like a tiny man.

1406. The Iroquois people believed that the world was perched on the back of a gigantic turtle.

1407. Victorians believed that *fasting girls* did not have to eat or drink and survived off of the love of God alone.

1408. The ancient Romans didn't believe Britain existed until Julius Caesar invaded it.

1409. To cure the Black Death, peasants would tie a chicken to the ankle of the diseased so the chicken would take in the illness, not the person.

1410. Vikings believed the sea was salty because of a salt mill that sat at the bottom of the ocean grinding for eternity.

1411. Egyptians believed that the sun god Ra died every night, and every sunrise was his rebirth.

1412. People in the Middle Ages thought Wolfsbane would protect them from wolves and werewolves when really it is a poisonous plant.

1413. In the 1950s, some people believed and even wrote books saying that you could pray your fat away.

1414. Plato believed the lost city of Atlantis had been on the Greek island of Santorini.

1415. Ancient Romans believed that by drinking the blood or eating the livers of fallen gladiators they would absorb their strength.

1416. Even today, some people believe ancient aliens built the pyramids even though there is plenty of evidence the Egyptians built them.

1417. Elephant puke was used by ancient Chinese doctors to get rid of bad breath.

1418. People in ancient Greece who died by lightning were thought to not deserve a burial because the gods had killed them.

Holiday Celebrations

1419. It is estimated that 46 million turkeys are eaten on Thanksgiving, which makes for 4.8 billion lbs of meat being consumed (Leffler, 2023).

1420. "Silent Night" is the most recorded Christmas carol in history, with 733 different versions copyrighted since 1978 (Fogle, 2020).

1421. At the Pumpkin Festival in Germany in 2021, the world's largest jack-o-lantern debuted at 2,684 lbs—1,217 kg. That's the weight of a small car! (McAfee, 2021)

1422. A chocolate bunny with diamond eyes became the most expensive Easter bunny at $49,000 (McDonough & Corbett, 2020).

1423. On average, Americans spend $1,000 on Christmas presents, which is about one week of work (Howarth, 2022).

1424. Most Hanukkah foods are fried because using the oil to cook is celebrating the oil that kept the lanterns lit.

1425. Kwanza was created in the 1960s as a way to celebrate African-American communities and unite people over a shared heritage.

1426. Ten days before the actual Hindu festival of Holi begins, kids throw water balloons and use water pistols filled with colored water to hit passers-by.

1427. In Japan, it is a tradition to eat KFC for Christmas. It's so popular that orders need to be placed two months in advance.

1428. Rather than just putting coal in your stocking, in Germany, there is a Christmas tradition that a demon Krampus will come eat a child if they've misbehaved.

Green Facts

1429. Every year, 10 million trees are cut down just to make toilet paper (*25+ Fascinating Facts*, 2023).

1430. Styrofoam and other kinds of plastic can take up to 1,000 years to decompose, making them key pollutants (*25+ Fascinating Facts*, 2023).

1431. The United States is the world's largest trash-producing nation, as it accounts for 30% of all the trash on Earth (*25+ Fascinating Facts*, 2023).

1432. Renewable energy consumption is predicted to rise by 78% between now and 2040, and there are more jobs in renewable energy than in fossil fuels (*Renewable Energy Fact*, 2023).

1433. The world will run out of fossil fuel reserves—which come from decayed organic matter—by 2052.

1434. Solar energy is almost 200 years old but was first used industrially by NASA in the 1950s (Brunel, 2021).

1435. Almost 100% of the energy in Iceland is produced by its geothermal power plants and hydro reserves (Brunel, 2021).

1436. Though 70% of the Earth is covered by water, only 2.5% of it is freshwater, and only 1% of that can be consumed by humans (*30 Interesting Facts About Sustainability*, 2023).

1437. If all the paper used in a year, 417 million t, was recycled, we would be able to save 7,089 trees (*30 Interesting Facts About Sustainability*, 2023).

1438. The average person now buys 60% more clothes than they did 15 years ago, and less than 1% of those clothes are recycled (Yorke, 2022).

Interesting Occupations

Past

1439. In the modern age, lamps are electric, but in 1920s London, someone would be paid £2 a week to light and clean the lamps.

1440. Whipping boys were peasant boys who were brought into Medieval courts to be beaten in place of the prince when he did something wrong.

1441. Billy Boys were younger men on worksites whose job was to supply the adult workers with hot beverages all day in the '50s and '60s.

1442. Crossing sweepers kept walkways clean so they did not soil upper-class garments and not tipping them had possibly been a criminal offense.

1443. Witch finding was a selective profession in the Middle Ages, complete with a Witchfinder General, one of which killed 230 people in 3 years (Cain, 2016).

1444. Now, we have music and podcasts, but in the 19th-century factories, a lector would stand on a podium to read the newspaper or books to the workers.

1445. Resurrectionists did the nasty work of digging up corpses so that medical students and scientists could study them, but the job was also illegal.

1446. Flautists professionally passed gas to musical cues or as punchlines to jokes and were known to perform at royal courts.

1447. Back in the day, you could have surgery in the same place where you got your hair cut because a barber was also a surgeon.

1448. Before alarm clocks, knocker-ups would go from door to door to wake people up by banging on the doors, but who woke them up?

1449. Sin-eaters were people who came to the houses of the recently deceased to eat a meal that symbolized their sins so the dead person could go to heaven.

1450. You didn't always have to push your own buttons in an elevator; the contraptions used to be driven by an elevator operator who controlled the speed and let you out.

1451. If you have trouble remembering names, you could use a *nomenclator* whose job was to tell their master the names of guests or remind them of conversations.

1452. Before indoor plumbing, necessary women would go through the homes of noblemen and empty their chamber pots by hand, but they were paid a cushy £60 a week (Cain, 2016).

1453. Vomit collectors in Ancient Rome had to collect the sick of the wealthy nobles who made themselves ill at dinner parties so they could eat more.

1454. Nowadays, bowling pins are automatically swept away, but before 1936, pin-setters had to manually set up and organize the pins.

Present

1455. At a hotel in Finland, a professional sleeper has been hired to test the comfort of the beds and write reviews about each one.

1456. Dog food tasters have to try all of the dog food that a company produces so it can be accurately marketed and compete with other companies.

1457. In an underwater hotel in Florida, an underwater pizza delivery man has to scuba dive to deliver the food.

1458. You can be hired as a legal bank robber whose job is to test the security of a bank by attempting to break into it.

1459. Build-a-Bear employs teddy bear surgeons who will sew the arms and legs back onto your stuffed friends and clean them.

1460. Paper towel sniffers have to smell each roll that goes out to be sold to ensure they don't have weird smells.

1461. Snake milking isn't for the faint of heart, as workers are hired to collect snake venom so it can be made into antidotes.

1462. Breath odor evaluators work for gum or toothpaste companies to make sure the product really helps get rid of bad breath.

1463. Human scarecrows are hired to scare birds off farmlands, sometimes playing instruments or shouting to chase them off.

1464. Professional queuers are hired by the rich to stand in line for them, but at £20 an hour, it's not too bad a gig (Elgueta, 2022).

1465. Babysitting baby pandas is a job in a Chinese zoo, but to be hired, candidates have to go through three elimination rounds and a media contest.

1466. Car sitters are people who charge around ¢0.50 to watch your car while you're out and make sure it doesn't get robbed.

1467. Haunted mazes and zombie films have made being a professional zombie a decent job, with the top pay being $41,000 a year (Culp, 2023).

1468. At a hotel in the United Kingdom, you can be hired as a bed warmer and sleep in a guest's bed in a fleece suit before they arrive so it's nice and toasty for them.

1469. Some Chinese companies hire Americans for $1,000 a week to be fake businessmen to make the company look more international (Noack, 2015).

Spies and Espionage

1470. *Spy* isn't a job itself; normally, spies are doing other jobs, and then they volunteer or are recruited to spy.

1471. The 1917 Espionage Act in the United States made spying a capital offense, but only Julius and Ethel Rosenberg were executed according to this act in 1953 for Soviet–Russian spying.

1472. The International Spy Museum in Washington D.C. receives 600,000 visitors a year and is a part of the Smithsonian Museum System (Jacob & Benzkofer, 2018).

1473. Most spies drive normal cars and wear regular clothes because the goal is to blend in; maybe you even know a spy!

1474. The earliest spies are thought to be from Ancient Egypt and were hired to discover military secrets of neighboring empires.

1475. The CIA has employed magicians and had even paid one $3,000 in the 1970s to write a handbook on deception and trickery (SpyScape, 2023).

Famous Spies

1476. Sir Francis Walsingham is thought to be the father of modern spying as he developed a network of double agents and codes to protect Queen Elizabeth I.

1477. James Bond made the British Secret Service a household name, but the British government pretended the agency didn't exist until 1994.

1478. In 2000, it was discovered that 10 Russian agents had been gathering secrets in the United States for decades.

1479. Though famous for books like *Charlie and the Chocolate Factory* or *Matilda*, Roald Dahl started his career as a British spy in the World Wars.

1480. A spy's pay depends on the assignment; such as in the 1980s, an American spying for the Soviet Union was paid $4 million.

1481. Robert Hanssen's leaks to the Soviet Union are considered the most damaging in United States history because he shared nuclear secrets (*The Most Famous Spies*, 2021).

1482. Harriet Tubman is considered the first female spy in the United States because, after her work on the Underground Railroad, she used her network to spy on the Confederacy.

1483. World War I spy Mata Hari was a dancer in Paris when she was recruited to be a spy, but in 1917, she was falsely accused of being a double agent and executed.

1484. Peggy Shippen was one of the most successful spies in American history as she went undetected for 150 years and even convinced George Washington she wasn't spying.

1485. Cher Ami was a pigeon who received the Cross of War medal in France for sneaking through enemy lines to free French prisoners in 1918.

1486. Sidney Reilley, who was active in World War I, is considered the inspiration behind James Bond because he was known as a ladies' man and the *Ace of Spies*.

1487. The United States first started using spies in the American Revolution, and George Washington was the first head of espionage.

1488. Virginia Hall was a spy in World War II, and she passed along German information which gave her the reputation of *the most dangerous Allied spy*.

1489. When Russian spy Melita Norwood was caught after a lifetime of selling nuclear secrets at age 87, she said, "Oh dear. I thought I had got away with it."

1490. In the 19th century, a monkey found in military dress on a French ship was tried and hanged as a spy by the English.

Gadgets

1491. In the 1960s, the CIA attempted to use a cat to spy on a conversation between Russian officials, but the cat was not able to behave as trained.

1492. Like something out of a film, a Bulgarian agent used an umbrella dart gun to assassinate an *enemy of the state* in 1978.

1493. Spy balloons are used today to collect pictures of military secrets, and they fly at about the same altitude as commercial planes.

1494. Pigeons weren't just used to carry messages, some also had cameras attached to them to take pictures of enemy bases in the World Wars.

1495. In 1946, Moscow schoolchildren gave an American official a wooden replica of the American seal and it wasn't until years later a listening device was found in it.

1496. *Dead-drop* canisters were used in the 1970s to transmit secret messages, and they were disguised as poop so no one would touch them.

1497. The *Kiss of Death* was a small pistol hidden in a lipstick tube used by Soviet spies in the Cold War.

1498. Minox cameras, which saw the most action in the Cold War, are able to take 50 pictures in a minute and focus on the smallest details (National Geographic, 2014).

Spy Myths

1499. James Bond's *license to kill* is not something any spy has in real life, as there are laws against that in international law.

1500. On average, spying is more paperwork and quietly watching than it is the stunts and glamour of James Bond.

1501. It's a myth that spies beat up bad guys or do incredible stunts; in fact, if a spy ever did anything that dangerous, they would probably be fired.

Accidents, Crimes, and Scams

1502. The art heist at the Isabella Stewart Gardener Museum in 1990 was the most expensive in history at $500 million (Neill, 2021).

1503. Archaeologists argue that the first evidence of murder was 430,000 years ago, which would make it the world's oldest cold case.

1504. In 2003, the Central Bank of Iraq was robbed of $920 million, which became the largest bank robbery in history (Campbell, 2019).

1505. Ponzi schemes are named for Charles Ponzi, who convinced investors they would receive high returns on his shady investments.

1506. Al Capone was the most successful gangster in history, as before his death, he had a net worth of $3 billion (Davidson, 2021).

1507. In 2021, there were a total of 1,964 bank robberies in the United States, which is about 5 bank robberies a day (*Bank Crime*, 2021).

1508. DNA testing was invented in 1984, and before that, all someone needed to do to get away with a crime was be out of there when the cops came.

1509. The longest prison sentence ever given was to Chamoy Thipyaso in Thailand. He received 141,000 years for fraud (Widya, 2022).

1510. John Patrick Hannan is the most successful prison fugitive in history, as he has been on the run from the police for 60 years (Boyle, 2016).

1511. Over 400,000 pickpocketing incidents occur over a year, that's over 1,000 every single day (*Some Interesting Pickpocket*, 2016).

Snakes and Vultures

Snakes

1512. Only six countries on Earth do not have snakes, most famously Ireland, because St. Patrick banished them from the Green Isle (Graham, 2023).

1513. Nocturnal snakes tend to have slitted pupils, while snakes who hunt during the day have rounded pupils.

1514. There is enough venom in a king cobra bite to kill an elephant (Sartore, 2010).

1515. Black Mambas can move up to 12 mph—19 kph—which is a bit faster than the average human running speed (Silverman, 2023).

1516. The Saw Scaled Viper is the world's most dangerous snake, as it kills 5,000 people a year in India alone (Williams, 2023).

1517. Escaped pet Burmese pythons are now an invasive species in Florida.

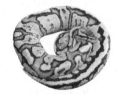

1518. Snakes shed their skin 4–12 times a year, and the only reason humans don't do that is we're shedding skin cells all the time (*Why Do Snakes Shed*, 2015).

1519. King cobras can reach up to 18 ft—5 m—and can *stand up* to a human's height when threatened (Sartore, 2010).

1520. Ball pythons are the most popular pet snake; just make sure you're not of the faint of heart when it comes to feeding time.

1521. Snake Charming is not a cobra loving the flute; it's the snake being put on the defensive but conditioned through pain not to harm the musician.

1522. You can tell the difference between sea and land snakes by the clubbed tail all sea snakes have.

1523. The venom in one bite of the Inland Taipan from Australia is enough to kill 100 humans, making it the most venomous snake (Williams, 2023).

1524. Reticulated pythons are the largest snakes on Earth at 20 ft—6.25 m—which is as tall as a two-story house (Osterloff, 2023).

1525. Snakes have an average of 10,000–15,000 muscles, while humans have 700–800 muscles (WordPress.com, 2018).

1526. In Christianity, snakes are a symbol of evil, but around the world, snakes are a symbol of medicine because of their ability to rejuvenate themselves.

Vultures

1527. Vultures have bare heads and necks, so blood doesn't mat their feathers when they feed on animal carcasses.

1528. There are 23 different species of vulture, and they are divided between Old and New World vultures (Bassett, 2023).

1529. The vultures in Disney's *The Jungle Book* were originally designed to be voiced by the Beatles, but the band declined.

1530. It's a myth that vultures know to encircle dying animals; like any other bird of prey, they are only looking for food.

1531. In ancient Egypt, vultures were worshipped as symbols of motherhood.

1532. The stomachs of vultures are more acidic than most creatures because they are designed to break down the bacteria found on corpses.

1533. In South America, the Andean Condor is the largest species of vulture with a wingspan of 10 to 11 ft—3 to 3.3 m. A human's average wingspan is 6 ft—1.8 m (Mayntz, 2022).

1534. The first Sunday in September is celebrated as International Vulture Day to bring awareness to what these birds do for the environment.

1535. Vultures help prevent the spread of disease by eating corpses no other animals can eat.

1536. Unlike their bird relatives, the raptors, vultures are social birds that hunt and feed in flocks.

1537. When threatened, vultures vomit to lessen their weight so they can fly away faster.

1538. Scientists are considering using vultures at crime scenes for body detection and seeing how quickly they can consume the body.

1539. Poachers sometimes intentionally use poison in illegally hunted animals so that vultures will not bring attention to the carcasses.

1540. African vultures eat 25,000 t of meat a year, which is more than any other predator on the continent (*Vultures*, 2023).

1541. Vultures are endangered because they often consume the human-made toxins left behind in rotting livestock.

1542. Turkey vultures are known to have better senses of smell than most dogs.

Paranormal Activity and Cryptids

1543. Savannah, Georgia, is thought to be the most haunted city in the United States; you can book ghost tours in its many haunted buildings (Perman, 2010).

1544. You can visit Dracula's Castle, Bran Castle, in Transylvania, as well as the church where Dracula arrived in England in Whitby.

1545. Nearly every American state has had a bigfoot sighting, but Washington state pulls ahead with a total of 710 reports (Clarridge, 2023).

1546. The most haunted place on Earth is the Château de Brissac in Maine-et-Loire, France, where the ghosts of the wealthy long gone can be seen (Team Wanderlust, 2023).

1547. There is a festival to celebrate the West Virginian Mothman every third weekend in September, where people can celebrate their favorite cryptid.

1548. The Loch Ness Monster is worth £41 million to the local Scottish economy because of all the tourism it brings in (Scottish Press and Journal, 2018).

1549. Around 40% of Americans believe in ghosts and credit them as one of their major fears (Kambhampaty, 2021).

1550. As of today, the Chupacabra has been blamed for over 150 animal deaths across Central America (Williams, 2023).

1551. The Winchester Mystery House has 160 rooms, and it took over 38 years to build. It is said to be filled with the ghosts of people killed by the Winchester rifle.

1552. Exorcism calls rose during 2020 because of the paranoia of the pandemic and the increased amount of time inside (Crary, 2020).

Probability, Luck

1553. When you flip an American penny, it's more likely you'll land on tails because its center of mass is slightly more on the head's side (Meno, 2023).

1554. There's a one-in-a-million chance you are hit by lightning, and then you have a 90% of surviving (Meno, 2023).

1555. Winning the lottery is a one-in-fourteen-million chance; you're more likely to become a saint of the Catholic church (Allingham, 2018).

1556. If you're in a group of 23 people, there's a 50% chance 2 of you share the same birthday (Moosbrugger, 2021).

1557. Every time you shuffle a deck of cards you are most likely looking at a combination of cards that has never been seen before (B, 2020).

1558. You are more likely to become a movie star at a one-in-a-million chance than you are to be attacked by a shark at a one-in-three million chance (Long, 2018).

1559. There is a 1-in-250 chance of being born a twin, though it helps if there are other twins in your family (Kay, 2020).

1560. On average, you have a 1-in-578,508 chance of getting rich, but this is highly dependent on where you're from and how long you stay in school (Hallman, 2018).

1561. In the UK, 3 in 4 people live within 15 minutes of their hometown, and they are more likely to value relationships (MacFarlane, 2017).

1562. Being born as you are is a 1-in-400 trillion chance (Meno, 2023).

Conclusion

Develop a passion for learning. If you do, you will never cease to grow. –Anthony J. D'Angelo

You have now learned 1,500+ facts.

What Next?

If you liked this book and can't wait to get more, there are plenty of resources to check out!

First, try your local library. Anyone of any age can get a library card, and libraries are completely free. You can sometimes even find clubs or groups that meet at libraries that interest you.

Some great resources can also be found online. For example, on the NASA website, you can see live cameras from the different rovers and missions to the planets in our solar system.

Museums are also a great place to learn new things, and museum personnel are always happy to answer your questions. If you are into the weird things people used to believe, a history museum may be for you, but if you love dinosaurs, there are paleontology museums all over the world.

Sometimes, you also just need to get outside! If the national parks or amazing places caught your interest, try researching the closest ones to you and make a family trip of it. Even your local park is a great place to start because you can find all sorts of plants and animal species in them.

Really, what's important is to keep learning; don't let it stop here! Go with your friends and family to see the things you've read about, and just stay curious.

A Weird, Wonderful World

Hopefully, this book has taught you that the world is a weird and fascinating place. You'll now know everything about poisons in nature and if pirates really buried treasure. With 1,500 facts in your head, you're one smart cookie!

If you stay in school, explore the world around you, and continue to read, you'll always be able to be confident in your brain. But more important than being smart is caring for and being interested in the world around you.

Things matter because we care about them, so it's up to you if any of this matters—if the dolphins in the sea, the people living in the biggest cities, or the lions in Africa matter. By learning, you are deciding to save the world.

So, keep going out there and saving the world with your super phrase, *Did you know?*

References

1903 Wright Flyer. (2023). National Air and Space Museum. https://airandspace.si.edu/collection-objects/1903-wright-flyer/nasm_A19610048000#:~:text=Brief%20Description

ABOUT PUGS. (2023). Dutch Pug Sisters. https://www.thedutchpugsisters.com/pugs#:~:text=In%20France%2C%20Josephine%20Bonaparte%20had

A Brief History of Vaccination. (2023). World Health Organization. https://www.who.int/news-room/spotlight/history-of-vaccination/a-brief-history-of-vaccination#:~:text=Dr%20Edward%20Jenner%20created%20the

Accommodation. (2023). The Manta Resort. https://themantaresort.com/the-resort/accommodation/

Achiam, J. (2016, February 24). *Toilet Paper: Luxury's Final Frontier*. Into the Gloss. https://intothegloss.com/2014/07/black-toilet-paper/

Ackerman, J. (2016, May 3). *Describing Someone as "Birdbrained" Is Misguided, Unless You're Talking About Emus*. Smithsonian Magazine. https://www.smithsonianmag.com/science-nature/describing-someone-birdbrained-misguided-unless-youre-talking-about-emus-180958981/#:~:text=Birds%20are%20smart%2C%20good%20at

Active Wild Admin. (2018, November 8). *The Triassic Period Facts For Kids & Adults: Animals, Climate, Geography*. Active Wild. https://www.activewild.com/triassic-period-facts/

Acuna, K. (2012, April 24). *RANKING: Check Out The 15 Richest Fictional Characters*. Business Insider. https://www.businessinsider.com/here-are-the-wealthiest-fictional-characters-from-the-simpsons-to-iron-man-2012-4?r=US&IR=T#1-smaug-15

Adelaide Robotics Academy. (2016, April 26). *History of Robots*. Adelaide Robotics Academy. https://www.roboticsacademy.com.au/history-of-robots/#:~:text=The%20first%20electronic%20autonomous%20orobots

Admin NG. (2016, November 25). *10 Facts about Hurricanes!* National Geographic Kids. https://www.natgeokids.com/uk/discover/geography/physical-geography/hurricanes/#:~:text=Hurricanes%20form%20over%20warm%20ocean

Admin. (2017, June 26). *Ocean facts!* National Geographic Kids. https://www.natgeokids.com/uk/discover/geography/general-geography/ocean-facts/#

Admin. (2018, January 29). *10 Interesting Facts About Warthogs* - Shamwari Private Game Reserve. Shamwari Private Game Reserve . https://www.shamwari.com/10-interesting-facts-about-warthogs/

Admin. (2021, May 31). *List of Deserts in the World* . Allsubjects4you. https://www.allsubjects4you.com/list-of-deserts-in-the-world/

Admin. (2022, May 9). *History's Mistaken Mermaids*. South Carolina Aquarium. https://scaquarium.org/historys-mistaken-mermaids/#:~:text=Manatees%20were%20often%20mistaken%20for

Admin Hogtown Mascots. (2020, November 3). *The 4 Most Common Bird Mascots and What They Symbolize*. Hogtown Mascots. https://hogtownmascots.com/the-4-most-common-bird-mascots-and-what-they-symbolize/#:~:text=Eagles%20%7C%20Courage%20and%20Power

Age of Mammals. (2023).USRA. https://www.lpi.usra.edu/education/timeline/gallery/slide_63.html

Agence France-Presse. (2023, August 14). *World's Deadliest Wildfires*. Voice of America. https://www.voanews.com/a/world-s-deadliest-wildfires-/7224983.html

Agnew, M. E. (2021, November 5). *Medieval Body Hair And The Curious Practice Of Forehead Plucking*. Eternal Goddess. https://www.eternalgoddess.co.uk/posts/medieval-body-hair-and-the-curious-practice-of-forehead-plucking

Agriculture and Aquaculture: Food for Thought. (2021, March 8). US EPA. https://www.epa.gov/snep/agriculture-and-aquaculture-food-thought#:~:text=A%20single%20cow%20produces%20between

Ahmed, Z. (2023, July 7). *Watch: The Fastest Ship In The World That Beats Metro Trains In Terms Of Top Speed*. Marine Insight. https://www.marineinsight.com/videos/watch-the-fastest-ship-in-the-world-that-beats-metro-trains-in-terms-of-top-speed/#:~:text=We%20know%20that%20ships%20are

Air traffic by the numbers. (2022, August 31). Federal Aviation Administration. https://www.faa.gov/air_traffic/by_the_numbers

Akshatha. (2018, August 30). *7 Interesting Facts About Hawa Mahal in Jaipur*. Https://Www.nativeplanet.com. https://www.nativeplanet.com/travel-guide/interesting-facts-about-hawa-mahal-001739.html

Albuquerque International Balloon Festival. (2023, April 11). *Hot Air History*. Balloonfiesta. https://balloonfiesta.com/Hot-Air-History

Alldridge, M. (2021, December 10). *Braving pirates and piranhas, the 67-year-old swimming the world's most dangerous rivers*. CNN. https://edition.cnn.com/travel/article/martin-strel-slovenia-distance-swimmer-spc-intl/index.html

Allingham, T. (2018, February 5). *Save the Student*. Save the Student; Save the Student. https://www.savethestudent.org/save-money/things-more-likely-than-winning-lottery.html

Amazing Facts You Didn't Know About Your Brain (Infographic). (2020, December 28). Cleveland Clinic. https://health.clevelandclinic.org/brain-teasers-infographic/

Amazon Aid. (2023). *The Amazon and Water*. Amazon Aid Foundation. https://amazonaid.org/resources/about-the-amazon/the-amazon-and-water/

AMDRO. (2023). *Fun Facts on Cockroaches*. Www.amdro.com. https://www.amdro.com/learn/household-pests/fun-facts-on-cockroaches

American Bear Association. (2023). *Hiking & Camping*. American Bear Association. Www.americanbear.org. https://www.americanbear.org/education-awareness/hiking-camping/

American Gem Society. (2021, May 11). *Diamond Facts for Kids and Adults | Learn Interesting Facts About Diamonds*. American Gem Society. https://www.americangemsociety.org/diamond-facts-for-kids-and-adults/

Americans Are Eating More Alligator. (2015, May 11). Food Republic. https://www.foodrepublic.com/2015/05/11/americans-are-eating-more-alligator/

Amicus Travels. (2019, November 19). *15 FACTS ABOUT MONGOLIAN GOBI DESERT*. Amicus Travel Mongolia. https://www.amicusmongolia.com/15-facts-about-mongolian-gobi-desert.html

Ancestry. (2017, April 19). *6 Weird But True Facts About DNA* - Ancestry Blog. Ancestry Blog. https://blogs.ancestry.com/cm/weird-but-true-facts-about-dna/

Anderson, M. (2023, October 25). *Interesting Facts About Computer Most People Don't Know*. 365 Technologies Inc. https://www.365tech.ca/interesting-facts-about-computer-most-people-dont-know/

Andrews, E. (2017, June 22). *The World's Most Catastrophic Floods, in Photos*. HISTORY. https://www.history.com/news/worlds-most-catastrophic-floods-in-photos

Andrews, E. (2018a, April 23). *9 Blades that Forged History*. HISTORY. https://www.history.com/news/knives-that-changed-history

Andrews, E. (2018b, August 23). *What was the dancing plague of 1518?*. HISTORY. https://www.history.com/news/what-was-the-dancing-plague-of-1518

Andrews, E. (2018c, August 29). *11 Things You May Not Know About Ancient Egypt*. HISTORY. https://www.history.com/news/11-things-you-may-not-know-about-ancient-egypt

Angulo, S. (2023, June 3). *10 Seriously Strange Beliefs Humans Held Throughout History*. Listverse. https://listverse.com/2023/06/03/10-seriously-strange-beliefs-humans-held-throughout-history/

Aniol, T. (2020). *Bayerische Schlösserverwaltung | Neuschwanstein Castle | Tourist info*. Neuschwanstein.de. https://www.neuschwanstein.de/englisch/tourist/

Annis, R. (2021, September 22). *11 Ways to Start a Fire*. Family Handyman. https://www.familyhandyman.com/article/ways-to-start-a-fire/

Antonov AN-225 Mriya. (2023). Air Charter Service. https://www.aircharterservice.com/aircraft-guide/cargo/antonov-ukraine/antonovan-225#:~:text=The%20Antonov%20AN%2D225%20Mriya

Appleton, S. (2022, September 29). *Roman Aqueducts | National Geographic Society*. Education.nationalgeographic.org; National Geographic. https://education.nationalgeographic.org/resource/roman-aqueducts/

Aprea, J. (2021, November 10). *The Early History of Human Excreta*. JSTOR Daily. https://daily.jstor.org/the-early-history-of-human-excreta/

Are Salamanders Dangerous? (2021, June 5). B.O.G. Pest Control. https://www.bogpestcontrol.com/pest-control/are-salamanders-dangerous/

Asbjørnsen, P. C., & Moe, J. (2023, January 1). *Why the Sea is Salt*. Tales from the Enchanted Forest. https://talesfromtheenchantedforest.com/2023/01/01/why-the-sea-is-salt/

Asia London Palomba. (2023, July 16). *6 Amazing Facts About Florence's Cathedral of Santa Maria del Fiore*. America Domani. https://americadomani.com/6-facts-about-cathedral-of-santa-maria-del-fiore/

Astaiza, R. (2012, September 20). *11 Crazy Things People Used To Think Were Healthy*. Business Insider. https://www.businessinsider.com/crazy-things-people-used-to-think-were-healthy-2012-9?r=US&IR=T#radioactive-drinks-1

Asteroid Impact that Killed Dinosaurs Triggered "Mega-earthquake" that Lasted Months. (2022, October 19). Montclair State University. https://www.montclair.edu/newscenter/2022/10/19/asteroid-impact-killed-dinosaurs-triggered-mega-earthquake-lasted-months/#:~:text=When%20the%206%2Dmile%2Dwide

Asturpesca. (2023). *The most fish-consuming countries in the world | Asturpesca*. The Most Fish-Consuming Countries in the World. https://asturpesca.com/en/2021/11/19/the-most-fish-consuming-countries-in-the-world/

Atkins, H. (2018). *10 Facts About Napoleon*. History Hit. https://www.historyhit.com/facts-about-napoleon/

Atlantic Dawn: The Ship from Hell. (2012, July 18). British Sea Fishing. https://britishseafishing.co.uk/atlantic-dawn-the-ship-from-hell/

Atlantic Productions and Zoo. (2023, October 19). *Quetzalcoatlus*. Education.nationalgeographic.org. https://education.nationalgeographic.org/resource/quetzalcoatlus-flight/

Atmosphere. (2023, April 14). National Oceanic and Atmospheric Administration. https://www.noaa.gov/jetstream/atmosphere

Atuna. (2023). *Tuna - World's Most Consumed Fish | Pages| ATUNA*. Atuna.com. https://atuna.com/pages/tuna-world-s-2nd-most-consumed-fish-2#:~:text=Tuna%20%2D%20World

Augustyn, A. (2018). U-2 | United States aircraft. In *Encyclopædia Britannica*. https://www.britannica.com/technology/U-2

Austin, C. (2021, December 31). *What is the greatest scientific discovery of all time?*. Carbon Scientific. https://www.carbonscientific.co.uk/blogs/news/what-are-the-greatest-scientific-discoveries-of-all-time

Austin, D. (2021, July 22). *The History of the World's First Cruise Ship Built Solely for Luxurious Travel*. Smithsonian Magazine. https://www.smithsonianmag.com/history/history-worlds-first-cruise-ship-built-solely-luxurious-travel-180978254/

Avian Adaptations. (2018, April 5). Montana Natural History Center. https://www.montananaturalist.org/blog-post/avian-adaptations/#:~:text=This%20bone%20specialization%20isn%27t

B, M. (2020, August 28). *3 Statistical Facts That Seem Outrageous at First*. Science Times. https://www.sciencetimes.com/articles/27066/20200827/3-statistical-outrageous.htm

Bachman, C. (2023). *Do Bears Really Hibernate?*. National Forest Foundation. Www.nationalforests.org. https://www.nationalforests.org/blog/do-bears-really-hibernate

Baddour, D. (2019, March 21). *Colombia's river of five colours*. Www.bbc.com. https://www.bbc.com/travel/article/20190320-colombias-river-of-five-colours

Badgamia, N. (2023, May 22). *Did you know there are more sheep than people in New Zealand?*. WION. https://www.wionews.com/world/sheep-outnumber-people-by-less-than-five-to-one-in-this-country-595162

Bagley, M. (2014, February 11). *Triassic Period Facts: Climate, Animals & Plants*. Live Science; Live Science. https://www.livescience.com/43295-triassic-period.html

Bailey, J. (2015, November 25). *10 hot air balloon world records*. Bailey Balloons. Www.baileyballoons.co.uk. https://www.baileyballoons.co.uk/2015/11/25/10-hot-air-balloon-world-records/

Baird, C. (2013, September 18). *How much water can a camel store in its hump?*. Science Questions with Surprising Answers. https://www.wtamu.edu/~cbaird/sq/2013/09/18/how-much-water-can-a-camel-store-in-its-hump/

Ballard-Whyte, P. (2023, July 11). *The Panzer VIII Maus: The Heaviest Tank Ever Built*. Warfare History Network. https://warfarehistorynetwork.com/article/the-panzer-viii-maus-the-heaviest-tank-ever-built/

Bank Crime Statistics 2021. (2021). Federal Bureau of Investigation. https://www.fbi.gov/file-repository/bank-crime-statistics-2021.pdf/view

Bantock, J. (2022, December 2). *The incredible true story of the time an astronaut played golf on the moon*. CNN. https://edition.cnn.com/2022/12/02/golf/alan-shepard-moon-golf-apollo-remastered-photo-spt-scn-spc/index.html

Baraniuk, C. (2016, November 29). *What it's like to sail a giant ship on Earth's busiest seas*. Www.bbc.com. https://www.bbc.com/future/article/20161128-what-its-like-to-sail-colossal-ships-on-earths-busiest-sea

Barrie, N. (2019, May 22). *10 deadly parasites*. Www.sciencefocus.com. https://www.sciencefocus.com/nature/10-deadly-parasites

Bartlett, J. (2022, October 29). *How a desert bloomed in the driest place on Earth*. The Observer. https://www.theguardian.com/world/2022/oct/29/desert-bloomed-in-chile-atacama-driest-place-on-earth

Bass Angler. (2022, July 26). *5 Interesting Facts You Didn't Know About Fishing as a Sport*. Bass Angler Magazine. https://bassanglermag.com/5-interesting-facts-you-didnt-know-about-fishing-as-a-sport/

Bassett, D. (2023). *Vultures of the world guide: how many species there are, and why they're important*. Www.discoverwildlife.com. https://www.discoverwildlife.com/animal-facts/birds/facts-about-vultures

Bauhaus, J. M. (2018, October 2). *How Many Dog Breeds Are There?*. Hill's Pet Nutrition. https://www.hillspet.com/dog-care/behavior-appearance/how-many-dog-breeds-are-there?lightboxfired=true#

Bauza, V. (2023, May 12). *Methuselah: Still the world's oldest tree?*. Www.conservation.org. https://www.conservation.org/blog/methuselah-still-the-worlds-oldest-tree#:~:text=In%20eastern%20California%2C%20a%20Great

BBC Bitesize. (2023). *The remarkable items that have been used as currency*. BBC Bitesize. https://www.bbc.co.uk/bitesize/articles/zfx2m39

BBC Newsround. (2023, February 23). *World's oldest toilet: 2,400-year-old loo discovered in China*. BBC Newsround. https://www.bbc.co.uk/newsround/64741409

BBC Science Focus. (2023). *Will you die if you eat a polar bear's liver?*. Www.sciencefocus.com. https://www.sciencefocus.com/the-human-body/will-you-die-if-you-eat-a-polar-bears-liver

BBC Wildlife Magazine. (2023, January 23). *What's the largest amphibian?* Discover Wildlife. https://www.discoverwildlife.com/animal-facts/amphibians/whats-the-largest-largest-amphibian

BBC. (2012, March 30). *What are spies really like?*. BBC News. https://www.bbc.co.uk/news/magazine-17560253

BBC. (2017, March 29). *How a giant python swallowed an Indonesian woman*. BBC News. https://www.bbc.co.uk/news/world-asia-39427462

BBC. (2019). *The life cycle of a star - AQA - Revision 1 - GCSE Physics (Single Science)*. BBC Bitesize. BBC Bitesize. https://www.bbc.co.uk/bitesize/guides/zpxv97h/revision/1

BBC. (2020, January 22). *Earth's oldest asteroid impact "may have ended ice age."* BBC News. https://www.bbc.co.uk/news/world-australia-51201168

BBC. (2023, September 7). *Saharan dust cloud sweeps over UK covering cars in an orange powder*. BBC Newsround. https://www.bbc.co.uk/newsround/66734529

Beckman, J. (2023, September 8). *90+ Fascinating Information Technology Statistics for 2023*. The Tech Report. https://techreport.com/statistics/information-technology-statistics/

Beheler, T. (2022, April 27). *10 Strange Medical Practices from History | Headlines and Heroes*. Blogs.loc.gov. https://blogs.loc.gov/headlinesandheroes/2022/04/10-strange-medical-practices-from-history/

Bell, J. (2021, August 7). *17 Facts to Know About Axes - Common Questions | Axe & Tool*. Axeandtool.com. https://axeandtool.com/axe-facts/

Bellis, M. (2019, December 3). *The Escalator Was Once an Amusement Park Ride*. ThoughtCo. https://www.thoughtco.com/history-of-escalator-4072151

Beltrao, A. (2021, August 12). *Why is blackcurrant banned in America?*. The Sun. https://www.thesun.co.uk/news/15847881/why-blackcurrant-banned-america/

Bender, K. (2023, March 16). *What's Next for Gunther, the World's Richest Dog? Offering to "Buy Nicolas Cage's Island."*. People Magazine . https://people.com/pets/gunther-millions-worlds-richest-dog-offers-to-buy-nicolas-cage-island/#:~:text=Gunther%20the%20German%20shepherd%20is

Bennett, E. (2020, December 14). *Fun facts about the Quokka, the happiest animal on earth*. Real Word. https://www.trafalgar.com/real-word/facts-about-the-quokka/

Benson, T. (2014, May 13). *Brief History of Rockets*. Nasa.gov; NASA. https://www.grc.nasa.gov/www/k-12/TRC/Rockets/history_of_rockets.html

Bentoli. (2017, October 31). *The 6 Weirdest Farming & Agriculture Facts You've Never Heard Before*. Bentoli. https://www.bentoli.com/agriculture-facts-weird/

Bhutto, S. (2020, January 9). *15 Weirdly Interesting Facts About Farming You Must Know*. 15 Weirdly Interesting Facts about Farming You Must Know. https://mmnews.tv/15-weirdly-interesting-facts-about-farming-you-must-know/

Bieber, C. (2023, April 24). *Motorcycle Accident Statistics & Numbers For 2023*. Forbes Advisor. Www.forbes.com. https://www.forbes.com/advisor/legal/motorcycle-accident-statistics/

Biography. (2021, October 29). *William Kidd - Ship, Death & Facts*. Www.biography.com. https://www.biography.com/history-culture/william-kidd

Bird Note. (2018, September 17). *Get to Know the Bee Hummingbird, the World's Smallest Bird*. Audubon. https://www.audubon.org/news/get-know-bee-hummingbird-worlds-smallest-bird

Birdfact. (2022, September 25). *How Fast Is A Roadrunner?*. Birdfact. https://birdfact.com/articles/how-fast-is-a-roadrunner

Birds. (2022, October 2). BirdLife International. https://www.bird-life.org/birds/#:~:text=There%20are%20more%20than%2011%2C000

Birds = Dinosaurs, and Other Survivors of K-T Extinction. (2023). American Museum of Natural History. https://www.amnh.org/exhibitions/dinosaurs-ancient-fossils/extinction/dinosaurs-survive#:~:text=Alligators%20%26%20Crocodiles%3A%20These%20sizeable%20reptiles

Black, R. (2012, May 11). *The Idiocy, Fabrications and Lies of Ancient Aliens*. Smithsonian; Smithsonian.com. https://www.smithsonianmag.com/science-nature/the-idiocy-fabrications-and-lies-of-ancient-aliens-86294030/

Blake, M. (2018, May 1). *Best Selling Candy Bars Around the World*. LoveToKnow. https://www.lovetoknow.com/food-drink/ingredients-supplies/best-selling-candy-bars#:~:text=Snickers

Blakemore, E. (2015, June 30). *How Many Craters Are There On Earth?*. Smithsonian Magazine. https://www.smithsonianmag.com/smart-news/how-many-craters-are-earth-180955771/

Blakemore, E. (2020, March 31). *What did people do before toilet paper?*. History. https://www.nationalgeographic.com/history/article/what-people-do-before-toilet-paper

Blakemore, E. (2023, May 1). *The gory history of Europe's mummy-eating fad*. History. https://www.nationalgeographic.com/history/article/mummy-eating-medical-cannibalism-gory-history

Blazenhoff, R. (2012, July 24). *World Record: See's Candies Creates the World's Largest Lollipop, Weighs 7,003 Pounds*. Laughing Squid. https://laughingsquid.com/world-record-sees-candies-creates-the-worlds-largest-lollipop-weighs-7003-pounds/

Blazeski, G. (2017, January 23). *In Ancient Rome, a slave would continuously whisper "Remember you are mortal" in the ears of victorious generals as they were paraded through the streets after coming home, triumphant, from battle*. The Vintage News. Thevintagenews. https://www.thevintagenews.com/2017/01/23/in-ancient-rome-a-slave-would-continuously-whisper-remember-you-are-mortal-in-the-ears-of-victorious-generals-as-they-were-paraded-through-the-streets-after-coming-home-triumphant-from-battle/

Blocksdorf, K. (2011, April 3). *15 Facinating Facts About Horses*. The Spruce Pets; TheSprucePets. https://www.thesprucepets.com/facts-about-horses-1887392

Bloom, J., Motlagh, M., & Czyz, C. N. (2021). *Anatomy, Head and Neck, Eye Iris Sphincter Muscle*. PubMed; StatPearls Publishing. https://www.ncbi.nlm.nih.gov/books/NBK532252/#:~:text=The%20iris%20sphincter%20muscle%2C%20also

Blue Whale | Species. (2023). World Wildlife Fund. https://www.worldwildlife.org/species/blue-whale#:~:text=The%20blue%20whale%20is%20the

Boater's Insurance. (2021, October 31). *Interesting Facts About Boats*. The Sena Group. https://www.thesenagroup.com/2021/10/31/interesting-facts-about-boats/

Boatsetter Team. (2020, July 29). *10 Facts About Fishing Most People Don't Know*. Boatsetter. https://www.boatsetter.com/boating-resources/ten-facts-fishing-boat-rental

Boeckmann, C. (2022, February 2). *Flower Meanings: The Language of Flowers*. Old Farmer's Almanac. https://www.almanac.com/flower-meanings-language-flowers

Boeckmann, C. (2023, September 11). *10 Burning Facts About the Sun*. Almanac.com. https://www.almanac.com/10-burning-facts-about-sun

Bolles, D. (2023, September 3). *Moons: Facts - NASA Science*. Science.nasa.gov. https://science.nasa.gov/solar-system/moons/facts/

Bones. (2012, October 31). *Better Health Channel*. https://www.betterhealth.vic.gov.au/health/conditionsandtreatments/bones

Bonsai: A Brief History. (2022, March 22). Birmingham Botanical Gardens. https://www.birminghambotanicalgardens.org.uk/blog/news/bonsai-a-brief-history/

Bowers, F. (1997, October 29). *Building a 747: 43 Days and 3 Million Fasteners*. Christian Science Monitor. https://www.csmonitor.com/1997/1029/102997.us.us.2.html#:~:text=Building%20an%20airplane%20is%20a

Boxing News Staff. (2021, March 7). *Editor's Pick: The longest fight in boxing history*. Boxing News. https://boxingnewsonline.net/the-longest-fight-in-boxing-history/

Boy Scouts of America. (2018, October 1). *Meet the Biggest Dinosaur of the Jurassic Period*. Heads up by Scout Life. https://headsup.scoutlife.org/meet-the-biggest-dinosaur-of-the-jurassic-period/

Boyd, I. (2023, February 7). *Analysis: How spy balloons work, and what information they can gather*. PBS NewsHour. https://www.pbs.org/newshour/nation/analysis-how-spy-balloons-work-and-what-information-they-can-gather

Boyle, D. (2016, January 4). *World's most successful prison fugitive has been on the run for 60 years*. The Telegraph. https://www.telegraph.co.uk/news/uknews/law-and-order/12080016/John-Patrick-Hannan-on-run-from-Verne-Prison-Dorset-60-years.html#:~:text=The%20world%27s%20most%20successful%20fugitive

Bradley, M. (2023, February 1). *11 Fastest Motorcycles In The World (Top Speed List)*. Luxe Digital. https://luxe.digital/lifestyle/cars/fastest-motorcycles/

Brain Institute. (2023). *Understanding Headaches and Migraines | Brain Institute | OHSU*. Www.ohsu.edu. https://www.ohsu.edu/brain-institute/understanding-headaches-and-migraines#:~:text=The%20brain%20itself%20doesn%27t

Bran Castle. (2023, July 14). *Welcome to Bran Castle! - History, Schedule & Tickets Online*. Bran Castle. https://bran-castle.com/

Braswell, K. (2023, August 11). *11 of the Most Expensive Hotels in the World*. Veranda. https://www.veranda.com/travel/g44796520/most-expensive-hotels-in-world/

Bressan, D. (2016, December 4). *What Are The Most Common Minerals On Earth?*. Forbes. https://www.forbes.com/sites/davidbressan/2016/12/04/what-are-the-most-common-minerals-on-earth/?sh=74126280615c

Breyer, M. (2022, March 31). *11 Wondrous Facts About Praying Mantises.* Treehugger. https://www.treehugger.com/wondrous-facts-about-praying-mantises-4858807
Bridges, M. (2021, September 19). *A Treasury of Pirate Facts.* Www.southwestern.edu. https://www.southwestern.edu/live/news/14973-a-treasury-of-pirate-facts#:~:text=Pirates%20wore%20earrings%20to%20commemorate
Brink, J. G., & Hassoulas, J. (2009). *The first human heart transplant and further advances in cardiac transplantation at Groote Schuur Hospital and the University of Cape Town.* Cardiovascular Journal of Africa, 20(1), 31–35. https://www.ncbi.nlm.nih.gov/pmc/articles/PMC4200566/#:~:text=Christiaan%20Barnard%20with%20his%20team
Broad, L. (2022, June 5). *Why toilets were a feminist issue.* Songs of Sunrise. https://leahbroad.substack.com/p/why-toilets-were-a-feminist-issue
Brunel. (2021). *Did you know? Fascinating renewable energy facts.* Brunel; Brunel. https://www.brunel.net/en-au/blog/renewable-energy/fascinating-renewable-energy-facts
Bruning, K. (2023, August 11). *12 Of The Best Tech Gadgets That You Didn't Know Existed.* SlashGear. https://www.slashgear.com/1360527/best-tech-gadgets-2023/
Bryan, M. (2021, July 13). *30 Triceratops Facts About The Three-Horned Dinosaur.* Facts.net. https://facts.net/triceratops-facts/
Bryan, M. (2023, September 23). *50 Desert Facts Too Hot To Handle. Turn Your Curiosity into Discovery.* Facts.net. https://facts.net/desert-facts/
Buckles, S. (2011). *25 Interesting Facts About Sailing You Probably Don't Know.* ImproveSailing. https://improvesailing.com/tips/interesting-sailing-facts
Burgin, C. J., Colella, J. P., Kahn, P. L., & Upham, N. S. (2018). *How many species of mammals are there?*, Journal of Mammalogy, 99(1), 1–14. https://doi.org/10.1093/jmammal/gyx147
Burgueño Salas, E. (2023, September 22). *Flood deaths per year worldwide 1960-2022.* Statista. https://www.statista.com/statistics/1293207/global-number-of-deaths-due-to-flood/#:~:text=The%20effects%20of%20flooding&text=For%20example%2C%20more%20than%2054
Burke, D. (2022, July 28). *101 Art History Facts.* Fine Art Restoration Company. https://fineart-restoration.co.uk/news/one-hundred-and-one-art-history-facts/
Burket, J. (2019, July 22). *22 Facts About the Brain | World Brain Day.* Dent Neurologic. https://www.dentinstitute.com/22-facts-about-the-brain-world-brain-day/
Burns, J. (2016, October 30). *Monsters, Magic, and Monkshood.* Chicago Botanic Garden. Www.chicagobotanic.org. https://www.chicagobotanic.org/blog/plants_and_gardening/monsters_magic_and_monkshood#:~:text=Frightened%20folks%20turned%20to%20growing
Burns, K. (2007). *War Production.* The War | Ken Burns | PBS. https://www.pbs.org/kenburns/the-war/war-production
Butcher, A. (2023). *History of Birthstones.* International Gem Society. https://www.gemsociety.org/article/history-of-birthstones/
Butler, R. (2019, July 1). *Countries with the most amphibian species.* Mongabay. https://rainforests.mongabay.com/03amphibian.htm
Butler, R. (2021, September 12). *10 Rainforest Facts for 2018.* Mongabay.com. https://rainforests.mongabay.com/facts/rainforest-facts.html
Butterfly Conservation. (2022, October 17). *12 Magnificent Moth Facts.* Butterfly-Conservation.org. https://butterfly-conservation.org/news-and-blog/12-magnificent-moth-facts
Byrne, G. (2023, May 17). *Top ten farming facts for kids.* Little Farmers. https://craigieslittlefarmers.co.uk/top-farming-facts-for-kids/#:~:text=Farming%20is%20the%20oldest%20industry%20in%20the%20world&text=These%20crops%20were%20cultivated%20around
Cabin, "EXPLORER II". (2023). National Air and Space Museum. https://airandspace.si.edu/collection-objects/cabin-explorer-ii/nasm_A19370060000#:~:text=Launched%20on%20November%2011%2C%201935
Cain, F. (2016, October 16). *10 Interesting Facts About Volcanoes - Universe Today.* Universe Today. https://www.universetoday.com/32185/10-interesting-facts-about-volcanoes/
Cain, Á. (2016, June 20). *Here are 24 of history's weirdest jobs.* Business Insider. https://www.businessinsider.com/weird-jobs-that-no-longer-exist-2016-6?r=US&IR=T#whipping-boy-5
California.com Team. (2023, September 14). *5 Mindblowing Fun Facts About Hollywood.* Www.california.com. https://www.california.com/5-mindblowing-fun-facts-about-hollywood/
Cambal, A. (2023, March 27). *15 Most Expensive Swords and Daggers in History.* Sword Encyclopaedia. https://swordencyclopedia.com/most-expensive-swords/
Camel. San Diego Zoo Wildlife Alliance. (2019). https://animals.sandiegozoo.org/animals/camel
Campbell, C. (2019, December 3). *The Top 10 Biggest Bank Robberies of All Time.* Www.chards.co.uk. https://www.chards.co.uk/guides/the-top-10-biggest-bank-robberies-of-all-time/1121
Campbell, E. M., Burdin, M., Hoppler, S., & Bowman, A. S. (2010). *Role of an aquaporin in the sheep tick Ixodes ricinus: Assessment as a potential control target,* International Journal for Parasitology, 40(1), 15–23. https://doi.org/10.1016/j.ijpara.2009.06.010
Carr, H. (2018). *10 Facts About Medieval Castles.* History Hit. https://www.historyhit.com/facts-about-medieval-castles/
Carroll, R. (2001, September 16). *Tuscany's Excalibur is the real thing, say scientists.* The Guardian. https://www.theguardian.com/world/2001/sep/16/rorycarroll.theobserver
Cartwright, M. (2022, July 25). *The Gold of the Conquistadors.* World History Encyclopedia. https://www.worldhistory.org/article/2045/the-gold-of-the-conquistadors/
Casale, S. (2023, September 7). *10 Most Haunted Hotels in the World.* Travel + Leisure. https://www.travelandleisure.com/trip-ideas/fall-vacations/worlds-most-haunted-hotels
Cassidy, M. (2022, June 1). *What happens on board fishing vessels?.* Global Seafood Alliance. https://www.globalseafood.org/blog/fishing-vessels/
Castelow, E. (2017). World War One Zeppelin Raids. Historic UK. https://www.historic-uk.com/HistoryUK/HistoryofBritain/World-War-One-Zeppelin-Raids/
Castiello, L. (2021, March 2). Moray Eel Bite: What to Do, Causes, Treatment, and More. Healthline. https://www.healthline.com/health/moray-eel-bite#symptoms
Catron, E. (2018a, June 5). *30 Facts About the World's Oceans That Will Blow Your Mind.* Best Life; Best Life. https://bestlifeonline.com/crazy-ocean-facts/
Catron, E. (2018b, June 7). *20 Bizarre Sea Creatures That Look Like They're Not Real.* Best Life; Best Life. https://bestlifeonline.com/bizarre-sea-creatures/
Catton, C. (1995). *Man & Marine Mammals - Dolphins In Ancient Mythology | A Whale Of A Business | FRONTLINE | PBS.* Www.pbs.org. https://www.pbs.org/wgbh/pages/frontline/shows/whales/man/myth.html#:~:text=They%20are%20saved%20from%20drowning
CBS News. (2011, January 5). *15 Most Bizarre Medical Treatments Ever.* Cbsnews.com. https://www.cbsnews.com/pictures/15-most-bizarre-medical-treatments-ever/9/
CBS News. (2012, April 8). *The Sport of Kings: Polo.* Cbsnews.com. https://www.cbsnews.com/news/the-sport-of-kings-polo-08-04-2012/
CBC News. (2021, March 28). *8 other times ships have run into problems in the Suez Canal.* CBC. https://www.cbc.ca/news/world/suez-canal-ships-delays-history-1.5964551
CDC. (2019). *History of Quarantine* . CDC. https://www.cdc.gov/quarantine/historyquarantine.html
Center for Food Safety and Applied Nutrition. (2020, September 17). *GMO Crops, Animal Food, and Beyond.* FDA. https://www.fda.gov/food/agricultural-biotechnology/gmo-crops-animal-food-and-beyond#:~:text=Most%20GMO%20plants%20are%20used
Chadwick, J. (2020, February 28). *5,000-year-old Anatolian sword is one of the world's oldest weapons.* Mail Online. https://www.dailymail.co.uk/sciencetech/article-8055409/The-worlds-oldest-weapon-5-000-year-old-Anatolian-sword-discovered-Armenian-Monastery-Venice.html
Chakra, H. (2023, April 11). *10 Oldest Ships In The World Which Have Survived To This Day - About History.* About History. https://about-history.com/10-oldest-ships-in-the-world-which-have-survived-to-this-day/
Chalasani, R., & Gornstein, L. (2015, July 31). *The most notorious spies in history.* Www.cbsnews.com. https://www.cbsnews.com/pictures/the-most-notorious-spies-in-history/4/
Chaliakopoulos, A. (2021, September 6). *The Myth of Daedalus and Icarus: Fly Between the Extremes.* The Collector. https://www.thecollector.com/daedalus-and-icarus/
Chamary, J. (2023, February 8). *Parasites: what they are, where they live and how parasites are transmitted.* Www.discoverwildlife.com. https://www.discoverwildlife.com/animal-facts/parasites-guide
Chameleon. (2019). San Diego Zoo Wildlife Alliance. https://animals.sandiegozoo.org/animals/chameleon
Chandler, N. (2015, July 11). *Why did Thomas Edison electrocute an elephant?.* HowStuffWorks. https://science.howstuffworks.com/innovation/science-questions/why-did-thomas-edison-electrocute-elephant.htm
Chaouali, N., Gana, I., Dorra, A., Khelifi, F., Nouioui, A., Masri, W., Belwaer, I., Ghorbel, H., & Hedhili, A. (2013). *Potential Toxic Levels of Cyanide in Almonds (Prunus amygdalus), Apricot Kernels (Prunus armeniaca), and Almond Syrup.* ISRN Toxicology, 2013, 1–6. https://doi.org/10.1155/2013/610648
Chelsea Flower Show. (2019, April 25). *Top 10 Most Popular Flowers in the World. Chelsea Flowers.* https://chelseaflowers.co.uk/top-10-most-popular-flowers-in-the-world/
Chivers, T. (2010, May 10). *The 10 weirdest physics facts, from relativity to quantum physics.* Independent.ie. https://www.independent.ie/regionals/herald/the-10-weirdest-physics-facts-from-relativity-to-quantum-physics/27951001.html
Choi, C. (2008, June 30). *Huge Tunguska Explosion Remains Mysterious 100 Years Later.* Space.com. https://www.space.com/5573-huge-tunguska-explosion-remains-mysterious-100-years.html
Choice DNA Testing. (2023, March 9). *Interesting Fun Facts about DNA.* Choice DNA. https://www.choicedna.com/12-interesting-fun-facts-about-dna/
Chromosome Information. (2023). Mount Sinai Health System. https://www.mountsinai.org/health-library/special-topic/chromosome
Čirjak, A. (2020, July 6). *The Biggest Thunderstorm Ever Recorded.* WorldAtlas. https://www.worldatlas.com/articles/the-biggest-thunderstorm-ever-recorded.html
City of Chicago. (2023). *Tree Planting.* Www.chicago.gov. https://www.chicago.gov/city/en/depts/streets/provdrs/forestry/svcs/tree_planting.html#:~:text=The%20Street%20Tree%20Planting%20Program
Clarridge, C. (2023, April 26). *Bigfoot loves Washington too, sightings suggest.* Axios. https://www.axios.com/local/seattle/2023/04/26/bigfoot-washington-sightings
Classes for Curious Minds. (2019, August 1). *10 Fascinating & Fun Science Facts: DNA.* Little House of Science. https://www.littlehouseofscience.com/10_fascinating__fun_science_facts_dna
Clegg, B. (2013, January 27). *20 amazing facts about the human body.* The Guardian; The Guardian. https://www.theguardian.com/science/2013/jan/27/20-human-body-facts-science
Climans, K. (2019, April 2). *Ruthless Facts About Ching Shih, China's Cunning Pirate Queen.* Factinate. https://www.factinate.com/people/facts-ching-shih
Coburg Banks. (2023, June 21). *10 Of The Strangest Jobs You'll EVER Read About | Coburg Banks IT Recruitment Agency Blog.* Www.coburgbanks.co.uk. https://www.coburgbanks.co.uk/it-recruitment-agencies/10-of-the-strangest-jobs-youll-ever-read-about
Cochrane, C. (2023, March 16). *13 things rich people buy that you've never heard of.* MoneyWise. https://moneywise.com/life/lifestyle/things-rich-people-buy-you-never-knew-existed
Coffey, J. (2015, December 24). *What Is The Largest Island In The World - Universe Today.* Universe Today. https://www.universetoday.com/73880/what-is-the-largest-island-in-the-world/
Cofresi, D. (1999, April 18). *Alien Empire ~ Mayflies | Nature | PBS.* Nature. https://www.pbs.org/wnet/nature/alien-empire-mayflies/3413/
Cohen, J. (2013, October 30). *Sulphur Springs's Glass-Walled Public Toilet Vies to Succeed Buc-ees as "America's Best Restroom.".* Texas Monthly. https://www.texasmonthly.com/the-daily-post/sulphur-springss-glass-walled-public-toilet-vies-to-succeed-buc-ees-as-americas-best-restroom/#:~:text=Sulphur%20Springs%20has%20the%20only
Cohn, L. (2023, January 13). *10 of the Smallest Islands in the World.* Reader's Digest. https://www.rd.com/list/smallest-islands-in-the-world/
Confucius Institute for Scotland. (2023). *1, 2, 3 - the Legend of Pangu. Confucius Institute for Scotland.* https://www.confuciusinstitute.ac.uk/1-2-3-the-legend-of-pangu/
Conlon, A. M. (2023). *How long can you go without sleep?* New Scientist. https://www.newscientist.com/question/how-long-can-you-go-without-sleep/#:~:text=The%20longest%20time%20a%20human
Cooke, P. (2021, December 1). *The Quest to Shoot an Arrow Farther Than Anyone Has Before.* Smithsonian Magazine. https://www.smithsonianmag.com/innovation/quest-shoot-arrow-farther-anyone-has-before-180979009/

Cooper, R. (2019, January 11). *6 Ways to Identify Spoiled Food.* Taste of Home; Taste of Home. https://www.tasteofhome.com/collection/how-to-tell-if-food-is-spoiled/

Copley, J. (2022, May 7). *12 of the weirdest deep-sea creatures that lurk in the oceans' depths.* Www.sciencefocus.com. https://www.sciencefocus.com/nature/deep-sea-creatures

Cornell University. (2018). *Cornell University Department of Animal Science.* Cornell.edu. https://poisonousplants.ansci.cornell.edu/toxicagents/ricin.html

Cowan, A. (2023, October 19). *Misunderstood Microbes | National Geographic Society.* Education.nationalgeographic.org. https://education.nationalgeographic.org/resource/misunderstood-microbes/

Craib, R. (2022, May 21). *The Brief Life and Watery Death of a '70s Libertarian Micronation.* Slate. https://slate.com/news-and-politics/2022/05/michael-oliver-republic-of-minerva-history-libertarian-micronations-tonga.html

Crary, D. (2020, October 31). *Exorcism: Increasingly frequent, including after US protests.* AP NEWS. https://apnews.com/article/portland-san-francisco-oregon-cff13a56cd41997553ea3e9a8fc21384

Crazy Critters. (2019, May 23). *OVER 50 Amazing Plant Facts!* Crazy Plants Crazy Critters. https://crazycrittersinc.com/over-50-amazing-plant-facts/

Creek. (2011, March 4). *31 Random Survival Number Facts.* WillowHavenOutdoor Survival Skills. https://willowhavenoutdoor.com/31-random-survival-number-facts/

Crigger, D. (2022, May 12). *10 Freezingly Fascinating Facts About Ice Hockey.* The Fact Site. https://www.thefactsite.com/ice-hockey-facts/

Critter Squad. (2023). *How High Can Frogs Jump?.* C.S.W.D. https://www.crittersquad.com/portfolio/how-high-can-frogs-jump/#:~:text=The%20largest%20jump%20in%20the

Croteau, J. (2022, May 3). *23 Fascinating Dolphin Facts for Kids.* We Are Teachers. https://www.weareteachers.com/dolphin-facts-for-kids/

Crystal the Monkey. (2023). IMDB. https://www.imdb.com/name/nm2640714/

Culp, A. (2023, October 2). *Top 10 Weirdest Jobs in The World - Let's Find Out!.* Employment Security Commission. https://www.ncesc.com/weirdest-jobs-world/

Cutmore, J. (2023, July 10). *Top 10 fastest planes in the world 2023.* Www.sciencefocus.com. https://www.sciencefocus.com/future-technology/fastest-plane-in-the-world

Cuttings. (2023). *The Top 5 Most Popular Gems Used in Jewellery | Cuttings the Jeweller.* Cuttingsjewellers.co.uk. https://cuttingsjewellers.co.uk/blog/top-5-most-popular-gems-used-jewellery#:~:text=Diamond

Daily Mail Reporter. (2014, May 1). *Average American spends $1,200 every year on fast food.* Mail Online. https://www.dailymail.co.uk/news/article-2617493/Average-American-spends-1-200-year-fast-food.html

Daley, J. (2016, April 6). *Sneak a Peek at the Multi-Million Dollar Meteorites Soon up for Sale.* Smithsonian Magazine. https://www.smithsonianmag.com/smart-news/sneak-peek-multi-million-dollar-meteorite-soon-sale-180958622/

Daly, N. (2019, April 25). *Meet the animals that survive extreme desert conditions.* Animals. https://www.nationalgeographic.com/animals/article/extreme-animals-that-live-in-deserts

Dan, M. (2018, August 2). *5 More Weird Weapons of World War I.* History and Headlines. Www.historyandheadlines.com. https://www.historyandheadlines.com/august-2-1916-5-more-weird-weapons-of-world-war-i/

Darling, G. (2021, November 2). *13 Most Expensive Houses In the World.* Luxe Digital. https://luxe.digital/lifestyle/home/most-expensive-houses/

Darren. (2023, April 5). *Thrones Fit for Royalty.* Westside Bathrooms. https://www.westsidebathrooms.co.uk/blog/thrones-fit-for-royalty/#:~:text=The%20toilet%20bowl%20got%20its

Darwin's finches. (2023). Galapagos Conservation Trust. https://galapagosconservation.org.uk/species/darwins-finches/

Dattani, S., & Spooner, F. (2022, October 20). *How many people die from the flu?.* Our World in Data. https://ourworldindata.org/influenza-deaths

Davenport, M. (2016). *Why bearcats smell like popcorn.* C&EN Global Enterprise, 94(17), 11–11. https://pubs.acs.org/doi/10.1021/cen-09417-scicon004#:~:text=Researchers%20have%20ferreted%20out%20whyDuke%20University%20and%20Thomas%20E.

Davidson, L. (2021, October 12). *10 of the Most Infamous Mob Bosses in History.* History Hit. https://www.historyhit.com/the-most-infamous-mob-bosses-in-history/#:~:text=1.

Davis, A. (2022, June 10). *What Are the 5 Mammals That Lay Eggs?.* Treehugger. https://www.treehugger.com/mammals-that-lay-eggs-5101526

Dawson, D. (2022, January 13). *The Seven Summits vs the Seven Second Summits.* How do they compare. Expedreview.com. https://www.expedreview.com/blog/2022/01/comparing-seven-summits-and-seven-second-summits

Day, F. (2022, November 16). *Wonders of God: the strange phenomenon of fasting girls.* HistoryExtra. https://www.historyextra.com/period/victorian/victorian-fasting-girls/

De Graaf, J. (2020, February 24). *100 History Facts They Didn't Teach You At School.* The Fact Site. https://www.thefactsite.com/100-history-facts/

De Luce, I., & Baer, D. (2019, November 14). *From leech collectors to knocker-ups, here are 16 weird jobs that no longer exist.* Business Insider. https://www.businessinsider.com/weird-jobs-that-no-longer-exist-2014-9#pinsetter-2

Deepa. (2023, April 9). *All About Sweet Juliet Rose, the World's Most Expensive Flower.* Dengarden. https://dengarden.com/gardening/The-Most-Expensive-Rose-in-the-World-Sweet-Juliet-Rose

Deering, S. (2015, February 6). *The 10 Weirdest Jobs in the World.* Undercover Recruiter. https://theundercoverrecruiter.com/weirdest-jobs-world/

Dentistry by Dery. (2022, November 17). *The largest teeth ever.* Dentistry by Dery. https://www.dentistrybydery.com/blog/the-largest-teeth-ever-2/#:~:text=The%20African%20elephant%20has%20the

Department of European Paintings. (2019). *Vincent van Gogh (1853–1890).* Metmuseum. https://www.metmuseum.org/toah/hd/gogh/hd_gogh.htm

Desai, K. (2022, March 17). *23 Fun Facts About Your DNA. School of Continuing Studies.* University of Toronto. https://learn.utoronto.ca/curiousu-blog/curiosity/23-fun-facts-about-your-dna

DeSalle, R., & Perkins, S. (2021). *Microbes A-Z: Your Questions Answered.* AMNH. https://www.amnh.org/explore/microbe-facts

DeSoto, L. (2022, April 30). *To eat or to skip breakfast? What the science says.* Www.medicalnewstoday.com. https://www.medicalnewstoday.com/articles/is-breakfast-really-the-most-important-meal-of-the-day

Devanney, J. (2023, February 24). *The most dangerous substance known to man - Works in Progress.* Worksinprogress.co. https://worksinprogress.co/issue/the-most-dangerous-substance-known-to-man

Dhalleine, T. (2023). *Why Geodesic Domes Are Such Incredible Structures.* Www.ecocamp.travel. https://www.ecocamp.travel/blog/why-geodesic-domes-are-incredible-structures#:~:text=Domes%20are%20in%20fact%20the

Dhar, M. (2022, May 20). *Ichthyosaur: Apex predator of the dinosaur-era seas.* Livescience.com. https://www.livescience.com/ichthyosaur-facts

Diabetes UK. (2023). *100 years of insulin.* Diabetes UK. https://www.diabetes.org.uk/our-research/about-our-research/our-impact/discovery-of-insulin#:~:text=23%20January%201923%20%E2%80%93%20%22insulin%20belongs

Dierickx, K. (2015). *59 Fun Facts About Our National Parks.* Outdoor Project. https://www.outdoorproject.com/articles/59-fun-facts-about-our-national-parks

DiMarco, S. (2023, March 1). *These Are the 10 Most Expensive Paintings in the World.* Veranda. https://www.veranda.com/luxury-lifestyle/artwork/g43012775/most-expensive-paintings-in-the-world/

Dinosaurs in "Jurassic Park" were not from Jurassic Period. (2021, January 14). My Dinosaurs. https://www.mydinosaurs.com/blog/dinosaurs-jurassic-park-not-jurassic-period/

Discover 9 of the strangest deep sea creatures. (2022). Monterey Bay Aquarium. https://www.montereybayaquarium.org/stories/deep-sea-creatures

Discovering the Origins of Pizza: Who Invented Pizza? (2023, February 27). Cinquecento. https://cinquecentopizzeria.com/who-invented-pizza-and-more-of-the-history-of-pizza/

Dobrijevic, D. (2021, September 22). *Meteor showers and shooting stars: Formation, facts and discovery.* Space.com. https://www.space.com/meteor-showers-shooting-stars.html

Dobson, J. (2021, April 9). *The 27 Most Active Volcanoes In The World And What Could Erupt Next.* Forbes. https://www.forbes.com/sites/jimdobson/2021/04/09/the-27-most-active-volcanoes-in-the-world-and-what-could-erupt-next/?sh=4bd7298c7836

Dog Bark Park Inn. (2023, April 7). https://www.dogbarkpark.com/

Domestication Timeline. (2020). American Museum of Natural History. https://www.amnh.org/exhibitions/horse/domesticating-horses/domestication-timeline#:~:text=Most%20of%20the%20domestic%20animals

Donegan, B. (2020, April 23). *13 Things You Might Not Know About Thunderstorms | The Weather Channel - Articles from The Weather Channel | weather.com.* The Weather Channel. https://weather.com/safety/thunderstorms/news/2020-04-23-things-you-might-not-know-about-thunderstorms

Donvito, T. (2023, January 24). *The Most Incredible Undersea Treasures Ever Found.* Reader's Digest. https://www.rd.com/list/incredible-undersea-treasures/

Dorn, L. (2022, February 17). *How Disney Issued Its Own Legal Currency for 29 Years.* Laughing Squid. https://laughingsquid.com/how-disney-issued-its-own-legal-currency/

Dowling, S. (2014, May 22). *World's worst planes: The aircraft that failed.* Www.bbc.com. https://www.bbc.com/future/article/20140522-are-these-the-worlds-worst-plane

Doyle, A. (2015, March 17). *There are 228,450 known species in the ocean — and as many as 2 million more that remain a total mystery.* Business Insider. https://www.businessinsider.com/r-oceans-yield-1500-new-creatures-many-others-lurk-unknown-2015-3?r=US&IR=T#:~:text=There%20are%20228%2C450%20known%20species

Dr. Chris and Dr. Xand. (2023). *16 of the weirdest and wackiest facts on the human body.* Penguin. https://www.penguin.co.uk/articles/childrens-article/16-weird-and-wacky-facts-on-the-human-body

Dreher, B. (2022, December 23). *10 Spooky Facts You Never Knew About the Moon.* Reader's Digest. https://www.rd.com/list/moon-facts/

DSF. (2022, July 6). *The Greatest Undiscovered Mythical Treasures Of All Times.* DSF Antique Jewelry. https://dsfantiquejewelry.com/blogs/interesting-facts/the-greatest-undiscovered-mythical-treasures-of-all-times

Ducksters. (2019). *Geography for Kids: Islands.* Ducksters.com. https://www.ducksters.com/geography/islands.php

Dulin, J. (2018, March 29). *36 Incredibly Fun Facts About Money I Bet You Didn't Know.* MoneySmartGuides.com. https://www.moneysmartguides.com/fun-facts-about-money-i-bet-you-didnt-know

Dunn, K. (2014, February 19). *10 Fun Facts about Ancient Rome for Kids (plus cool places to visit)|10 Fun Facts about Ancient Rome for Kids (plus cool places to visit).* Eating Europe. https://www.eatingeurope.com/blog/ancient-rome-for-kids/

Dwarf Sperm Whale. (2022, September 15). *NOAA Fisheries.* https://www.fisheries.noaa.gov/species/dwarf-sperm-whale

Dyvik, E. (2023a, October 9). *Topic: Global megacities.* Statista. https://www.statista.com/topics/4841/megacities/#topicOverview

Dyvik, E. (2023b, August 25). *Countries with the largest share of women 2021.* Statista. https://www.statista.com/statistics/1238987/female-population-share-by-country/

Dyvik, E. (2023c, September 1). *Countries with the smallest population 2022.* Statista. https://www.statista.com/statistics/1328242/countries-with-smallest-population/#:~:text=The%20Vatican%20City%2C%20often%20called

Easy Irrigation. (2023). *A History of Agricultural Irrigation : Easy Irrigation, Watering and Irrigation.* Www.easy-Irrigation.co.uk. https://www.easy-irrigation.co.uk/a-history-of-agricultural-page-29?zenid=872a44vu2gt4nr2sad3n62eus0#:~:text=The%20earliest%20known%20systems%20of

EasyDNA. (2023). *Where and how was Forensic DNA Analysis invented? | EasyDNA UK.* Easydna.co.uk. https://easydna.co.uk/knowledge-base/history-of-forensic-dna-analysis/#:~:text=DNA%20forensics%20was%20first%20reported

Eden. (2023). *Flood Facts | Earth | Nature | Eden Channel*. Eden.uktv.co.uk. https://eden.uktv.co.uk/nature/earth/article/flood-facts/

Editorial Staff. (2015, November 24). *34 Interesting Facts About Toilets - Page 2 of 2*. The Fact File. https://thefactfile.org/toilets-facts/2/

Editorial Staff. (2016, December 5). *27 Interesting Facts About Holi*. The Fact File. https://thefactfile.org/holi-facts/

Editorial Staff. (2016, February 15). *15 Things You Might Not Know About Competitive Fishing*. Www.mentalfloss.com. https://www.mentalfloss.com/article/75364/15-things-you-might-not-know-about-competitive-fishing

Editorial Staff. (2021, July 6). *45 Interesting Facts About Computers*. The Fact File. https://thefactfile.org/computer-facts/

Editorial Team. (2019, November 4). *24 Fascinating London Facts For Kids*. THE LONDON MOTHER. https://www.thelondonmother.net/london-facts-for-kids/

Editorial Team. (2023, January 1). *The 15 Valuable Gemstones in the World (Ranking)*. Luxe Digital. https://luxe.digital/lifestyle/jewelry/most-valuable-gemstones/#:~:text=1.,is%20a%20natural%20blue%20diamond.

Edwards, S. (2015). *Nightmares and the Brain*. Hms.harvard.edu. https://hms.harvard.edu/news-events/publications-archive/brain/nightmares-brain

Ehrhardt, M., Barr, K., Ion, F., & Liszewski, A. (2023, January 9). *The Best, Coolest, and Weirdest Gadgets at CES 2023*. Gizmodo. https://gizmodo.com/the-best-coolest-and-weirdest-gadgets-at-ces-2023-1849957334/slides/29

Ehrlich. (2023a). *12 fascinating facts about mice you need to know*. Ehrlich Pest Control. https://www.jcehrlich.com/help-and-advice/blog/rodents/12-fascinating-facts-about-mice-you-need-to-know

Ehrlich. (2023b). *Top 10 deadliest insects in the world*. Ehrlich. https://www.jcehrlich.com/help-and-advice/blog/pests-in-the-headlines/top-10-deadliest-insects-in-the-world

8 Fun Giant Tube Worm Facts. (2017). Fact Animal. https://factanimal.com/giant-tube-worm/

Eight Interesting Facts About Salamanders. (2016, March 2). Forest Preserves of Cook County. https://fpdcc.com/eight-interesting-facts-about-salamanders/

8 Interesting platypus facts. (2021, May 31). WWF Australia. https://wwf.org.au/blogs/8-interesting-platypus-facts/

11 Facts About Oil. (2015). Do Something. https://www.dosomething.org/us/facts/11-facts-about-oil

11 fun facts about your brain. (2019, October). Northwestern Medicine. https://www.nm.org/healthbeat/healthy-tips/11-fun-facts-about-your-brain

Elgueta, A. (2022, January 14). *I'm a professional queuer and I earn £160 a DAY standing in line for rich people*. The Sun. https://www.thesun.co.uk/money/17322242/professional-queuer-stands-in-line-for-rich-people/

Elhassan, K. (2018, March 2). *These 10 Truly Bizarre Beliefs From History Will Keep You Laughing All Night*. History Collection. https://historycollection.com/10-truly-bizarre-beliefs-history-will-keep-laughing-night/

Elodie. (2016, October 20). *10 Bizarre Reasons People Were Accused of Witchcraft During the Salem Witch Trials*. The SparkNotes Blog. https://www.sparknotes.com/blog/10-bizarre-reasons-people-were-accused-of-witchcraft-during-the-salem-witch-trials/

Elsbury, W. (2022, July 18). *Research Guides: The Machine Gun: Its History, Development and Use: A Resource Guide: Introduction*. Guides.loc.gov. https://guides.loc.gov/machine-gun-its-history-development-and-use

Emergency Disinfection of Drinking Water. (2015, November 18). US EPA. https://www.epa.gov/ground-water-and-drinking-water/emergency-disinfection-drinking-water#:~:text=Boil%20water%2C%20if%20you%20do

Encyclopaedia Britannica Editor. (2023). *Lake Titicaca summary | Britannica*. Www.britannica.com. https://www.britannica.com/summary/Lake-Titicaca#:~:text=Lake%20Titicaca%2C%20South%20American%20lake

Enjoy Travel. (2023). *7 Interesting Facts About Kyoto*. Www.enjoytravel.com. https://www.enjoytravel.com/au/travel-news/interesting-facts/interesting-facts-kyoto

Enriquez, K. C. (2022, October 13). *Captain Chuck Yeager: Breaking the Sound Barrier*. The Unwritten Record. https://unwritten-record.blogs.archives.gov/2022/10/13/captain-chuck-yeager-breaking-the-sound-barrier/#:~:text=On%20October%2014%2C%201947%2C%20USAF

Envirotech. (2021, March 4). *How Much Water Does Farming Use?*. Envirotech Online. https://www.envirotech-online.com/news/water-wastewater/9/breaking-news/how-much-water-does-farming-use/54505

Epifani, M. (2019, August 1). *The First Dinosaur Fossil Was Named Before We Had A Word For Dinosaurs*. Discovery. https://www.discovery.com/science/First-Dinosaur-Fossil-Name

Ettinger, Z. M., Zoë. (2021, June 7). *16 creatures from the bottom of the ocean that will give you nightmares*. Insider. https://www.insider.com/strange-deep-sea-creatures-trivia-facts-2018-4#hagfish-are-known-for-their-repulsive-feeding-habits-lacking-jaws-they-consume-the-decaying-carcasses-of-other-sea-creatures-by-burrowing-into-them-with-tooth-like-structures-2

Evans, C. (2022, July 15). *What makes people so afraid of sharks? "Jaws," some scientists say*. Www.cbsnews.com. https://www.cbsnews.com/news/what-makes-people-so-afraid-of-sharks-jaws-scientists/

Evers, J. (2023a, October 19). *Island | National Geographic Society*. Education.nationalgeographic.org. https://education.nationalgeographic.org/resource/island/

Evers, J. (2023b, October 19). *meteor | National Geographic Society*. Education.nationalgeographic.org. https://education.nationalgeographic.org/resource/meteor/

Fabry, M. (2018, May 1). *What Was the First Sound Ever Recorded by a Machine? Time*. Time. https://time.com/5084599/first-recorded-sound/

Facts About The Blue Lagoon (And 20+ Tips To Make The Most Of Your Visit) | Blue Lagoon Iceland Reviews. (2015, July 27). Just Go Places. https://www.justgoplacesblog.com/facts-about-the-blue-lagoon/

Falcon 9. (2023). SpaceX. https://www.spacex.com/vehicles/falcon-9/

Family Medicine. (2022, July 12). *Should You Pee on a Jellyfish Sting?*. Cleveland Clinic. https://health.clevelandclinic.org/pee-jellyfish-sting/#:~:text=Remember%20that%20if%20you%27re

Fantozzi, J. (2018, May 23). *Facts You Didn't Know About Your Favorite Junk Foods*. Mashed.com. https://www.mashed.com/123737/facts-didnt-know-favorite-junk-foods/

Fantozzi, J. (2020, March 13). *30 food facts that will blow your mind*. Insider. https://www.insider.com/amazing-food-facts-2017-12#scientists-can-turn-peanut-butter-into-diamonds-7

FAO Regional Office for Asia and the Pacific. (2023). *Future Smart Food & Mountain Agriculture. Organisation des Nations Unies pour l'alimentation et l'agriculture*. g. https://www.fao.org/asiapacific/perspectives/zero-hunger/future-smart-food/fr/

Farmhands. (2020, March 7). *7 interesting facts about agriculture*. Farmbrite. https://www.farmbrite.com/post/7-interesting-facts-about-agriculture

Fascinating Dolphin Facts. (2015). Fact Animal. https://factanimal.com/dolphins/

Feather & Black. (2020, July 24). *10 Curious Facts About Sleep*. Feather & Black. https://www.featherandblack.com/inspiration/10-curious-facts-about-sleep

Fenker, H. (2023). *Questions and Answers - Why are electrons so far away from the nucleus of an atom?*. Education.jlab.org. https://education.jlab.org/qa/atomicstructure_05.html#:~:text=Electrons%20are%20indeed%20far%20away

Ferguson, S. (2019, November 22). *Saving Lives, One Toilet at a Time*. UNICEF USA. https://www.unicefusa.org/stories/saving-lives-one-toilet-time#:~:text=Around%2060%20percent%20of%20the

Fieseler Fi 156D-1 "Storch". (2023). Planes of Fame Air Museum. https://planesoffame.org/aircraft/plane-Fi-156D-1

15 Facts About Boats & Ships That Will Surprise You! (2023). Boat Names Australia. https://www.boatnames.com.au/boat-fun-facts

15 Random Car Facts To Impress Your Friends & Family. (2023, January 20). | *Easterns*. Easterns Automotive Group. https://www.easterns.com/2023/01/20/15-random-car-facts-that-will-impress-your-friends-and-family/

Fifty physics mind blowing facts - complete information. (2020, June 26). The Mega Guide. https://www.themegaguide.com/2020/06/Mind-blowing-facts.html

51 Fun & Interesting Facts About New York. (2023, January 30). CuddlyNest. https://www.cuddlynest.com/blog/facts-about-new-york/

Filippone, P. (2019). *Everything You Wanted to Know About Pineapples*. The Spruce Eats. https://www.thespruceeats.com/history-of-the-pineapple-1807645

Finney, L. (2017, February 22). *FRI 2020 Fire-Rescue International*. CBRNE Central. https://cbrnecentral.com/five-of-the-most-explosive-non-nuclear-chemicals-ever-made/10598/

Finnis, A. (2023, May 5). *What the Crown Jewels are, how much they're worth and how they're involved in Queen's funeral*. Inews.co.uk. https://inews.co.uk/news/crown-jewels-what-how-much-royal-family-regalia-worth-history-explained-1864753#:~:text=The%20Crown%20Jewels%20are%20considered

Fish, T. (2021, October 27). *12 Mind-blowing facts about your body*. Newsweek. https://www.newsweek.com/mind-blowing-facts-about-your-body-human-1638872

Fisher, K. (2021, January 18). *Top 12 Iconic Dome Of The Rock Facts | Ultimate List*. Art Facts. https://art-facts.com/dome-of-the-rock-facts/

Fisher, L. (2023). *Are any bacteria visible to the naked eye?*. Www.sciencefocus.com. https://www.sciencefocus.com/the-human-body/are-any-bacteria-visible-to-the-naked-eye

5 Facts About The Internet. (2023, October 1). SysGen. https://sysgen.ca/five-facts-internet/

5 Fun Frog Facts. (2023, March 14). WCS. https://www.wcs.org/get-involved/updates/5-fun-frog-facts

5 Interesting Facts About Physics for Kids and its Importance. (2023, May 13). EuroSchool. https://www.euroschoolindia.com/blogs/interesting-facts-about-physics-for-kids/

5 most interesting shipwreck treasure hauls. (2023). Boat International. https://www.boatinternational.com/destinations/most-interesting-shipwreck-treasure-hauls--25603

5 Things You Never Knew About The Power Of Touch. (2016, February 16). Power of Positivity: Positive Thinking & Attitude. https://www.powerofpositivity.com/5-mind-blowing-things-you-never-knew-about-touch/

Here are our top 10 facts about dolphins. 2023). World Wildlife Fund. https://www.wwf.org.uk/learn/fascinating-facts/dolphins?psafe_param=1&utm_source=Grants&utm_medium=PaidSearch-Brand&pc=AWD014007&gclid=Cj0KCQjwhfipBhCqARIsAH9msbnuTXWJccrBsh3de0dk2ZeUGrlFCUss8asg7va6QkTDpyuI8K990vwaAlGWEALw_wcB&gclsrc=aw.ds

Here are our top 10 facts about whales. (2023). World Wildlife Fund. https://www.wwf.org.uk/learn/fascinating-facts/top-10-facts-about-whales?psafe_param=1&utm_source=Grants&utm_medium=PaidSearch-Brand&pc=AWD014007&gclid=Cj0KCQjwhfipBhCqARIsAH9msblOU5Rfgr-XgaH0UexBx_jPibewKVA8N5P7bAEKfLuie683LpTRwAkaArP9EALw_wcB&gclsrc=aw.ds

Five of the World's Rarest Dog Breeds. (2021, November 25). Pet Plan. https://www.petplan.co.uk/pet-information/blog/rare-dog-breeds/

Nunez, C. (2019, February 26). *Desert Information and Facts*. National Geographic. https://www.nationalgeographic.com/environment/article/deserts

Nuwer, R. (2013, December 30). *Dolphins Seem to Use Toxic Pufferfish to Get High*. Smithsonian Magazine. https://www.smithsonianmag.com/smart-news/dolphins-seem-to-use-toxic-pufferfish-to-get-high-180948219/

O, D. (2019, September 9). *30 Incredible Facts About Pirates That Are 100 Percent True*. Best Life. https://bestlifeonline.com/pirate-facts/

Oakley, F. (2023). *1378 The Great Papal Schism*. Christian History | Learn the History of Christianity & the Church. https://www.christianitytoday.com/history/issues/issue-28/1378-great-papal-schism.html

Off-Highway Trucks From Largest to Smallest. (2023). Construction Equipment Guide. https://www.constructionequipmentguide.com/equipment-features/largest-payload-off-highway-trucks#:~:text=The%20BelAZ%2075710%20is%20currently

Ofgang, E. (2021, May 28). *Who invented the hamburger? Biting into the messy history of America's iconic sandwich.* Washington Post. https://www.washingtonpost.com/food/2021/05/28/hamburger-origin-story/

Oishya. (2017, February 7). *Top 10 Most Expensive Knives In The World.* Oishya. https://oishya.com/journal/top-10-expensive-knives-world/

Okafor, J. (2022a, July 9). *23 Ocean Facts Exploring Our Planet's Vast Blue Expanse.* TRVST. https://www.trvst.world/environment/ocean-facts/

Okafor, J. (2022b, January 9). *21 Interesting Turtle Facts.* TRVST. https://www.trvst.world/biodiversity/turtle-facts/

Okafor, J. (2022c, October 12). *21 Cool Bug Facts For Creepy Crawly Appreciation.* TRVST. https://www.trvst.world/biodiversity/cool-bug-facts/

Okuda, J., & Kiyokawa, R. (2000). *[Snake as a symbol in medicine and pharmacy - a historical study].* Yakushigaku Zasshi, 35(1), 25–40. https://pubmed.ncbi.nlm.nih.gov/11640204/#:~:text=Snakes%20have%20been%20used%20for

Old Farmer's Almanac. (2023). *How exactly does a cactus live without water?.* Old Farmer's Almanac. https://www.almanac.com/fact/how-exactly-does-a-cactus-live-without#:~:text=Because%20it%20has%20no%20leaves

Oldest.org. (2017, October 30). *8 Oldest Sports in the World.* Oldest.org. https://www.oldest.org/sports/sports/

Oliver, M. (2017, January 3). *10 Truly Disgusting Facts About Ancient Greek Life.* Listverse. https://listverse.com/2017/01/03/10-disgusting-facts-about-ancient-greek-life/

Omlet. (2017, November 18). *Top 7 Largest Cat Breeds | Choosing The Right Cat For You | Cats | Guide.* Www.omlet.co.uk. https://www.omlet.co.uk/guide/cats/choosing_the_right_cat_for_you/top_7_largest_cat_breeds/#:~:text=Maine%20Coons%20are%20considered%20by

100 Fun Chemistry Facts (With Awesome Explanations!) (2019, July 18). Chemistry Hall. https://chemistryhall.com/fun-chemistry-facts/

One Hundred and One Amazing Cat Facts: Fun Trivia About Your Feline Friend (2018). Charlottesville Cat Care Clinic. https://cvillecatcare.com/veterinary-topics/101-amazing-cat-facts-fun-trivia-about-your-feline-friend/

Online Etymology Dictionary. (2020). Robot. In *etymonline.com.* https://www.etymonline.com/word/robot

Online Etymology Dictionary. (2023a). Amphibian | *Etymology, origin and meaning of amphibian by etymonline.* In etymonline.com. https://www.etymonline.com/word/amphibian

Online Etymology Dictionary. (2023b). Castle. In *etymonline.com.* https://www.etymonline.com/word/castle

Online Etymology Dictionary. (2023c). Meteor. In etymonline.com. https://www.etymonline.com/word/meteor

Online Etymology Dictionary. (2023d). Toilet.In etymonline.com. https://www.etymonline.com/word/toilet

Opfer, C., & Gleim, S. (2013, October 2). *15 Worst Hurricanes of All Time.* HowStuffWorks. https://science.howstuffworks.com/nature/natural-disasters/10-worst-hurricanes.htm#pt15

Orkin. (2023). *Termite Damage Statistics & Costs | Orkin.* Www.orkin.com. https://www.orkin.com/pests/termites/termite-statistics

Osborn, J. (2023, February 15). *Amazing Statistics About How Many Cats Are in the World.* WAF. https://worldanimalfoundation.org/cats/how-many-cats-are-in-the-world/

Osborne, S. (2021, November 17). *25 Crazy Facts About the Human Body.* TutorOcean. https://corp.tutorocean.com/25-crazy-facts-about-the-human-body/

Oskin, B. (2014, September 30). *5 Surprising Facts About Lakes.* Livescience.com. https://www.livescience.com/48064-surprising-facts-about-lakes.html

Osmond, C. (2016, October 13). Bring home the bacon Idiom Definition. Grammarist. https://grammarist.com/idiom/bring-home-the-bacon/

Osterloff, E. (2019, September 23). *Immortal jellyfish: the secret to cheating death.* Www.nhm.ac.uk. https://www.nhm.ac.uk/discover/immortal-jellyfish-secret-to-cheating-death.html

Osterloff, E. (2020, September 14). *Planet Venus.* National History Museum . https://www.nhm.ac.uk/discover/planet-venus.html?gclid=CjwKCAjwv-2pBhB-EiwAtsQZFGjU_V3x5YB86mv27ZnZ2Vve_v5wCZ65EWmeEgpB2lI4IAiJRQ-sLhoC-psQAvD_BwE

Osterloff, E. (2023a). *Coconut crabs: the bird-eating behemoths thriving on isolated tropical islands.* Www.nhm.ac.uk. https://www.nhm.ac.uk/discover/coconut-crabs-bird-eating-giants-on-tropical-islands.html#:~:text=Coconut%20crabs%27%20broad%20diets%20have

Osterloff, E. (2023b). *What is the biggest snake in the world?.* Www.nhm.ac.uk. https://www.nhm.ac.uk/discover/what-is-the-biggest-snake-in-the-world.html

Outdoors.com. (2023, April 24). *100 Amazing Facts About America's National Parks.* Outdoors with Bear Grylls. https://outdoors.com/facts-about-americas-national-parks/

O'Neill, T. (2015, April 23). *Did the People of Middles Ages Era England Really Toss Their Feces Out of the Window?.* HuffPost. https://www.huffpost.com/entry/did-the-people-of-middles_b_7129084

Paddison, L. (2023, June 12). *The planet's coldest, saltiest ocean waters are heating up and shrinking, report finds.* CNN. https://edition.cnn.com/2023/06/12/world/antarctic-deep-ocean-water-shrinking-climate-scn-intl/index.html#:~:text=%E2%80%9CAntarctic%20bottom%20water%E2%80%9D%20is%20the

Padway, M. (2018, March 16). *38 Motorcycle Facts That Will Blow Your Mind.* Motorcycle Legal Foundation. https://www.motorcyclelegalfoundation.com/motorcycle-facts/

Pal, M. (2023, August 7). *Top 20 Smallest Dog Breeds – Forbes Advisor.* Www.forbes.com. https://www.google.com/url?q=https://www.forbes.com/advisor/pet-insurance/pet-care/smallest-dog-breeds/&sa=D&source=docs&ust=1699054810927380&usg=AOvVaw1pO63EmME-RSl0dg40CvxG

Palacio de Sal. (2023). https://palaciodesal.com.bo/

Pallardy, R. (2015). *Anne Bonny | Irish American pirate.* In Encyclopædia Britannica. https://www.britannica.com/biography/Anne-Bonny

Pappas, S. (2023, February 28). *Is the Alpha Wolf Idea a Myth?.* Scientific American. https://www.scientificamerican.com/article/is-the-alpha-wolf-idea-a-myth/#:~:text=But%20it%20turns%20out%20that

Paragon Bank. (2022, March 27). *The Origins of the Piggy Bank | Paragon Bank.* Www.paragonbank.co.uk. https://www.paragonbank.co.uk/blog/origins-of-the-piggy-bank#:~:text=The%20invention%20of%20the%20piggy

Parry, W. (2023, June 25). *How a Human Smell Receptor Works Is Finally Revealed.* Wired. https://www.wired.com/story/how-a-human-smell-receptor-works-is-finally-revealed/#:~:text=Researchers%20think%20that%20human%20noses

Patowary, K. (2016, May 14). *Devon Island: Mars on Earth.* Www.amusingplanet.com. https://www.amusingplanet.com/2016/05/devon-island-mars-on-earth.html

Patterson, T. (2013, December 31). *5 surprising facts about the Goodyear blimp.* CNN. https://edition.cnn.com/travel/article/goodyear-blimp-five-things/index.html

PBS. (2015). *Wayfinders : Polynesian History and Origin.* Www.pbs.org. https://www.pbs.org/wayfinders/polynesian2.html#:~:text=Nonetheless%2C%20the%20archaeological%20evidence%20indicates

PBS. (2023). *Borneo -- An Awesome Island.* Www.pbs.org. https://www.pbs.org/edens/borneo/awesome.html

Pearsall, M. (2017, July 17). *The National Archives - Wettin to Windsor: changing the royal name.* The National Archives Blog. https://blog.nationalarchives.gov.uk/wettin-windsor-changing-royal-name/

Peeples, L. (2009, July 13). *Manipulative meow: Cats learn to vocalize a particular sound to train their human companions.* Scientific American Blog Network. https://blogs.scientificamerican.com/news-blog/the-manipulative-meow-cats-learn-to-2009-07-13/

Pei, D. (2023). *Are Rosary Peas Poisonous?.* Poison.org. https://www.poison.org/articles/are-rosary-peas-poisonous-194

Pellegrino, S. (2022, September 12). *The Most Expensive Cruises in the World.* Elite Traveler. https://elitetraveler.com/travel/luxury-cruises/the-most-expensive-cruises-in-the-world

Pelling, E. (2020, December 31). *Sea Snake Facts: 12 Facts about Sea Snakes.* Blog.padi.com. https://blog.padi.com/sea-snake-facts/

Pendlebury, T. (2023, January 14). *The Most Ridiculous and Weird Tech Gadgets From the Last 25 Years.* CNET. https://www.cnet.com/tech/computing/the-most-ridiculous-and-weird-tech-gadgets-from-the-last-25-years/

Penn LPS. (2023, May 3). *7 Fascinating facts about neuroscience and the brain: How well do you know your brain? | Penn LPS Online.* Lpsonline.sas.upenn.edu. https://lpsonline.sas.upenn.edu/features/7-fascinating-facts-about-neuroscience-and-brain-how-well-do-you-know-your-brain

Perez, J. (2022, April 13). *20 most expensive cars in the world.* Motor1.com. https://uk.motor1.com/features/313656/most-expensive-new-cars-ever/

Perez, J. (2022, May 12). *5 Facts About Mudskippers.* Ocean Conservancy. https://oceanconservancy.org/blog/2022/05/12/5-facts-mudskippers/

Perman, C. (2010, October 12). *The 10 most haunted cities in America.* CNBC. https://www.cnbc.com/2010/10/12/The-10-Most-Haunted-Cities-in-America.html

Petruzzello, M. (2020). *Why Does Cilantro Taste Like Soap to Some People? | Britannica.* In Encyclopædia Britannica. https://www.britannica.com/story/why-does-cilantro-taste-like-soap-to-some-people

Petsko, E. (2019, February). *13 Facts About Genes.* Mentalfloss.com. https://www.mentalfloss.com/article/570647/gene-facts

Pevos, E. (2018, February 3). *20 things you didn't know about monster trucks as Monster Jam comes to Detroit.* Mlive. https://www.mlive.com/entertainment/2018/02/monster_truck_fun_facts_as_we.html

Pezzato, M. (2020, October 2). *Who's Afraid of the Big Bad Wolf? A Fearsome Beast in Tales Around the World.* Www.ancient-Origins.net. https://www.ancient-origins.net/myths-legends/beast-legends-tales-007472

Pflanzer, L. R. (2016, January 9). *8 genetic mutations that can give you "superpowers.".* Business Insider. https://www.businessinsider.com/genetic-mutations-that-make-you-more-awesome-2016-1?r=US&IR=T#actn3-and-the-super-sprinter-variant-1

Picard, G. (2023, June 27). *100 Best National Parks in the World 2023 - TourScanner.* Tour Scanner. https://tourscanner.com/blog/best-national-parks-in-the-world/

Piore, A. (2012, August 10). *20 Things You Didn't Know About Deserts. Discover Magazine.* https://www.discovermagazine.com/planet-earth/20-things-you-didnt-know-about-deserts

Piro, L., Picard, C., & Thomas, M. (2022, May 26). *25 Poisonous Plants That May Be Too Deadly to Keep at Home.* Good Housekeeping. https://www.goodhousekeeping.com/home/gardening/advice/g1174/deadly-poisonous-plants/?slide=6

Pistilli, M. (2021, August 2). *Top Silver Countries by Reserves | INN.* Investing News Network. https://investingnews.com/daily/resource-investing/precious-metals-investing/silver-investing/top-silver-countries-by-reserves/

Pletcher, P. (2014, September 17). *Belladonna: Remedy with a Dark Past.* Healthline. https://www.healthline.com/health/belladonna-dark-past#Medical-Uses

Plumer, B. (2014a, September 5). *What would happen if the Yellowstone supervolcano actually erupted?.* Vox; Vox. https://www.vox.com/2014/9/5/6108169/yellowstone-supervolcano-eruption

Plumer, B. (2014b, October 15). *Here's what 9,000 years of breeding has done to corn, peaches, and other crops.* Vox; Vox. https://www.vox.com/2014/10/15/6982053/selective-breeding-farming-evolution-corn-watermelon-peaches

Pocock, J. (2021, December 1). *10 interesting facts about your ears.* Www.hiddenhearing.co.uk. https://www.hiddenhearing.co.uk/hearing-blog/hearing-loss/10-interesting-facts-about-your-ears

Poland, G. (2021, September 3). *17 Interesting facts about cars.* Bridle Blog. https://www.bridlevehicleleasing.co.uk/blog/17-interesting-facts-about-cars

Pollinator Partnership. (2023). *About Pollinators.* Pollinator. https://www.pollinator.org/pollinators#:~:text=Somewhere%20between%2075%25%20and%2095

Pomeroy, R. (2020, September 3). *What Animals Are Most Likely to Prey Upon Humans?.* Real Clear Science. https://www.realclearscience.com/blog/2020/09/03/what_animals_are_most_likely_to_prey_upon_humans.html

Pomranz, M. (2017, June 22). *Your Salmon Might Be Lying To You: Farm-Raised Salmon Isn't Naturally Pink.* Food & Wine. https://www.foodandwine.com/news/your-salmon-might-be-lying-you-farm-raised-salmon-isn-t-naturally-pink#:~:text=Farm%2Draised%20salmon%20is%20naturally

Port, J. (2018, April 3). *The difference between mass and weight.* Cosmos Magazine. https://cosmosmagazine.com/science/physics/explainer-whats-the-difference-between-mass-and-weight/
Potter, A. (2023). *The world's tiniest tree | BBC Earth.* Www.bbcearth.com. https://www.bbcearth.com/news/the-worlds-tiniest-tree
Potter, J. (2022, March 18). *Why The Beatles didn't cameo in Disney film "The Jungle Book.".* Faroutmagazine.co.uk. https://faroutmagazine.co.uk/why-the-beatles-turned-down-jungle-book/
Powell, S. (2019, June 21). *The Elements And When They Were First Discovered.* Medium. https://sylviapowellnd.medium.com/the-elements-and-when-they-were-first-discovered-d591428f877d
Prada, P., & Furton, K. (2018, August 14). *Birds and Dogs: Toward a Comparative Perspective on Odor Use and Detection.* Frontiers. https://www.frontiersin.org/articles/10.3389/fvets.2018.00188/full
Press Office. (2001, February 11). *Ten facts from the Human Genome Project - Wellcome Sanger Institute.* Www.sanger.ac.uk. https://www.sanger.ac.uk/news_item/ten-facts-human-genome-project/
Pritchard, C. (2012, December 13). *Are you never more than 6ft away from a rat?.* BBC News. https://www.bbc.co.uk/news/magazine-20716625
Private Jet Charter Team. (2023). *The World's 5 Most Expensive Private Jets | Private Jet Charter.* Privatejetcharter.com. https://privatejetcharter.com/the-worlds-5-most-expensive-private-jets/
Pro Gas Admin. (2022, July 28). *Top 12 Mind Blowing Facts About Natural Gas.* Pro Gas, LLC-Products & Services. https://www.progasllc.com/12-facts-about-natural-gas/
Protein Data Bank in Europe. (2021, May 1). *The unzipping enzyme | Protein Data Bank in Europe.* ebi. https://www.ebi.ac.uk/pdbe/news/unzipping-enzyme#:~:text=The%20typical%20human%20chromosome%20has
Puffin Team. (2023). *15 fascinating facts about the ocean.* Www.penguin.co.uk. https://www.penguin.co.uk/articles/childrens-article/facts-about-the-ocean-for-kids
Puiu, T. (2016, June 27). *17 Amazing Chemistry Facts that will Blow Your Mind.* ZME Science. https://www.zmescience.com/feature-post/natural-sciences/chemistry-articles/applied-chemistry/amazing-chemistry-facts/
Purina. (2022). *Do Cats Always Land on Their Feet? | Purina.* Www.purina.co.uk. https://www.purina.co.uk/articles/cats/behaviour/common-questions/do-cats-land-on-their-feet#:~:text=Cats%20have%20an%20inbuilt%20balancing
Purina. (2023a). *10 of the World's Biggest Dog Breeds | Purina.* Www.purina.co.uk. https://www.purina.co.uk/find-a-pet/articles/dog-types/breed-size/biggest-dog-breeds
Purina. (2023b). *14 Mind-Blowing Facts about Cats | Purina.* Www.purina.co.uk. https://www.purina.co.uk/articles/cats/behaviour/common-questions/fun-facts-about-cats
Purina. (2023c). *Top 5 Smartest Dog Breeds | Purina.* Www.purina.co.uk. https://www.purina.co.uk/find-a-pet/articles/dog-types/breed-guides/top-11-smartest-dog-breeds#:~:text=Border%20Collie&text=Their%20intelligence%2C%20enthusiasm%20and%20willingness
Quaglia, S. (2023, February 17). *8 Facts You Didn't Know About Venom and Toxic Animals.* Discover Magazine. https://www.discovermagazine.com/planet-earth/7-facts-you-didnt-know-about-venom-and-toxic-animals
Quick Dose: Should You Wake Someone up While They Are Sleepwalking? (2022, March 1). Northwestern Medicine. https://www.nm.org/healthbeat/healthy-tips/quick-dose-should-you-wake-someone-sleepwalking#:~:text=There%20seems%20to%20be%20a
Radiator Admin. (2019, April 29). *10 Amazing Jellyfish Facts for Kids.* Bristol Aquarium. https://www.bristolaquarium.co.uk/education/10-amazing-jellyfish-facts-for-kids/
Radovanovic, K. L., Dragan. (2016, September 13). *10 survival myths that might get you killed.* Business Insider. https://www.businessinsider.com/common-survival-myths-and-facts-2016-9?r=US&IR=T#myth-you-can-suck-the-venom-out-of-a-snakebite-1
Raga, S. (2017, October 18). *50 Sweet Facts About Your Favorite Halloween Candies.* Mentalfloss.com. https://www.mentalfloss.com/article/507656/50-sweet-facts-about-your-favorite-halloween-candies
Rainforests explained: where they are, what they do, and why they're crucial for our planet. (2023, June 22). Global Witness. https://www.globalwitness.org/en/blog/rainforests-explained-where-they-are-what-they-do-and-why-theyre-crucial-for-our-planet/?gclid=CjoKCQjw4vKpBhCZARIsAOKHoWQUdDI3IdnDxvcE4X7FS2rbQZsfzXlBkumjN78nuaZrQVBJnfGYJGoaAgpUEALw_wcB
Rao, P. (2023, March 29). *Ranked: The 25 Poorest Countries by GDP per Capita.* Visual Capitalist. https://www.visualcapitalist.com/worlds-poorest-countries-2023-gdp-per-capita/
Rathi, A. (2017, October 12). *How 200,000 Homemade Lunches Get Delivered in Mumbai Every Weekday.* Food52. https://food52.com/blog/20676-how-mumbai-dabbawalas-deliver-lunch#:~:text=There%20are%20about%205000%20dabbawalas
Redif, Z. (2021, August 4). *Strange Things People Really Used To Believe About Medicine.* Health Digest. https://www.healthdigest.com/478326/strange-things-people-really-used-to-believe-about-medicine/
Redmond, A. (2021, September 23). *My French Country Home Magazine» 10 Facts About Mont-Saint-Michel.* My French Country Home Magazine. https://myfrenchcountryhomemagazine.com/10-facts-about-mont-saint-michel/
Regional Information Centre for Western Europe. (2022, November 15). *8 billion people: 10 facts on the world's population.* United Nations Western Europe. https://unric.org/en/8-billion-people-10-facts-on-the-worlds-population/
Renewable Energy Facts: Fun Stats About Clean Energy You Won't Believe. (2023). Inspire Clean Energy. https://www.inspirecleanenergy.com/blog/clean-energy-101/renewable-energy-facts
Renner, S. (2022, October 26). *The 15 Most Expensive Buildings In The World.* Luxurycolumnist.com. https://luxurycolumnist.com/the-most-expensive-buildings-in-the-world/
Renner, T. (2021, July 27). *Las Vegas Goes All In on Water Resources.* Wastewater Digest. https://www.wwdmag.com/home/article/10938544/las-vegas-goes-all-in-on-water-resources
Reuter, D. (2022, March 22). *Crude oil is selling for over $100 per barrel, but 200 years ago it was a plentiful resource used in medicine and cosmetics. Here are 15 surprising facts about the history of oil and gas.* Business Insider. https://www.businessinsider.com/surprising-facts-about-history-of-oil-and-gas-2022-5?r=US&IR=T#after-the-war-the-rush-to-produce-outpaced-demand-so-much-that-a-price-crash-in-the-1870s-made-oil-cheaper-than-drinking-water-for-households-in-the-oil-regions-8
Rice, J. (2008, October 23). *20 Things You Didn't Know About... Bacteria.* Discover Magazine; Discover Magazine. https://www.discovermagazine.com/health/20-things-you-didnt-know-about-bacteria
Richard, M. (2017, January 21). *10 Facts About Your Sense Of Touch That Will Really Surprise You - Listverse.* Listverse. https://listverse.com/2017/01/21/10-facts-about-your-sense-of-touch-that-will-really-surprise-you/
Riders Share. (2023, November 4). *Riders Share.* Www.riders-Share.com. https://www.riders-share.com/blog/article/number-motorcycles-world-top-countries#:~:text=The%20correct%20answer%3A%20about%20600
Riggs, C. (2022, September 26). *Tomb-raiding in ancient Egypt.* Apollo Magazine. https://www.apollo-magazine.com/short-history-of-tomb-raiding-maria-golia/
RingCentral Team. (2022, April 25). *National Telephone Day: 10 mind-blowing facts about phones.* RingCentral. https://www.ringcentral.com/us/en/blog/national-telephone-day/
Rinkesh. (2016, December 25). *35 Facts of Tropical RainForest.* Conserve Energy Future. https://www.conserve-energy-future.com/various-tropical-rainforest-facts.php
Ritchie, H. (2019a, February 4). *Which countries eat the most meat?.* BBC News. https://www.bbc.co.uk/news/health-47057341
Ritchie, H. (2019b, September 13). *The world now produces more seafood from fish farms than wild catch.* Our World in Data. https://ourworldindata.org/rise-of-aquaculture
River Turtle. (2023, March 30). A-Z-Animals. https://a-z-animals.com/animals/river-turtle/
Robbins, E. (2023, February 2). *9 Tips to Help You Choose a Perfect Campsite Every Time.* The Trek. https://thetrek.co/five-tips-to-help-you-choose-a-perfect-campsite-every-time/
Roberts, R. (1992, July 1). *Because It's There : Lake Titicaca Is So Cold It Sends Chills to the Muscles and Has Something That Leaves Swimmers With Bites; So, of Course, It's Ideal for Lynne Cox.* Los Angeles Times. https://www.latimes.com/archives/la-xpm-1992-07-01-sp-1211-story.html
Robinson, L. (2022, November 2). *The Smallest Bones In our Body Make a Big Difference.* Hearing Industries Association. https://betterhearing.org/newsroom/blogs/the-smallest-bones-in-our-body-make-a-big-difference/
Robinson, M. (2023, July 13). *A Brief Overview of Salvador Dalí's "Melting Clocks" Painting | Art & Object.* Www.artandobject.com. https://www.artandobject.com/news/salvador-dalis-melting-clocks-perfect-hot-summer-painting#:~:text=According%20to%20Dal%C3%AD%2C%20who%20used
Robotic milking. (2023, September 1). Dairy New Zealand. https://www.dairynz.co.nz/milking/new-dairy-technology/automatic-milking-systems/#:~:text=The%20most%20common%20automated%20milking
Rodgers, J. (2016). *Joshua Trees - Joshua Tree National Park (U.S. National Park Service).* Nps.gov. https://www.nps.gov/jotr/learn/nature/jtrees.htm
Rooney, J. (2013, April 13). *The 10 best real-life spies – in pictures.* The Guardian. https://www.theguardian.com/culture/gallery/2013/apr/13/10-best-real-life-spies
Roos, D. (2018, October 11). *Human Sacrifice: Why the Aztecs Practiced This Gory Ritual.* HISTORY; History.com. https://www.history.com/news/aztec-human-sacrifice-religion
Rose, S. (2023, July 9). *Rhubarb Grows So Fast That You Can Actually Hear It.* Food Republic. https://www.foodrepublic.com/1332068/forced-rhubarb-fruit-fast-growth-noises/
Rosicrucian Egyptian Museum. (2023). *Ra - Explore Deities of Ancient Egypt.* Egyptianmuseum.org. https://egyptianmuseum.org/deities-ra
Rothery, B. (2023). *12 amazing facts about butterflies and moths.* Www.penguin.co.uk. https://www.penguin.co.uk/articles/childrens-article/amazing-butterfly-facts-for-kids
Rotondi, J. P. (2022, July 20). *7 Mysterious Mass Illnesses That Defied Explanation.* HISTORY. https://www.history.com/news/mysterious-illnesses-mass-hysteria
Roy, D. (2023, February 10). *Can Amazon Countries Save the Rain Forest?* Council on Foreign Relations. https://www.cfr.org/backgrounder/can-amazon-countries-save-rain-forest
Royal Museums Greenwich. (2018). *Greek fire.* Www.rmg.co.uk. https://www.rmg.co.uk/stories/topics/greek-fire
Royal Museums Greenwich. (2019). *Ferdinand Magellan.* https://www.rmg.co.uk/stories/topics/ferdinand-magellan
Royal Museums Greenwich. (2022a). *The Golden Age of Piracy.* https://www.rmg.co.uk/stories/topics/golden-age-piracy
Royal Museums Greenwich. (2022b). *Steam power.* https://www.rmg.co.uk/stories/topics/steam-power
Royal Museums Greenwich. (2023a). *Is Venice Flooding Getting Worse? Cities & Climate Change.* https://www.rmg.co.uk/stories/topics/venice-flooding-climate-change-coastal-cities#:~:text=Venice
Royal Museums Greenwich. (2023b). *RMS Titanic facts.* https://www.rmg.co.uk/stories/topics/rms-titanic-facts
Royal Museums Greenwich. (2023c). *What do pirates do?* https://www.rmg.co.uk/stories/topics/what-do-pirates-do
Royal Museums Greenwich. (2023d). *Who were the real pirates of the Caribbean?* https://www.rmg.co.uk/stories/topics/who-were-real-pirates-caribbean
Rudy, L. J. (2022, July 8). *14 Amazing Facts About Alligators.* Treehugger. https://www.treehugger.com/alligator-facts-5119214
Rupp, R. (2015, January 8). *Are French Fries Truly French?.* Culture. https://www.nationalgeographic.com/culture/article/are-french-fries-truly-french
Russell, C. (2020, August 9). *The Film Radioactive Shows How Marie Curie Was a "Woman of the Future.".* Scientific American. https://www.scientificamerican.com/article/the-film-radioactive-shows-how-marie-curie-was-a-woman-of-the-future/

Ryan, M. (2023, January 1). *10 Largest Deserts in the World.* HowStuffWorks. https://science.howstuffworks.com/environmental/earth/geology/largest-desert-in-world.htm#:~:text=1.
Santiago, E. (2023). *Fireball or Contrail?.* American Meteor Society. https://www.amsmeteors.org/fireballs/fireball-or-contrail/#:~:text=A%20fireball%20is%20another%20term
Santorini-View.com. (2023). *The Black Sand Beach in Santorini - Santorini View.* Santorini-View.com. https://www.santorini-view.com/black-sand-beach/
Sartore, J. (2010, September 10). *King cobra, facts and photos.* Animals. https://www.nationalgeographic.com/animals/reptiles/facts/king-cobra
Satariano, A. (2019, March 11). *How the Internet Travels Across Oceans.* The New York Times. https://www.nytimes.com/interactive/2019/03/10/technology/internet-cables-oceans.html
Saunders, T. (2023a, July 12). *Who discovered electricity? Probably not who you're thinking.* Www.sciencefocus.com. https://www.sciencefocus.com/science/who-invented-electricty
Saunders, T. (2023b, September 25). *Top 10 longest rivers in the world 2023.* Www.sciencefocus.com. https://www.sciencefocus.com/planet-earth/longest-river-in-the-world
Scheffer, N. (2019, May 25). *Scary Facts about Lions.* Secret Africa. https://secretafrica.com/scary-facts-about-lions/
Schmidt, A. (2020, August 4). *Dolphin Fact Sheet | Blog | Nature | PBS.* Nature. https://www.pbs.org/wnet/nature/blog/dolphin-fact-sheet/#:~:text=Dolphins%20vary%20in%20size%20and
Schmidt, A. (2021, May 7). *Frog Fact Sheet | Blog | Nature | PBS.* Nature. https://www.pbs.org/wnet/nature/blog/frog-fact-sheet/#:~:text=Frog%3A%20any%20member%20of%20a
Schreiber, A. (2023, October 19). *Monkey Facts.* Education.nationalgeographic.org. https://education.nationalgeographic.org/resource/monkey-facts/
Science and Technology. (2023). *Airship R.34.* National Museums Scotland. https://www.nms.ac.uk/explore-our-collections/stories/science-and-technology/airship/
Science Museum. (2021, February 23). *How was penicillin developed?.* Science Museum. https://www.sciencemuseum.org.uk/objects-and-stories/how-was-penicillin-developed
Scotese, C. (2011). *Plesiosaurus.* Dinosaurpictures.org. https://dinosaurpictures.org/Plesiosaurus-pictures
Scottish Press and Journal. (2018, September 14). *Loch Ness Monster worth nearly £41m a year to Scottish economy.* Press and Journal. https://www.pressandjournal.co.uk/fp/news/highlands-islands/1562103/loch-ness-monster-worth-nearly-41m-a-year-to-scottish-economy/
Scurvy Pirate History. (2015, May 19). *Top 10 Pirate Facts - Pirate Show Cancun.* Blog - Pirate Show Cancun. https://www.pirateshowcancun.com/blog/scurvy-pirate-history/top-10-pirate-facts/
Seaway. (2022, November 30). *Which Are The 5 Busiest Shipping Routes?* Seaway Logistics. https://seawaylogistics.co.uk/which-are-the-5-busiest-shipping-routes/#:~:text=The%20English%20Channel%2C%20which%20lies
Sedgwick, I. (2020, June 16). *What Is The Witching Hour And Does It Exist?.* Medium. https://medium.com/@icy.sedgwick/what-is-the-witching-hour-and-does-it-exist-2127f25caaab
Seitz, D. (2020, February 5). *How to find drinkable water in the wild.* Popular Science. https://www.popsci.com/story/diy/find-drinkable-water-wild/
Sequoia & Kings Canyon National Parks. (2019). https://www.visitsequoia.com/
7 INTERESTING FACTS ABOUT DIPLODOCUS. (2023). Dinosaur World Live. https://dinosaurworldlive.com/blog/7-interesting-facts-about-diplodocus
7 Trucking Facts You May Not Know. (2022, May 2). AFP Global Logistics. https://afplus.com/7-trucking-facts-you-may-not-know/
Seventeen amazing facts about birds. (2023). Love the Garden. https://www.lovethegarden.com/uk-en/article/17-amazing-facts-about-birds
Shah, D. (2007, July 6). *19 million US Dollars for a space station toilet - Fareastgizmos.* Gadgets, Gizmos, and Tech from the East. https://fareastgizmos.com/uncategorized/19_million_us_dollars_for_a_space_station_toilet.php
Shank, I. (2017, August 1). *When Picasso Went on Trial for Stealing the Mona Lisa.* Artsy. https://www.artsy.net/article/artsy-editorial-picasso-trial-stealing-mona-lisa
Shapley, D. (2015, March 10). *35 Utterly Weird Sea Animals.* Popular Mechanics; Popular Mechanics. https://www.popularmechanics.com/science/animals/g210/strange-sea-animals-2/
Sharma, P. (2022, May 27). *Who Invented Motorcycles? The Story Of The First Motorcycle.* TopSpeed. https://www.topspeed.com/motorcycles/motorcycle-news/who-invented-motorcycles-the-story-of-the-first-motorcycle/
Sharma, S. (2021, March 5). *Top 20 Agricultural Facts That Will Amaze You.* Krishijagran.com. https://krishijagran.com/agripedia/top-20-agricultural-facts-that-will-amaze-you/
Shaw, J. (2007, January 1). *Figs Were First.* Harvard Magazine. https://www.harvardmagazine.com/2007/01/figs-were-first-html#:~:text=New%20archaeobotanical%20evidence%20pushes%20the,Jericho%20began%20propagating%20seedless%20figs.
Shawna. (2022, January 28). *50 Fun Reptile Facts Your Kids Will Love.* Different by Design Learning. https://differentbydesignlearning.com/fun-reptile-facts-kids/
Shenker, J. (2016, August 15). *Lost cities #6: how Thonis-Heracleion resurfaced after 1,000 years under water.* The Guardian; The Guardian. https://www.theguardian.com/cities/2016/aug/15/lost-cities-6-thonis-heracleion-egypt-sunken-sea
Sherifi, M. (2021, November 23). *15 FUN Facts About Cricket That Will Amaze You!.* Fun Facts About. https://www.funfactsabout.com/fun-facts-about-cricket/#10_The_longest_cricket_match_lasted_14_days
Sherrin, H. (2021, September 22). *10 of the Coolest Spy Gadgets in Espionage History.* History Hit. https://www.historyhit.com/coolest-spy-gadgets-in-espionage-history/
Shiffman, D. S. (2021). *What are the biggest sharks?.* Save Our Seas Foundation. https://saveourseas.com/worldofsharks/what-are-the-biggest-sharks
Shiga, Y. (2021, July 15). *Manila's $25bn traffic headache looms as 2022 election issue.* Nikkei Asia. https://asia.nikkei.com/Business/Transportation/Manila-s-25bn-traffic-headache-looms-as-2022-election-issue#:~:text=The%20work%20is%20designed%20to
Shukla, K. (2023, September 2). *World's Most Expensive Phones: Top 10 World's Most Expensive Smartphones in 2023.* MySmartPrice. https://www.mysmartprice.com/gear/worlds-most-expensive-phones/
Shvili, J. (2020, September 16). *The Most Popular Sports in the World.* WorldAtlas. https://www.worldatlas.com/articles/what-are-the-most-popular-sports-in-the-world.html
Siegel, E. (2020, May 25). *This Is Where The 10 Most Common Elements In The Universe Come From.* Forbes. https://www.forbes.com/sites/startswithabang/2020/05/25/this-is-where-the-10-most-common-elements-in-the-universe-come-from/?sh=1e80762dd24b
Silk, E. (2023, February 21). *7 Amazing Facts About The Sea Of Stars In The Maldives.* Hoo. https://justhooit.com/blog/sea-of-stars-maldives
Silverman, L. (2020, December 10). *All of The Facts You Never Knew About Hanukkah.* Town & Country. https://www.townandcountrymag.com/leisure/arts-and-culture/g13787924/hanukkah-facts-history-story/
Silverman, S. (2023, February 7). *February's Featured Animal: The Black Mamba.* Animal World and Snake Farm. https://www.awsfzoo.com/februarys-featured-animal-the-black-mamba/#:~:text=Since%20the%20black%20mamba%20is
Simmons, S. (2022, July 22). *This Is Why Lemons Float but Limes Sink – LifeSavvy.* Www.lifesavvy.com. https://www.lifesavvy.com/126859/this-is-why-lemons-float-but-limes-sink/
Singh, B. (2022, March 4). *Stag Beetle: World's Most Expensive Insect That Can Make You A Millionaire Overnight.* IndiaTimes. https://www.indiatimes.com/trending/environment/stag-beetle-worlds-most-expensive-insect-563643.html
Singh, S. (2022, April 6). *A Look At The Safest Airliners Of All Time.* Simple Flying. https://simpleflying.com/safest-airliners-all-time/
Sistine Chapel. (2023). *The Sistine Chapel ceiling of Michelangelo.* Www.thesistinechapel.org. https://www.thesistinechapel.org/sistine-chapel-ceiling
Site Editor. (2020, July 20). *20 Strange But True Facts About Ancient Rome.* Kickassfacts.com. https://www.kickassfacts.com/20-strange-but-true-facts-about-ancient-rome/
Sivak, M. (2019, September 30). *Actual fuel economy of cars and light trucks: 1966-2017.* Green Car Congress. https://www.greencarcongress.com/2019/09/20190930-sivak.html
61 facts you need to know about the rainforest. (2016, December 1). *OVO Energy.* https://www.ovoenergy.com/blog/ovo-foundation-real-benefits-for-local-communities/61-facts-you-need-to-know-about-the-rainforest
Skinner, M., & Parker, B. (2020). *How many corms do I need to plant an acre?* https://www.uvm.edu/~saffron/Old/Workshops/Saffron%20Workshop%202020/Saffron%20by%20the%20numbers%202020.pdf
Skiver, K. (2023, July 4). *Nathan's Hot Dog Eating Contest records: Who has eaten the most hot dogs on July 4?.* Www.sportingnews.com. https://www.sportingnews.com/us/other/news/nathans-hot-dog-eating-contest-records/1jlk76v3c2l051u8sajwnavzov
Smallpox. (2022). World Health Organization. https://www.who.int/health-topics/smallpox#tab=tab_1
Smart Traveller. (2023, January 4). *Reducing the risk of kidnapping.* Smartraveller.gov.au. https://www.smartraveller.gov.au/before-you-go/safety/kidnapping
Smit, J. L. (2019, July 14). *10 Unusual Studies And Stories About Dogs.* Listverse. https://listverse.com/2019/07/14/10-unusual-studies-and-stories-about-dogs/
Smith, B. (2023, June 8). *5 unsettling facts you might not know about the ocean.* The Daily. https://thedaily.case.edu/5-unsettling-facts-you-might-not-know-about-the-ocean/
Smith, F. (2023, September 4). *Trucks With the Best Towing Capacity for 2023.* Road & Track. https://www.roadandtrack.com/rankings/g44993239/best-towing-capacity-trucks/
Smithsonian Institution. (2013, June 19). *Microwave Oven.* Smithsonian Institution. https://www.si.edu/newsdesk/snapshot/microwave-oven
Smithsonian Magazine. (2022, March 29). *Scientists Are Making Cochineal, a Red Dye From Bugs, in the Lab.* Smithsonian Magazine. https://www.smithsonianmag.com/innovation/scientists-are-making-cochineal-a-red-dye-from-bugs-in-the-lab-180979828/
Smithsonian. (2022). *How Big are Great White Sharks?* Smithsonian Ocean. https://ocean.si.edu/ocean-life/sharks-rays/how-big-are-great-white-sharks#:~:text=The%20biggest%20great%20white%20sharks
Smithsonian. (2023a). *Biomimicry Shark Denticles* Smithsonian Ocean. https://ocean.si.edu/ocean-life/sharks-rays/biomimicry-shark-denticles#:~:text=Shark%20skin%20is%20covered%20by
Smithsonian. (2023b). *Fun Facts About Bugs.* Smithsonian Institution. https://www.si.edu/spotlight/buginfo/fun-facts-bugs
Sociéte d'Exploitation de la tour Eiffel. (2020, March 4). *15 essential things to know about the Eiffel Tower.* La Tour Eiffel. https://www.toureiffel.paris/en/news/history-and-culture/15-essential-things-know-about-eiffel-tower
Sohn, E. (2019, January 15). *Why the Great Molasses Flood Was So Deadly.* HISTORY. https://www.history.com/news/great-molasses-flood-science
Sokol, T. (2022, September 4). *Late Stuntman Alex Harvill Holds World Record for Motorcycle Jump.* News Radio 560 KPQ. https://kpq.com/late-stuntman-alex-harvill-holds-world-record-for-motorcycle-jump/
Some Interesting Pickpocket Statistics. (2016, February 9). Clever Travel Company. https://www.clevertravelcompanion.com/blogs/news/14502437-some-interesting-pickpocket-statistics
Sood, S. (2012, April 27). *Birth and spread of the world's national parks.* Www.bbc.com. https://www.bbc.com/travel/article/20120426-travelwise-birth-and-spread-of-the-worlds-national-parks
Sophia. (2020, August 6). *60 Delicious Facts About Breakfast Around The World.* Facts.net. https://facts.net/breakfast-around-the-world/
Sowden, M. (2013, January 30). *Remote islands: 7 of the world's hardest-to-reach outposts.* CNN. https://edition.cnn.com/travel/article/most-remote-islands/index.html#:~:text=Tristan%20da%20Cunha%20is%20the
Space Enthusiast. (2022, September 25). *Do you know these 17 facts about rockets?.* Orbital Today. https://orbitaltoday.com/2022/09/25/17-amazing-facts-about-rockets-you-may-not-know/

Space for Kids - Meteors. (2017, April 12). ESA Kids. https://www.esa.int/kids/en/learn/Our_Universe/Comets_and_meteors/Meteors

Spanner, H. (2023, April 29). *Top 10: Which animals have the strongest bite?.* Www.sciencefocus.com. https://www.sciencefocus.com/nature/top-10-which-animals-have-the-strongest-bite

Specialists in Potato Chips Projects. (2018, January 4). *Fun Facts about Potato Chips, Interesting Potato Chip Facts.* CHIPS MACHINE. https://potato-chips-machine.com/chips-making-news/fun-facts-about-potato-chips.html

Spencer, E. (2022, April 28). *Tongue-Eating Louse Actually Eats Tongues.* Ocean Conservancy. https://oceanconservancy.org/blog/2022/04/28/tongue-eating-louse-eats-tongues/

Sportspodium. (2017, October 3). *How many sports are there in the world.* Steemit. https://steemit.com/sport/@sportspodium/how-many-sports-are-there-in-the-world#:~:text=There%20is%20roughly%20200%20sports

SpyScape. (2023). *CIA Secrets: Five Quirky Facts about the Spy Agency.* Spyscape.com. https://spyscape.com/article/cia-secrets-five-quirky-facts-about-the-spy-agency

SS-Admin. (2021, April 22). *10 Facts About Gemstones You Didn't Know.* Seized Sales. https://seizedsales.com/10-facts-about-gemstones-you-didnt-know/

Stacey, S. (2023, February 25). *This Belle Époque public restroom in Paris has been restored to its former glory, but costs about $2 to use.* Business Insider. https://www.businessinsider.com/photos-belle-epoque-public-restroom-paris-restored-former-glory-2023-2

Staff Writer. (2023). *Desert Facts for Kids | Deserts for Kids.* Geography | World Deserts. Www.kids-World-Travel-Guide.com. https://www.kids-world-travel-guide.com/desert-facts.html

Staff. (2021, October 15). *Ask Astro: How much of the universe can we observe?* Astronomy Magazine. https://www.astronomy.com/science/ask-astro-how-much-of-the-universe-can-we-observe/

Staff. (2023, September 8). *2023 Motorcycle of the Year.* Rider Magazine. https://ridermagazine.com/2023/09/08/2023-motorcycle-of-the-year/

Stainton, H. (2020, November 26). *The history of the hotel industry | Understanding tourism - Tourism Teacher.* Tourism Teacher. https://tourismteacher.com/the-history-of-the-hotel-industry-understanding-tourism/

Stamp, J. (2014, June 20). *From Turrets to Toilets: A Partial History of the Throne Room.* Smithsonian Magazine; Smithsonian Magazine. https://www.smithsonianmag.com/history/turrets-toilets-partial-history-throne-room-180951788/

Statista Research Department. (2019). *Global ocean cruise industry: passengers 2009-2019 | Statista.* Statista; Statista. https://www.statista.com/statistics/385445/number-of-passengers-of-the-cruise-industry-worldwide/

Statista Research Department. (2023, August 30). *Countries with largest gold reserves 2022.* Statista. https://www.statista.com/statistics/267998/countries-with-the-largest-gold-reserves/#:~:text=The%20United%20States%20has%20the

Statoil Contributor. (2015, January 12). *Statoil BrandVoice: 16 Amazing Facts About Natural Gas.* Forbes. https://www.forbes.com/sites/statoil/2015/01/12/16-amazing-facts-about-natural-gas/?sh=b088b756b4e4

Staveley-Wadham, R. (2022, January 12). *The British Newspaper Archive Blog Lost Occupations | The British Newspaper Archive Blog.* Blog.britishnewspaperarchive.co.uk. https://blog.britishnewspaperarchive.co.uk/2022/01/12/seven-unusual-or-lost-occupations-from-history/

Steen, E. (2022, January 28). *5 most confusing train stations in Tokyo.* Time out Tokyo. https://www.timeout.com/tokyo/things-to-do/most-confusing-train-stations-in-tokyo

Steenblik Hwang, L. (2023, July 31). *50 years ago, scientists thought they had found Earth's oldest rocks.* Science News. https://www.sciencenews.org/article/50-years-ago-earth-oldest-rocks#:~:text=At%20about%204.3%20billion%20years

Stegosaurus. (2014). Natural History Museum. https://www.nhm.ac.uk/discover/dino-directory/stegosaurus.html

Stein, J. (2023, July 5). *Most Expensive Production Motorcycles You Can Buy.* Cycle World. https://www.cycleworld.com/bikes/most-expensive-production-motorcycles-you-can-buy/

Stein, V. (2022, March 2). *25 Weirdest Facts About the Solar System.* Space.com. https://www.space.com/35695-weirdest-solar-system-facts.html#section-5-mars-boasts-a-volcano-bigger-than-the-entire-state-of-hawaii

Strauss, B. (2018, February 23). *10 Fast Facts About Amphibians.* ThoughtCo. https://www.thoughtco.com/facts-about-amphibians-4069409

Stromberg, J. (2012, July 25). *When the Olympics Gave Out Medals for Art.* Smithsonian Magazine; Smithsonian Magazine. https://www.smithsonianmag.com/arts-culture/when-the-olympics-gave-out-medals-for-art-6878965/

Stromberg, J. (2014, June 11). *Don't freak out, but there are thousands of mites living all over your face.* Vox. https://www.vox.com/2014/6/11/5799992/these-mites-live-on-your-face-and-come-out-to-have-sex-at-night

Sullivan, B. (2013, July 29). *The History of the Lavatory - Old House Journal Magazine.* Old House Journal Magazine - Renovation DIY and Old-House Restoration, Traditional Styles, Period Kitchens, Historical Decorating, Period Gardens, from Colonial and Victorian through Arts & Crafts and Mid-Century Modern: All from Old-House Journal Magazine and Special-Interest Titles Old-House Interiors, New Old House, and Early Homes. https://www.oldhouseonline.com/kitchens-and-baths-articles/the-history-of-the-toilet/

Suni, E. (2020, November 4). *Common myths and facts about sleep.* Sleep Foundation. https://www.sleepfoundation.org/how-sleep-works/myths-and-facts-about-sleep

Surfer Today. (2023). *The 53 most surprising facts about sharks.* Surfer Today. https://www.surfertoday.com/environment/the-most-surprising-facts-about-sharks

Switek, B. (2016, May 20). *How Do You Feed A T. Rex?.* FiveThirtyEight. https://fivethirtyeight.com/features/how-do-you-feed-a-t-rex/

Synan, M. (2013, June 26). *What is the holy grail?.* HISTORY. https://www.history.com/news/what-is-the-holy-grail

T, J. (2021, March 19). The Hardest Rock and Hardest Mineral on Earth - Rock and Mineral Planet. Rockandmineralplanet.com. https://rockandmineralplanet.com/the-hardest-rock-and-hardest-mineral-on-earth/

Tadashi. (2020, September 10). *100 Interesting Fish Facts That You Never Knew About.* Facts.net. https://facts.net/fish-facts/

Tang, C. (2014). *10 Forbidden City Facts You Should Know — Before Visiting.* China Highlights. https://www.chinahighlights.com/beijing/forbidden-city/forbidden-city-facts.htm

Tappity. (2023). *13 Best Human Body Facts, Videos, & Trivia for Kids | Tappity.* Tappity - the #1 Educational Science App for Kids 4-10. https://www.tappityapp.com/science-lessons/human-body

TasteAtlas. (2023, November 2). *Most Popular Insects in the World.* Www.tasteatlas.com. https://www.tasteatlas.com/most-popular-insects-in-the-world

Taylor, D. B. (2021, March 25). *America's Bald Eagle Population Has Quadrupled.* The New York Times. https://www.nytimes.com/2021/03/25/climate/how-many-bald-eagles-united-states.html

Tchakarov, V. (2020, June 17). *Lost Treasures of the World (Top 10).* TheCollector. https://www.thecollector.com/lost-treasures-of-the-world/

Tchakarov, V. (2020, September 3). *Here's Why Roman Architecture Stands the Test of Time (10 Facts).* TheCollector. https://www.thecollector.com/roman-architecture/

Teague, C. (2023, August 20). *What is the fastest car in the world in 2023?.* Autoblog. https://www.autoblog.com/article/what-is-the-fastest-car-in-the-world/#:~:text=on%20the%20leaderboard.-

Team Wanderlust. (2023, October 27). *The 20 Most Haunted Places in the World.* Wanderlust. https://www.wanderlust.co.uk/content/the-worlds-10-most-haunted-places/

Temescu, L. (2006, January 20). *20 Things You Didn't Know About... Meteors.* Discover Magazine. https://www.discovermagazine.com/the-sciences/20-things-you-didnt-know-about-meteors

10 amazing DNA facts you may not know. (2022, September 20). AlphaBiolabs. https://www.alphabiolabs.com/blog/10-amazing-dna-facts-you-may-not-know/

Ten Cool Facts About Penguins. (2023). City of Albuquerque. https://www.cabq.gov/artsculture/biopark/news/10-cool-facts-about-penguins

10 Facts about cane toads. (2019, September 23). WWF Australia. https://wwf.org.au/blogs/10-facts-about-cane-toads/

10 Facts About Flooding. (2016). American Rivers. https://www.americanrivers.org/rivers/discover-your-river/10-facts-about-flooding/

10 Fun Facts About Money. (2022, August 1). TransferGo. https://www.transfergo.co.uk/facts-about-money

10 Fun Reptile Facts. (2017, July 22). Noah's Ark Zoo. Www.noahsarkzoofarm.co.uk. https://www.noahsarkzoofarm.co.uk/blog/fun-reptile-facts

10 Interesting Facts About Fishing You Probably Didn't Know. (2023). Mariner Marine. https://www.marinermarine.com/10-Interesting-Facts-About-Fishing-You-Probably-Didn-t-Know-1-15680.html

10 things you didn't know about sharks. (2023). Zoological Society of London. https://www.zsl.org/what-we-do/species/sharks/shark-facts

10 things you didn't know about the world's population. (2015). United Nations Population Fund. https://www.unfpa.org/news/10-things-you-didn%E2%80%99t-know-about-world%E2%80%99s-population

10 Wildfire Facts for Kids. (2023, January 25). Western Fire Chiefs Association. https://wfca.com/articles/wildfire-facts-for-kid/

Tendu, B. (2022, August 21). *Ranking the 15 most expensive sports in the world right now.* SportsBrief - Sport News. https://sportsbrief.com/other-sports/22038-ranking-15-expensive-sports-world-now/

Tennis Court Dimensions & Size. (2020, March 27). Harrod Sport. https://www.harrodsport.com/advice-and-guides/tennis-court-dimensions

Terra. (2023). *Gulper Eel.* New Zealand Encyclopaedia . https://teara.govt.nz/en/photograph/5269/gulper-eel#:~:text=The%20open%20mouth%20is%2011,where%20food%20appears%20only%20rarely

Texas Parks and Wildlife. (2023). *TPWD: Horned Lizard Facts.* Tpwd.texas.gov. https://tpwd.texas.gov/huntwild/wild/wildlife_diversity/texas_nature_trackers/horned_lizard/#:~:text=Its%20horny%20appearance%20and%20coloration

The 10 Biggest Birds In The World. (2020, November 8). BirdSpot. https://www.birdspot.co.uk/bird-numbers/the-10-biggest-birds-in-the-world

The 10 dog breeds with the best sense of smell. (2015, July 27). Dogtime. https://dogtime.com/dog-health/general/18724-10-dog-breeds-with-the-best-sense-of-smell

The 10 Most Common Dreams and Their Interpretations. (2023, March 29). ViscoSoft. https://viscosoft.com/blogs/dream-journal/the-10-most-common-dreams-and-their-interpretations

The Blitz around Britain. (2018). Imperial War Museums. https://www.iwm.org.uk/history/the-blitz-around-britain

The Capital of São Paulo has the largest fleet of helicopters in the world. (2022, May 9). BisAviation Group. https://bisaviation.com.br/the-capital-of-sao-paulo-has-the-largest-fleet-of-helicopters-in-the-world/#:~:text=The%20Fleet%20of%20the%20Capital

The Cornell Lab. (2009, April 1). *Why can't penguins fly?* All about Birds. https://www.allaboutbirds.org/news/why-cant-penguins-fly/#:~:text=To%20dive%20deep%2C%20to%20catch

The Economist. (2019, January 3). *In the Middle Ages there was no such thing as childhood.* The Economist; The Economist. https://www.economist.com/special-report/2019/01/03/in-the-middle-ages-there-was-no-such-thing-as-childhood

The Editors of Encyclopaedia Britannica. (2019). *phrenology | History, Theory, & Pseudoscience.* In Encyclopædia Britannica. https://www.britannica.com/topic/phrenology

The Geological Society. (2023). *The Geological Society*. Www.geolsoc.org.uk. https://www.geolsoc.org.uk/Plate-Tectonics/Chap3-Plate-Margins/Convergent/Continental-Collision#:~:text=The%20Himalayan%20mountain%20range%20and

The History Press. (2023). *The History Press | 10 facts about Blackbeard*. Www.thehistorypress.co.uk. https://www.thehistorypress.co.uk/articles/10-facts-about-blackbeard/

The History of Airships in Commercial Aviation. (2021, August 5). Air Charter Service. https://www.aircharterserviceusa.com/about-us/news-features/blog/the-history-of-airships-and-airship-travel-in-commercial-aviation#:~:text=In%201852%2C%20French%20engineer%20Henri

The International Spy Museum. (2023). *Espionage Facts*. International Spy Museum. https://www.spymuseum.org/education-programs/spy-resources/espionage-facts/#:~:text=In%20the%20intelligence%20world%2C%20a

The Kruger Safari Co. (2020, September 15). *30 Interesting Facts about Kruger National Park*. Kruger Park Travel. https://www.krugerpark.travel/kruger-park-facts

The longest traffic jam in history occurred in China and lasted 12 days. (2023, September 2). Arabia Weather. https://www.arabiaweather.com/en/content/the-longest-traffic-jam-in-history-occurred-in-china-and-lasted-12-days#:~:text=On%20August%2014%2C%202010%2C%20something

The Most Common Birds in the World. (2018, June 5). WorldAtlas. https://www.worldatlas.com/articles/most-populous-bird-species-in-the-world.html#:~:text=The%20domestic%20chicken%20is%20the

The most famous spies in history. (2021, August 18). Chicago Tribune. https://www.chicagotribune.com/featured/sns-ws-most-famous-spies-20210818-jo3wgceaxrdqpot3i7bzhoga4y-photogallery.html

The Most Poisonous Animals in The World. (2023). Fact Animal. https://factanimal.com/animal-facts/most-poisonous-animals-in-the-world/

The Origin and History of Breakfast. (2023, April 4). Filthy Flats. https://filthyflats.com/lifestyle/the-origin-and-history-of-breakfast/

The Parthenon: 10 Surprising Facts about the Temple. (2020, September 16). Greek Travel Tellers. https://greektraveltellers.com/blog/the-parthenon-facts

The Planets. (2014). *Meteorite Facts: Interesting Facts about Meteorites*. The Planets. https://theplanets.org/meteorites/

The Royal Mint. (2023). *Sir Isaac Newton | The Royal Mint*. Www.royalmint.com. https://www.royalmint.com/discover/uk-coins/sir-isaac-newton/

These are the top 5 fastest Supercomputers in the world; Check out the list. (2023, May 23). HT Tech. https://tech.hindustantimes.com/tech/news/these-are-the-top-5-fastest-supercomputers-in-the-world-check-out-the-list-71684856958969.html

The Spruce Official. (2012). *12 Most Popular Cat Breeds*. The Spruce Pets. https://www.thesprucepets.com/personalities-of-popular-cat-breeds-554219

The Sun. (2021). *World's largest "treasure hoard" worth over $20 billion may soon be found*. In NEW YORK POST. https://nypost.com/2021/11/02/worlds-largest-treasure-hoard-worth-over-20-billion-may-soon-be-found/

The Top 10 Causes of Death. (2020, December 9). World Health Organization. https://www.who.int/news-room/fact-sheets/detail/the-top-10-causes-of-death

The Way of Pirates. (2020). *Real Pirates - Facts about Real and Fictional Pirates*. Thewayofthepirates.com. http://www.thewayofthepirates.com/

The Way of Pirates. (2023). *Calico Rackham Jack - Famous Pirate - The Way of the Pirates*. Www.thewayofthepirates.com. http://www.thewayofthepirates.com/famous-pirates/calico-rackham-jack/

The World's Highest-Paid Athletes 2023. (2023, May 16). Forbes. https://www.forbes.com/lists/athletes/?sh=775409a05b7e

The World's Most Linguistically Diverse City. (2018, July 30). World Atlas. https://www.worldatlas.com/articles/which-is-the-most-linguistically-diverse-city-in-the-world.html#:~:text=Papua%20New%20Guinea%2C%20with%20roughly

3 Surprising Facts About Parasites and How You Can Help. (2016, September 14). WayFM. https://wayfm.com/content/faith-life/3-surprising-facts-about-parasites-and-how-you-can-help/

13 Awesome Facts About Bats. (2018, October 24). U. S. Department of the Interior. https://www.doi.gov/blog/13-facts-about-bats

30 Interesting Facts about Sustainability. (2023). SUMAS. https://sumas.ch/sustainability-facts/

30 mind-blowing facts about the microbes that live inside of you. (2021, July 26). Business Insider. https://www.businessinsider.in/science/30-mind-blowing-facts-about-the-microbes-that-live-inside-of-you/slidelist/49696157.cms

37 Interesting Cruise Ship Facts that Will Surprise You. (2021, May 31). Life Well Cruised. https://lifewellcruised.com/cruise-ship-facts/

Thompson & Morgan. (2023). *Edible Flowers Guide | Thompson & Morgan*. Www.thompson-Morgan.com. https://www.thompson-morgan.com/edible-flowers

Thomson, L. (2019, May 30). *The ten most expensive military aircraft ever built | Airforce-technology.com*. Airforce Technology. https://www.airforce-technology.com/features/most-expensive-military-aircraft/?cf-view

Tillman, N. (2018, July 26). *What Is the Biggest Star?*. Space.com. https://www.space.com/41290-biggest-star.html

Time Magazine. (2019). *Top 10 Things You Didn't Know About Money*. Time Magazine USA. https://content.time.com/time/specials/packages/article/0,28804,1914560_1914558_1914593,00.html

Timeless Knowledge. (2019). *Sunrise and Sunset*. Stanford.edu. http://solar-center.stanford.edu/AO/sunrise.html

Tiwari, S. (2022, September 30). *Pride Of US Navy: The Largest & Most Expensive Warship In The World, USS Gerald R Ford, Is Ready To Sail*. Latest Asian, Middle-East, EurAsian, Indian News. https://www.eurasiantimes.com/largest-most-expensive-warship-in-the-world-uss-gerald-r-ford/

Toilet. (2017, August 2). Water Footprint Calculator. https://www.watercalculator.org/posts/toilet/#:~:text=Get%20a%20low%2Dflow%20toilet

Toomer, J. (2020, October 21). *Giulia Tofana, the Italian serial poisoner who became a legend*. SYFY Official Site. https://www.syfy.com/syfy-wire/giulia-tofana-the-italian-serial-poisoner-who-became-a-legend

Top 15 Countries by GDP in 2022. (2022). Global PEO Services. https://globalpeoservices.com/top-15-countries-by-gdp-in-2022/

Top Olympic Medal Winners. (2010). TopEnd Sports. https://www.topendsports.com/events/summer/medal-tally/top-winners.htm

Top 10 Agricultural Producing Countries in The World. (2020, November 6). Tractor Junction. https://www.tractorjunction.com/blog/top-10-agricultural-producing-countries-in-the-world/

Top 10 facts about Beavers. (2023). WWF. https://www.wwf.org.uk/learn/fascinating-facts/beavers

Top 10 Facts About Bugs! (2023). Fun Kids - the UK's Children's Radio Station. https://www.funkidslive.com/learn/top-10-facts/top-10-facts-about-bugs/

Top 10 facts about elephants. (2022). WWF. https://www.wwf.org.uk/learn/fascinating-facts/elephants

Top 10 facts about marine turtles. (2023). World Wildlife Fund. https://www.wwf.org.uk/learn/fascinating-facts/marine-turtles?utm_source=Grants&utm_medium=PaidSearch-Brand&pc=AWD014007&gclid=Cj0KCQjwhfipBhCqARIsAH9msblW-vE8vSRB0AioMDIdA9UK5rnOdcpZWRtIIt11pnmpK4RHcWL0P1QaAnpGEALw_wcB&gclsrc=aw.ds

Top 10 facts about mountain gorillas. (2023). WWF. https://www.wwf.org.uk/learn/fascinating-facts/gorillas?psafe_param=1&utm_source=Grants&utm_medium=PaidSearch-Brand&pc=AWD014007&gclid=Cj0KCQjwhfipBhCqARIsAH9msbm1_4dlM8R5KlNHgpN9r4Ml74Lf0-8TdcDyCD4jj68sy34Jglth30kaArjkEALw_wcB&gclsrc=aw.ds

Top 10 facts about polar bears. (2023). WWF. https://www.wwf.org.uk/learn/fascinating-facts/polar-bears#:~:text=Beneath%20all%20that%20thick%20fur

Top 10 facts about rhinos. (2023). WWF. https://www.wwf.org.uk/learn/fascinating-facts/rhinos

Top 10 facts about sharks. (2019). WWF. https://www.wwf.org.uk/learn/fascinating-facts/sharks

Top 10 facts about Sloths. (2023). WWF. https://www.wwf.org.uk/learn/fascinating-facts/sloth?pc=AUT005007&utm_source=Grants&utm_medium=PaidSearch-Brand&pc=AWD014007&gclid=Cj0KCQjwhfipBhCqARIsAH9msbkrg0Q623DtqCM4jqGc3Hs31jVcwQPZ7ZTZ4HJDABzKL2cHk7_UTa4aAnqrEALw_wcB&gclsrc=aw.ds

Top Facts about the Amazon. (2023). WWF. https://www.wwf.org.uk/learn/fascinating-facts/amazon

Top 10 Interesting Facts about Trucks. (2019, June 22). 360 MAGAZINE.https://www.the360mag.com/top-10-interesting-facts-about-trucks/

Top Ten Most Expensive Items Of Jewelry in the World. (2023). My Gemma. https://mygemma.com/en-gb/blogs/news/top-10-expensive-items-jewelry

Top 10 Rare Diseases in the World You Never Heard About. (2023, February 15). Regency Healthcare Ltd. https://regencyhealthcare.in/blog/top-10-rare-diseases-in-the-world-you-never-heard-about/#:~:text=RPI%20Deficiency

Top 10 weird facts about space rockets. (2023, July 23). Fun Kids - the UK's Children's Radio Station. https://www.funkidslive.com/learn/top-10-facts/top-10-weird-facts-about-rockets/

Top 12 Interesting Oil Facts. (2023). Rix. https://www.rix.co.uk/blog/post/top-12-interesting-oil-facts

Torgan, C. (2015, May 12). *Humans Can Identify More Than 1 Trillion Smells*. National Institutes of Health (NIH). https://www.nih.gov/news-events/nih-research-matters/humans-can-identify-more-1-trillion-smells#:~:text=Based%20on%20the%20test%20findings

Toscano, P. (2009, July 6). *The Weirdest Currencies In the World*. CNBC. https://www.cnbc.com/2009/07/06/The-Weirdest-Currencies-In-the-World.html

Towers, L. (2014, March 17). *Five Weird Fish Dishes from Around the World*. The Fish Site. https://thefishsite.com/articles/five-weird-fish-dishes-from-around-the-world

Townsend, L. (2023). *Tree time: 20 facts about trees you might not know*. CPRE. https://www.cpre.org.uk/discover/facts-about-trees/

Tran, C. (2018, November 5). *44 Unsanitary Facts About The History Of The Toilet*. Factinate. https://www.factinate.com/things/history-toilet

Tran, S. (2022, January 22). *Relatively Special Facts About Physics*. Factinate. https://www.factinate.com/things/32-relatively-special-facts-physics

Triceratops. (2023). Natural History Museum. https://www.nhm.ac.uk/discover/dino-directory/triceratops.html

Turgeon, A., & Morse, E. (2023, February 21). *Natural Gas | National Geographic Society*. Education.nationalgeographic.org. https://education.nationalgeographic.org/resource/natural-gas/

12 Shark Facts That May Surprise You. (2018, July 17). NOAA Fisheries. https://www.fisheries.noaa.gov/feature-story/12-shark-facts-may-surprise-you

20 Fun Dolphin Facts You Never Knew. (2019, April 17). Marco Island Dolphin Tour. https://marcoislanddolphintour.com/dolphin-facts/

25 Amazing Facts About Foxes. (2023). Country & Home. https://www.countryandhome.co.uk/blog/country-gifts/25-amazing-facts-about-foxes/

25 Fun Facts About Flowers. (2011, April 28). -Gardening Channel. https://www.gardeningchannel.com/25-fun-facts-about-flowers/

24 Mind-Blowing Facts About The Roman Colosseum (PICTURES). (2021). The Colosseum. https://www.thecolosseum.org/facts/

25+ Fascinating Facts About the Environment That Might Surprise You. (2023). Conserve Energy Future. Www.conserve-Energy-Future.com. https://www.conserve-energy-future.com/environment-facts.php

Twenty-two Fascinating Bird Facts About Our Feathered Friends. (2022, March 4). TRVST. https://www.trvst.world/biodiversity/bird-facts/

Tymann, M. (2023, July 3). *The Biggest Hotels in the World | Oyster*. Oyster.com. https://www.oyster.com/articles/largest-hotels-in-the-world/

Tyrannosaurus rex. (2018). American Museum of Natural History. https://www.amnh.org/dinosaurs/tyrannosaurus-rex

U.S. Department of Agriculture. (2020). *If You Get Lost | US Forest Service*. Usda.gov. https://www.fs.usda.gov/visit/know-before-you-go/if-you-get-lost

U.S. Department of Commerce. (2023, June 2). *Thunderstorm Hazards - Flash Floods*. National Oceanic and Atmospheric Administration. https://www.noaa.gov/jetstream/thunderstorms/flood

UN Water. (2023). *World Toilet Day*. UN-Water. https://www.unwater.org/our-work/world-toilet-day#:~:text=World%20Toilet%20Day%2C%20celebrated%20on

Unbelievable Facts. (2018, November 18). *10 Crazy Things Scientists Used to Believe*. Unbelievable Facts. https://unbelievable-facts.com/2018/11/crazy-things-scientists-used-to-believe.html

Uncommon Goods. (2015, May 26). *Uncommon Knowledge: Why do we wish upon stars? – The Goods*. Www.uncommongoods.com. https://www.uncommongoods.com/blog/2015/uncommon-knowledge-why-do-we-wish-upon-stars/

UNESCO World Heritage Centre. (2023a). *Salonga National Park*. UNESCO World Heritage Centre. https://whc.unesco.org/en/list/280/

UNESCO World Heritage Centre. (2023b). *Shark Bay, Western Australia*. UNESCO World Heritage Centre. https://whc.unesco.org/en/list/578/

United States Department of Commerce. (2023). *Tropical Cyclone Naming History and Retired Names*. Www.nhc.noaa.gov. https://www.nhc.noaa.gov/aboutnames_history.shtml

Population. (2022). United Nations. https://www.un.org/en/global-issues/population#:~:text=Our%20growing%20population&text=The%20global%20human%20population%20reached

University of Kansas. (2023). *Mesozoic Era (252 million years ago to 66 million years ago)*. GeoKansas. https://geokansas.ku.edu/mesozoic-era-252-million-years-ago-to-66-million-years-ago#:~:text=Mesozoic%20Era%20(252%20million%20years%20ago%20to%2066%20million%20years%20ago)

University of Queensland. (2019, January 30). *Understanding the brain: a brief history*. Uq.edu.au. https://qbi.uq.edu.au/brain/intelligent-machines/understanding-brain-brief-history

University of Rochester. (2023). *Taking Care of Cuts and Scrapes - Health Encyclopedia - University of Rochester Medical Center*. Www.urmc.rochester.edu. https://www.urmc.rochester.edu/encyclopedia/content.aspx?contenttypeid=1&contentid=2978#:~:text=Stop%20bleeding%20by%20putting%20pressure

UNRV. (2023). *Scutum – Roman Shield | Roman Military*. Www.unrv.com. https://www.unrv.com/military/scutum.php

US Department of Commerce, National Oceanic and Atmospheric Administration. (2019). *What is the world's smallest ocean?*. Noaa.gov. https://oceanservice.noaa.gov/facts/smallestocean.html

US Department of Commerce. (2023a). *The Black Sunday Dust Storm of April 14, 1935*. Www.weather.gov. https://www.weather.gov/oun/events-19350414#:~:text=The%20Black%20Sunday%20Dust%20Storm%20of%20April%2014%2C%201935

US Department of Commerce. (2023b, January 20). *Why is the ocean blue?*. Oceanservice.noaa.gov. https://oceanservice.noaa.gov/facts/oceanblue.html#:~:text=The%20ocean%20is%20blue%20because

Vamplew, A. (2020, August 19). *How to see the Milky Way*. BBC Sky at Night Magazine. https://www.skyatnightmagazine.com/advice/skills/how-to-see-the-milky-way

Van Niekerk, T. (2023, February 23). *How Many Cows Are in the World?*. (Global Distribution Data). WAF. https://worldanimalfoundation.org/advocate/how-many-cows-are-in-the-world/

Vedantu. (2023, November 6). *Bacteria: Parts of Bacteria and Interesting Facts about Them*. VEDANTU. https://www.vedantu.com/evs/interesting-facts-about-bacteria

Verasai, A. (2022, September 16). *10 Weirdest Jobs in the World*. The HR Digest. https://www.thehrdigest.com/10-weirdest-jobs-in-the-world/

Vicki Keith. (2023). Ontario Heritage Trust. https://www.heritagetrust.on.ca/pages/our-stories/exhibits/snapshots-of-ontarios-sport-heritage/connection-between-community-geography-and-sport/vicki-keith

Victoria, K. (2022, May 22). *60+ Cool Computer Facts That You Should Know*. Teach Your Kids Code. https://teachyourkidscode.com/com)puter-facts/

Victoria Falls. (2013). Zambia Tourism. https://www.zambiatourism.com/destinations/waterfalls/victoria-falls/

Victorian Fisheries Authority. (2023). *What to do if you're attacked by a shark*. VFA. https://vfa.vic.gov.au/education/shark-smart/first-aid-and-treatment

Vieira, Warren A., Wells, Kaylee M., & McCusker, Catherine D. (2019). *Advancements to the Axolotl Model for Regeneration and Aging*, Gerontology, 66(3), 1–11. https://doi.org/10.1159/000504294

Viktoria. (2019, March 5). *Puffins in Iceland - All You Need to Know About*. Arctic Adventures. https://adventures.is/blog/puffins-in-iceland/#:~:text=With%208%20to%2010%20million

Vinopal, L. (2023, July 31). *25 Truly Weird Facts About The Human Body*. Fatherly. https://www.fatherly.com/health/weird-facts-about-human-body

Vogel, T., Wasser, M., & Wright, E. (2022, October 13). *What You Need to Know About the Lunar Eclipse*. Moon: NASA Science. https://moon.nasa.gov/news/185/what-you-need-to-know-about-the-lunar-eclipse/#:~:text=During%20a%20lunar%20eclipse%2C%20the

Voss, N. (2019, March 21). *When Will Fossil Fuels Run Out?*. Infinity Renewables. https://infinity-renewables.com/162-2/#:~:text=So%2C%20if%20we%20continue%20at

Vultures. (2023). DK Find Out! https://www.dkfindout.com/uk/animals-and-nature/birds/vultures/

Walcott, W. (2015, December 3). *8 Super Cool Genetic Mutations Found In Humans*. HowStuffWorks. https://science.howstuffworks.com/life/genetic/8-super-cool-genetic-mutations-found-in-humans.htm

Wallin, L. (2021, August 8). *9 Fun Facts about Mount Fuji for Mountain Day*. Tokyo Weekender. https://www.tokyoweekender.com/travel/9-fun-facts-mount-fuji/

Water Science School. (1993). *The distribution of water on, in, and above the Earth*. Www.usgs.gov. https://www.usgs.gov/media/images/distribution-water-and-above-earth-0

Water Science School. (1999, October 3). *Lake Baikal from space, the largest, oldest, and deepest lake*. U.S. Geological Survey. https://www.usgs.gov/media/images/lake-baikal-space-largest-oldest-and-deepest-lake

Waxman, O. (2017, October 17). *3 Strange Treatments Doctors Used to Think Were Good for You*. Time. https://time.com/4982099/quackery-medicine-history/

Waxman, O. B. (2017, April 8). *The Bear Who Became a Cigarette-Smoking, Beer-Drinking World War II Hero*. Time; Time. https://time.com/4731787/wojtek-the-bear-history/

Weber, R. (2020, January 20). *8 old-fashioned medical remedies that are still being used*. Wexnermedical.osu.edu. https://wexnermedical.osu.edu/blog/old-fashioned-medicine-still-in-use

Webgo Admin. (2021, September 22). *The 10 most expensive dog breeds in the world*. Hundeo. https://www.hundeo.com/en/magazine/most-expensive-dog-breeds/#:~:text=1.-

Wecker, J. (2022, August 10). *Fascinating Facts About Hummingbirds and How to Attract Them to Your Yard*. Good Housekeeping. https://www.goodhousekeeping.com/home/gardening/g19632825/hummingbird-facts/

Wei-Haas, M. (2018, January 31). *Inside the First Solar-Powered Flight Around the World*. Smithsonian Magazine. https://www.smithsonianmag.com/innovation/inside-first-solar-powered-flight-around-world-180968000/#:~:text=After%2014%20months%20of%20travel

Welch, J. (2012, October 5). *University graduate finds work as human scarecrow*. BBC News. https://www.bbc.co.uk/news/uk-england-norfolk-19846642

Wells, D. (2017). *21 Fun Facts About the Brain*. Healthline. https://www.healthline.com/health/fun-facts-about-the-brain

Wenger, A. (2014, October 8). *11 Ancient Medical Treatments That Will Make Your Stomach Turn*. Healthline. https://www.healthline.com/health/old-medical-treatments-make-your-stomach-turn#Elephant-Bile-to-Treat-Bad-Breath

Western Exterminator Company. (2023). *Ouch! The top 5 most painful insect stings*. Western Exterminator Company. https://www.westernexterminator.com/help-and-advice/pest-insights/wasps/ouch-the-top-5-most-painful-insect-stings

What Are Meteorites? Ancient Clues to Our Solar System (2020). American Museum of Natural History. https://www.amnh.org/exhibitions/permanent/meteorites/meteorites/what-is-a-meteorite

When Was Candy Invented? (2023). Wonderopolis. https://wonderopolis.org/wonder/when-was-candy-invented

When were eyeglasses invented and by whom? (2022, November 2). Glasses.com. https://www.glasses.com/gl-us/blog/when-were-glasses-invented#:~:text=It%20is%20generally%20accepted%20that

Where is the highest tide? (2020). US Department of Commerce, National Oceanic and Atmospheric Administration. https://oceanservice.noaa.gov/facts/highesttide.html

Which were the biggest dinosaurs of all? (2009, February 8). The Observer. https://www.theguardian.com/science/2009/feb/08/biggest-dinosaurs-argentina#:~:text=The%20largest%20and%20heaviest

Whisker. (2023). *15 Famous Cats From World History | Learn more on Litter-Robot Blog*. Www.litter-Robot.com. https://www.litter-robot.com/blog/15-famous-cats-from-world-history/

Whitakers. (2023, April 13). *Fun Facts About Chocolate - Whitakers Chocolates | Our Blog*. Whitakers Chocolates | Our Blog - Keeping You up to Date with the Latest News, Products and Events in the World of Whitakers Chocolates. https://www.whitakerschocolates.com/blog/fun-facts-about-chocolate/

Whitman, M. (2023, July 31). *Climbing Denali – Highest Peak in North America (Complete Guide)*. Mountain IQ. https://www.mountainiq.com/guides/denali/

Why Do Snakes Shed Their Skin? (2015, August 15). Iowa Department of Natural Resources. https://www.iowadnr.gov/About-DNR/DNR-News-Releases/ArticleID/158/Why-Do-Snakes-Shed-Their-Skin#:~:text=While%20humans%20E2%80%9Cshed%E2%80%9D%20millions%20of

Widya, A. (2022, October 27). *The Craziest and Longest Prison Sentences in History*. Www.viva.co.id. https://www.viva.co.id/english/1537397-the-craziest-and-longest-prison-sentences-in-history?page=all

Wikramanayake, E. (2023). *Thar Desert*. One Earth. https://www.oneearth.org/ecoregions/thar-desert/#:~:text=The%20Thar%20Desert%20is%20undoubtedly

Williams, J. A. (2020, May 28). *What Was the Beast of Gévaudan?*. HISTORY. https://www.history.com/news/beast-gevaudan-france-theories

Williams, L. (2022, November 15). *10 of the world's most poisonous plants*. Www.discoverwildlife.com. https://www.discoverwildlife.com/plant-facts/worlds-most-poisonous-plants

Williams, L. (2023, June 5). *10 deadliest snakes in the world: meet the world's most venomous snakes and their lethal bite*. Www.discoverwildlife.com. https://www.discoverwildlife.com/animal-facts/reptiles/deadliest-snakes

Williams, L. (2023a). *Time Line*. Www.princeton.edu. https://www.princeton.edu/~accion/chupa21.html

Williams, L. (2023b, April 3). *9 most poisonous mushrooms: deadly fungi you don't want to mess with*. Www.discoverwildlife.com. https://www.discoverwildlife.com/plant-facts/fungi/poisonous-mushrooms

Williams, M. (2022, September 10). *Top ten highest goalscorers of all time: Ronaldo breaks Bican's mammoth record*. TalkSPORT. https://talksport.com/football/691008/highest-goalscorers-ever-cristiano-ronaldo-lionel-messi-josef-bican-pele-manchester-united-barcelona-juventus-psg/

Williamson, E. (2023, August 22). *What's Eating You? 5 Fascinating Facts About Parasites*. News.virginia.edu. https://news.virginia.edu/content/whats-eating-you-5-fascinating-facts-about-parasites

Wilson, D. R. (2021, July 27). *Poison ivy: Home remedies and how to recognize it*. Www.medicalnewstoday.com. https://www.medicalnewstoday.com/articles/318059#home-remedies

Winchester Mystery House. (2022, August 4). *Plan Your Visit - Winchester Mystery House*. Winchestermysteryhouse.com. https://winchestermysteryhouse.com/plan-your-visit/#:~:text=The%20Winchester%20Mystery%20House%20has

Winston, C. (2022, August 28). *14 Weird Facts About The Gates Of Hell In Turkmenistan*. TheTravel. https://www.thetravel.com/facts-about-the-gates-of-hell-in-turkmenistan/#previous-attempts-have-been-made-to-extinguish-the-crater

Wires, L. (2015, February 4). *Cormorants: the world's most hated bird?*. New Scientist. https://www.newscientist.com/article/mg22530071-100-cormorants-the-worlds-most-hated-bird/

Wise, J. (2017, February 1). *20 Survival Tips You Must Know*. Popular Mechanics. https://www.popularmechanics.com/adventure/outdoors/tips/a3114/how-not-to-die-20-survival-tips-you-must-know-16030884/

Wisevoter. (2023). *Richest Countries in the World 2023*. Wisevoter. https://wisevoter.com/country-rankings/richest-countries-in-the-world/#:~:text=Thus%2C%20the%20richest%20countries%20in

Wishart, A. (2017, August 21). *11 Interesting & Fun Facts About Castles You Probably Don't Know | LTR Castles*. Loyd & Townsend Rose. https://ltrcastles.com/facts-about-castles/

Wood, R. (2010, May). *Olympic Games Host Cities*. Www.topendsports.com. https://www.topendsports.com/events/summer/hosts/list.htm

Woodward, D. (2023, February 25). *The 10 most iconic jewels through history*. Www.bbc.com. https://www.bbc.com/culture/article/20230224-the-10-most-iconic-jewels-through-history

Woolley, J. (2022, January 31). *Green Planet: 5 mind-blowing facts we learned from the show*. Greenpeace UK. https://www.greenpeace.org.uk/news/green-planet-5-amazing-plant-facts/

WordPress.com. (2018, April 18). *Muscular System*. The Biomechanics of Snake Locomotion. https://snakelocomotion.wordpress.com/the-muscular-system/

World Health Organisation. (2020). *Malaria*. Www.who.int. https://www.who.int/health-topics/malaria#tab=tab_1

World Population Day. (2022). United Nations. https://www.un.org/en/observances/world-population-day

World's protected natural areas receive eight billion visits a year. (2015, February 24). University of Cambridge. https://www.cam.ac.uk/research/news/worlds-protected-natural-areas-receive-eight-billion-visits-a-year#:~:text=The%20world%27s%20national%20parks%20and

World Record Academy . (2023, June 5). *World's Largest Toilet: world record in Columbus, Indiana*. Www.worldrecordacademy.org. https://www.worldrecordacademy.org/2023/6/worlds-largest-toilet-world-record-in-columbus-indiana-423244#:~:text=Indiana%20is%20home%20to%20the

World's deepest hotel is now open to visitors. (2023, July 4). *The Times of India*. https://timesofindia.indiatimes.com/travel/travel-news/worlds-deepest-hotel-is-now-open-to-visitors/articleshow/101485371.cms

World's Largest Beaver Dam. (2022, November 25). Government of Canada Parks Agency. https://www.pc.gc.ca/pn-np/nt/woodbuffalo/nature/beaver_gallery

niakiewicz, P. (2023, August 9). *What causes a meteor shower?* https://www.skyatnightmagazine.com/space-science/what-causes-meteor-shower

WPS. (2023). *Interesting Facts About the Sahara Desert*. Global Adventure Challenges https://www.globaladventurechallenges.com/journal/facts-about-sahara-desert#:~:text=The%20Sahara%20Desert%20is%20the%20largest%20hot%20desert%20in%20the

Wurr, M. (2011). *How many days does the average person sleep for during their lifetime?*. The Guardian. https://www.theguardian.com/notesandqueries/query/0,5753,-50504,00.html#:~:text=How%20many%20days%20does%20the%20average%20person%20sleep%20for%20during%20their%20lifetime%3F,-Melissa%2C%20Glasgow%2C%20Scotland&text=If%20the%20average%20night%27s%20sleep,years%20asleep%2C%20or%209%2C125%20days.

WWII Aircraft Losses By Country. (2023). World War Wings. https://worldwarwings.com/wwii-aircraft-losses-by-country/

WWF & Goulding. (2020). *Amazon fish*. Panda. https://wwf.panda.org/discover/knowledge_hub/where_we_work/amazon/about_the_amazon/wildlife_amazon/fish/#:~:text=Amazon%20fish%20%7C%20WWF&text=While%20things%20may%20seem%20relatively

Xinhua. (2020, November 14). *Backgrounder: Yangtze River, China's longest, world's busiest waterway - Xinhua | English.news.cn*. Www.xinhuanet.com. https://www.xinhuanet.com/english/2020-11/14/c_139516079.htm

Xiong, M. (2023, January 30). *A Brief History of the Croissant | Institute of Culinary Education*. Www.ice.edu. https://www.ice.edu/blog/brief-history-croissant#:~:text=Records%20state%20that%20the%20kipferl

Xu, Q., Chen, L., Dijun Chen, R., Zhu, A., Chen, C., Bertrand, D., Jiao, W., Hao, B., Lyon, M., Chen, J., Gao, S., Xing, F., Lan, H., Chang, J., Ge, X., Lei, Y., Hu, Q., Miao, Y., and Ruan, Y. (2013). The draft genome of sweet orange (Citrus sinensis). *Nature Genetics*, 45(1), 59–66. https://doi.org/10.1038/ng.2472

Yellow Cab. (2023). NYC Taxi and Limousine Commission. https://www.nyc.gov/site/tlc/businesses/yellow-cab.page#:~:text=By%20law%2C%20there%20are%2013%2C587

Yew poisoning Information. (2023). Mount Sinai Health System. https://www.mountsinai.org/health-library/poison/yew-poisoning

Yong, E. (2016, October 27). *These Birds Fly Almost a Year Without Landing*. Animals. https://www.nationalgeographic.com/animals/article/swift-bird-10-month-migration

York, C. (2013, August 6). *This Is The World's Smallest Painting…* HuffPost UK. https://www.huffingtonpost.co.uk/2013/08/06/worlds-smallest-painting-mona-lisa-nanotechnology_n_3711377.html#:~:text=mini%20olisananotech-

Yorke, S. (2022, September 1). *Oxfam GB | 7 facts about sustainable fashion*. Oxfam GB. https://www.oxfam.org.uk/oxfam-in-action/oxfam-blog/7-facts-about-sustainable-fashion/

Yorkshire Dales National Park. (2023). *Rare Mosses in the Dales*. Yorkshire Dales National Park. https://www.yorkshiredales.org.uk/about/wildlife/species/mosses-liverworts/rare-mosses-in-the-dales/

Young, A. (2022, August 16). *36 Fun Fishing Facts That Will Blow Your Mind! • Panfish Nation*. 36 Fun Fishing Facts That Will Blow Your Mind! https://panfishnation.com/36-fun-fishing-facts/

Young, A. (2023, July 16). *The Fastest Firing Machine Guns in the World*. 24/7 Wall St. https://247wallst.com/special-report/2023/07/16/fastest-firing-machine-guns-in-the-world/

Young, E. (2021, December 20). *Fear Of Spiders May Have Its Evolutionary Roots In Aversion To Scorpions*. BPS. https://www.bps.org.uk/research-digest/fear-spiders-may-have-its-evolutionary-roots-aversion-scorpions

Young, L. (2020, August 21). *Why Scientists Say We Should Defend Parasites*. Science Friday. https://www.sciencefriday.com/articles/defend-parasites/

Zahn, A. (2023, March 10). *The 9 Smallest Cell Phones You Can Currently Buy*. SlashGear. https://www.slashgear.com/1224589/the-9-smallest-cell-phones-you-can-currently-buy/

Zeldovich, L. (2022, November 18). *8 Fascinating Facts About Toilets*. Mental Floss. https://www.mentalfloss.com/posts/toilet-facts-history

Zerkel, E. (2020, March 3). *The World's Smallest Desert Is in … Canada?* The Weather Channel. https://weather.com/science/environment/news/2018-06-22-smallest-desert-canada-yukon-carcross

Zimmer, P. (2014, June). *Japan's Underwater Aircraft Carriers*. Warfare History Network. https://warfarehistorynetwork.com/article/japans-underwater-aircraft-carriers/

Zuckerman, C. (2019, March 20). *Everything you wanted to know about stars*. National Geographic. https://www.nationalgeographic.com/science/article/stars

Zutshi, A. (2023). *22 Interesting Facts About Petra, Jordan - Holidify*. Www.holidify.com. https://www.holidify.com/pages/facts-about-petra-5995.html

Images cited

p.26 Hindenburg burning from Wikimedia Commons. Public Domain work of US Federal Government. https://commons.wikimedia.org/wiki/File:Hindenburg_burning.jpg

p.27 Christmas Bullet image from Wikimedia Commons. Public Domain. https://commons.wikimedia.org/wiki/File:Christmas_Bullet.jpg

p.27 Messerschmitt Me 163 V8 on the ground from Wikimedia Commons by Royal Air Force official photographer. Public Domain. https://commons.wikimedia.org/wiki/File:Messerschmitt_Me_163_V8_on_the_ground.jpg

p.31 Daimler Reitwagen by Wladyslaw from Wikimedia Commons. https://commons.wikimedia.org/wiki/File:Daimler_Reitwagen.JPG

p.32 Patent-Motorwagen Nr.1 Benz 2 by DaimlerChrysler AG from Wikimedia Commons. Altered to black and white and brightness adjusted from the original. Creative Commons Attribution-Share Alike 3.0 Unported. https://commons.wikimedia.org/wiki/File:Patent-Motorwagen_Nr.1_Benz_2.jpg

P.59 Gate of Hell Darvasa gas crater panorama by Tormod Sandtorv from Wikimedia Commons. Altered to black and white, and brightness adjusted from the original. Creative Commons Attribution-Share Alike 2.0 Generic. https://commons.wikimedia.org/wiki/File:Darvasa_gas_crater_panorama.jpg

p.63 I400 2 from Wikimedia Commons. Public domain. https://commons.wikimedia.org/wiki/File:I400_2.jpg

p.63 USS Gerald R. Ford (CVN-78) underway on 8 April 2017 by Mass Communication Specialist 2nd Class Ridge Leoni from Wikimedia Commons. Public domain work of U.S. federal government. https://commons.wikimedia.org/wiki/File:USS_Gerald_R._Ford_(CVN-78)_underway_on_8_April_2017.JPG

p.94 Metro-maus1 from Wikimedia Commons. Made public domain by the author Superewer. https://commons.wikimedia.org/wiki/File:Metro-maus1.jpg

p.94 Grand Panjandrum IWM FLM 1627 from Wikimedia Commons. Made public domain by the United Kingdom Government. https://commons.wikimedia.org/wiki/File:Grand_Panjandrum_IWM_FLM_1627.jpg

p.94 Image-Flechettes, probably French, c1914, Royal Armouries, Leeds from Wikimedia Commons. Made public domain by the author. https://commons.wikimedia.org/wiki/File:Image-Flechettes,_probably_French,_c1914,_Royal_Armouries,_Leeds.jpg

p.98 Chlamydoselachus anguineus1 from Wikimedia Commons. Author: R. Mintern. Public domain {{PD-old}} https://commons.wikimedia.org/wiki/File:Chlamydoselachus_anguineus1.jpg

p.98 Pacific hagfish Myxine from Wikimedia Commons. Author: Lmozero. Public domain work of U.S. National Oceanic and Atmospheric Administration. https://commons.wikimedia.org/wiki/File:Pacific_hagfish_Myxine.jpg

p.98 urypharynx pelecanoides from Wikimedia Commons. Pelican eel, "Eurypharynx pelecanoides". From plate 49 of "Oceanic Ichthyology" by G. Brown Goode and Tarleton H. Bean., published 1896. Public domain {{PD-old}} https://commons.wikimedia.org/wiki/File:Eurypharynx_pelecanoides.jpg

p.99 Goblin shark image Mitsu.jpg. from Wikimedia Commons. Hussakof L. A new goblin shark, Scapanorhynchus jordani, from Japan. Bulletin of the AMNH 26, 257-262. Public domain. https://commons.wikimedia.org/wiki/File:Mitsu.JPG

p.99 dumbo octopus image Dumbo-hires (cropped).jpg from Wikimedia Commons. Public domain work of U.S. National Oceanic and Atmospheric Administration. https://commons.wikimedia.org/wiki/File:Dumbo-hires_(cropped).jpg

p.99 atlantic Hagfish (Myxine glutinosa) from Wikimedia Commons. Author: Charles Keith. Public domain work of U.S. National Oceanic and Atmospheric Administration. https://commons.wikimedia.org/wiki/File:Atlantic_Hagfish_(Myxine_glutinosa).jpg

p.99 rabe cocotiers Birgus latro (Linnaeus 1777) from Wikimedia Commons. Author: Jebulon. The work was dedicated as public domain by the author. https://commons.wikimedia.org/wiki/File:Crabe_cocotiers_Birgus_latro_(Linnaeus_1777).jpg

p.99 unfish image GFNMS -- Mola Mola (35221024103) from Wikimedia Commons. Author: National Marine Sanctuaries. Public domain work of U.S. National Oceanic and Atmospheric Administration. https://commons.wikimedia.org/wiki/File:GFNMS_--_Mola_Mola_(35221024103).jpg

p.99 lamprey mouth from Wikimedia Commons. Public domain work of Environmental Protection Agency. https://commons.wikimedia.org/wiki/File:Lamprey_mouth.jpg

p.99 Triggerfish image Rhinecanthus rectangulus SI from Wikimedia Commons. Public domain work of Smithsonian Institution. https://commons.wikimedia.org/wiki/File:Rhinecanthus_ectangulus_SI.jpg

p.99 Whiplash squid image Mastigoteuthis sp from Wikimedia Commons. Public domain work of U.S. National Oceanic and Atmospheric Administration. https://commons.wikimedia.org/wiki/File:Mastigoteuthis_sp.jpg

p.99 Oarfish image Giant Oarfish.jpg from Wikimedia Commons. Public domain work of U.S. Navy. https://commons.wikimedia.org/wiki/File:Giant_Oarfish.jpg

p.99 Glass squid image Cranchiidae sp.jpg from Wikimedia Commons. Public domain work of U.S. National Oceanic and Atmospheric Administration. https://commons.wikimedia.org/wiki/File:Cranchiidae_sp.jpg

p.99 Fangtooth fish image Anoplogaster cornuta SI.jpg from Wikimedia Commons. Author: Sandra Raredon. Public domain work of Smithsonian Institution. https://commons.wikimedia.org/wiki/File:Anoplogaster_cornuta_SI.jpg

p.105 Roundworm image Ascaris lumbricoides.jpeg from Wikimedia Commons. Public domain work of Centers for Disease Control and Prevention. https://commons.wikimedia.org/wiki/File:Ascaris_lumbricoides.jpeg

p.105 Tapeworm image Taenia saginata adult 5260 lores.jpg from Wikimedia Commons. Public domain work of Centers for Disease Control and Prevention. https://commons.wikimedia.org/wiki/File:Taenia_saginata_adult_5260_lores.jpg

p.105 Tick image Adult deer tick.jpg from Wikimedia Commons. Public domain work of Agricultural Research Service. https://commons.wikimedia.org/wiki/File:Adult_deer_tick.jpg

p.108 Dermal denticle image Denticules cutanés du requin citron Negaprion brevirostris vus au microscope électronique à balayage.jpg from Wikimedia Commons. Author: Pascal Deynat/Odontobase. Creative Commons Attribution-Share Alike 3.0 Unported. https://commons.wikimedia.org/wiki/File:Denticules_cutan%C3%A9s_du_requin_citron_Negaprion_brevirostris_vus_au_microscope_%C3%A9lectronique_%C3%A0_balayage.jpg

p.108 Dwarf lanternshark image Etmopterus perryi SI cr.jpg from Wikimedia Commons. Public domain work of Smithsonian Institution. https://commons.wikimedia.org/wiki/File:Etmopterus_perryi_SI_cr.jpg

p.108 Megalodon jaw reconstruction image Carcharodon megalodon.jpg. from Wikimedia Commons. Public domain due to copyright expiration. https://commons.wikimedia.org/wiki/File:Carcharodon_megalodon.jpg

p.109 Blue whale image Anim1754 - Flickr - NOAA Photo Library.jpg from Wikimedia Commons. Public domain work of U.S. National Oceanic and Atmospheric Administration. https://commons.wikimedia.org/wiki/File:Anim1754_-_Flickr_-_NOAA_Photo_Library.jpg

p.109 Sperm whale image Physeter macrocephalus NOAA.jpg from Wikimedia Commons. Public domain work of U.S. National Oceanic and Atmospheric Administration. https://commons.wikimedia.org/wiki/File:Physeter_macrocephalus_NOAA.jpg

p.123 Burmese snake image Burmese Python (13), NPSPhoto, R. Cammauf (9101584016).jpg from Wikimedia Commons. Public domain work of National Park Service. https://commons.wikimedia.org/wiki/File:Burmese_Python_(13),_NPSPhoto,_R._Cammauf_(9101584016).jpg

p.112 Sistine Chapel image Secretary Pompeo Visits the Sistine Chapel (48840327766).jpg from Wikimedia Commons. Public domain work of United States Department of Service. https://commons.wikimedia.org/wiki/File:Secretary_Pompeo_Visits_the_Sistine_Chapel_(48840327766).jpg

p.112 The Birth of Venus image Sandro Botticelli 046.jpg from Wikimedia Commons. Public domain. https://commons.wikimedia.org/wiki/File:Sandro_Botticelli_046.jpg

p.112 Salvator Mundi image Leonardo da Vinci (attrib.) - Salvator Mundi.jpg from Wikimedia Commons. Public domain. https://commons.wikimedia.org/wiki/File:Leonardo_da_Vinci_(attrib.)_-_Salvator_Mundi.jpg

p.112 Van Gogh self portrait image Vincent van Gogh - Self-Portrait - Google Art Project (454045).jpg from Wikimedia Commons. Public domain. https://en.wikipedia.org/wiki/File:Vincent_van_Gogh_-_Self-Portrait_-_Google_Art_Project_(454045).jpg

p.112 Starry Night image VanGogh-starry night ballance1.jpg from Wikimedia Commons. Public domain. https://en.wikipedia.org/wiki/File:VanGogh-starry_night_ballance1.jpg

Disclaimer: Any of the cited images including public domain images from U.S. governmental agencies and other governmental agencies are not endorsing the content of this book.

Made in the USA
Monee, IL
08 March 2024

54695090R00079